Tongue-Tied America

Tongue-Tied America
Reviving the Art of Verbal Persuasion

Robert N. Sayler
Molly Bishop Shadel
University of Virginia School of Law

Wolters Kluwer
Law & Business

AUSTIN   BOSTON   CHICAGO   NEW YORK   THE NETHERLANDS

Aspen Publishers
Attn: Permissions Department
76 Ninth Avenue, 7th Floor
New York, NY 10011-5201

To contact Customer Care, e-mail customer.service@aspenpublishers.com, call 1-800-234-1660, fax 1-800-901-9075, or mail correspondence to:

Aspen Publishers
Attn: Order Department
PO Box 990
Frederick, MD 21705

Printed in the United States of America.

2 3 4 5 6 7 8 9 0

ISBN 978-0-7355-9859-1

Library of Congress Cataloging-in-Publication Data

Sayler, Robert N.
    Tongue-tied America : reviving the art of verbal persuasion / Robert N. Sayler, Molly Bishop Shadel.
        p. cm.
    Includes bibliographical references and index.
    ISBN 978-0-7355-9859-1
    1. Communication in law—United States. 2. Trial practice—United States. 3. English language—Rhetoric. 4. Persuasion (Rhetoric) 5. Public speaking. I. Shadel, Molly Bishop, 1969- II. Title.
    KF8915.S39 2011
    347.73'504—dc22
                                                                        2010052273

About Wolters Kluwer Law & Business

Wolters Kluwer Law & Business is a leading provider of research information and workflow solutions in key specialty areas. The strengths of the individual brands of Aspen Publishers, CCH, Kluwer Law International and Loislaw are aligned within Wolters Kluwer Law & Business to provide comprehensive, in-depth solutions and expert-authored content for the legal, professional and education markets.

CCH was founded in 1913 and has served more than four generations of business professionals and their clients. The CCH products in the Wolters Kluwer Law & Business group are highly regarded electronic and print resources for legal, securities, antitrust and trade regulation, government contracting, banking, pension, payroll, employment and labor, and healthcare reimbursement and compliance professionals.

Aspen Publishers is a leading information provider for attorneys, business professionals and law students. Written by preeminent authorities, Aspen products offer analytical and practical information in a range of specialty practice areas from securities law and intellectual property to mergers and acquisitions and pension/benefits. Aspen's trusted legal education resources provide professors and students with high-quality, up-to-date and effective resources for successful instruction and study in all areas of the law.

Kluwer Law International supplies the global business community with comprehensive English-language international legal information. Legal practitioners, corporate counsel and business executives around the world rely on the Kluwer Law International journals, loose-leafs, books and electronic products for authoritative information in many areas of international legal practice.

Loislaw is a premier provider of digitized legal content to small law firm practitioners of various specializations. Loislaw provides attorneys with the ability to quickly and efficiently find the necessary legal information they need, when and where they need it, by facilitating access to primary law as well as state-specific law, records, forms and treatises.

Wolters Kluwer Law & Business, a unit of Wolters Kluwer, is headquartered in New York and Riverwoods, Illinois. Wolters Kluwer is a leading multinational publisher and information services company.

Summary of Contents

Table of Contents

About the Authors

Robert N. Sayler studied Rhetoric and Trial Advocacy at Stanford University and Harvard Law School. He joined the law firm of Covington & Burling, LLP, in Washington, D.C., in 1962, where he specialized in trying complex multi-party cases, including product liability, antitrust, and intellectual property cases and cases seeking insurance coverage for mass liabilities arising from asbestos, breast implants, *Exxon-Valdez*, Superfund, and other environmental cleanup costs. He is a member of the American College of Trial Lawyers and has served as the Chair of the American Bar Association's Litigation Section. He has been named multiple times as one of the country's 100 Most Influential Lawyers by the *National Law Journal*; on American Lawyer's list of Top Ten D.C. Litigators; as Commercial Prosecutor of the Year by the *International Commercial Journal*; and as "the father" of insurance coverage litigation by Chambers International. In 1995, he was appointed the John Ewald Chair at the University of Virginia School of Law, where he teaches trial advocacy, rhetoric, and oral communications.

Molly Bishop Shadel studied English and Theater at Harvard University and directed plays professionally before entering law school. She earned her law degree at Columbia University, where she was a Notes Editor for the *Columbia Law Review*. She clerked for the Honorable Eugene Nickerson, U.S. District Court, Eastern District of New York, and practiced law at Covington & Burling and the United States Department of Justice. She joined the faculty of the University of Virginia School of Law in 2004, where she teaches oral advocacy and public speaking.

Acknowledgments

We are extremely grateful to our crackerjack research assistants, David Leahy and Henry Sire, who provided unflagging energy and terrific insights all along the way. We also owe a debt of thanks to our families, who have shown remarkable tolerance of and support for us and this project.

Copyright Acknowledgments

Permission to reprint copyrighted excerpts from the following is gratefully acknowledged:

Maya Angelou, Eulogy for Coretta Scott King, delivered on February 7, 2006. Copyright 2006 by Maya Angelou. Reprinted by Permission of the Helen Brann Agency, Inc.

William F. Buckley, Jr., *Torture on 60 Minutes,* Natl. Rev. Online, May 2, 2007, http://article.nationalreview.com/313807/torture-on-i60-minutesi/william-f-buckley-jr. Reprinted by permission of the National Review.

Mary Fisher, Address to the Republican National Convention, August 19, 1992. Reprinted by Permission of the Mary Fisher Clinical AIDS Research and Education (CARE) Fund at the University of Alabama at Birmingham.

Excerpts from Dr. Martin Luther King, Jr., "I've Been to the Mountaintop," speaking at Mason Temple, Memphis, Tennessee, on April 3, 1968. Reprinted by arrangement with The Heirs to the Estate of Martin Luther King Jr., c/o Writers House as agent for the proprietor New York, NY. Copyright 1968 Dr. Martin Luther King Jr; copyright renewed 1996 Coretta Scott King.

Brianna Rego, The History of Science Society, *The Polonium Brief: A Hidden History of Cancer, Radiation, and the Tobacco Industry,* 100 Isis 453, 454 (2009). © 2009 by The History of Science Society. All rights reserved. Reprinted by permission of the author.

Tongue-Tied America

Prologue

Too many Americans are ill-at-ease with public speaking. Many suffer from glossophobia,[i] or fear of public speaking, and avoid the exercise altogether. The small minority who are willing to make a speech may cling too tightly to notes, insisting on burying their faces in the text to read every word; pepper the presentation with "ah," "umm," "you know," and other meaningless filler sounds; mumble; stand frozen. The speech itself may be incomprehensible because of how it is written. The speaker's case may be overstated or unfairly argued, with scant attention paid to facts and logic, perhaps unfairly ripping at the heartstrings of the audience to disguise flaws in the argument, or perhaps boring listeners to tears as it plods through minutiae best resigned to a footnote. These failings crop up time and again in setting after setting, from informal discussions with family and friends to formal presentations when the stakes are high. This book addresses why the problem exists, why it matters, and what to do about it.

When public speaking is done well, there is usually a rich payoff. Take, as an example, Franklin Delano Roosevelt's first "Fireside Chat," delivered on March 12, 1933. America was in the grip of the Great Depression. Jobs were scarce; people were struggling to manage the basic necessities of life like keeping a roof over their heads or feeding their families. During early March 1933, runs on local banks became common as people feared that their paltry savings might be wiped out altogether. Roosevelt declared a national bank holiday, closing the banks for a short period in order to give them the breathing space they needed to respond to the situation. He then made a radio address to the nation to explain to the American people what had happened.

Franklin D. Roosevelt. AFP/AFP/Getty Images

The speech is remarkable for its pitch-perfect calm. Roosevelt's pace is measured and sure. His tone is steady, in sharp contrast with the "hysterical hoarders" that he describes. Roosevelt sounds like a straight-shooter, someone trustworthy, because he delivers the address to regular people, using everyday language. There is an intimacy to the address that makes it appealing: It is called a "fireside chat," as if Roosevelt were sitting by the hearth with his listeners, whom he calls "my friends," speaking directly to them. Finally, the speech is crystal clear. Roosevelt uses common, everyday words that people could understand. He explains complex ideas in straightforward language and takes his time so that the listeners can follow.

The result was profound. Roosevelt's speech calmed the panic and helped restore stability to the banking system. It gave the country hope at a time when it badly needed it.

Fast-forward 76 years, to February 10, 2009. America was once again devastated by a rocky economy. As a result of the recession, people saw their savings vanish in a matter of weeks. Many lost jobs. Others watched as their homes were sold in foreclosure. In February 2009, Treasury Secretary Timothy Geithner was charged with introducing the Financial Stability Plan, with which the Obama Administration hoped to turn things around.

Geithner's task was clear: He must calm a jittery stock market and win the support of the people.

Mr. Geithner, while clearly an expert on monetary policy, was less confident as a public speaker. Rather than speaking conversationally and directly, he read his script aloud, eyes darting from teleprompter to teleprompter as he performed. Shifting eyes (and the swaying that also overtook him) communicated nervousness, even dishonesty, to some in the audience. A speaker cannot hope to achieve emotional connection when he is focused on simply reading the text aloud. Mr. Geithner's presentation consequently lacked confidence and conviction, which the country needed to see. His case was also difficult to follow because of the complexity of the writing. The sentences were long, laden with jargon (like "the Federal Reserve's Term Asset Backed Securities Loan Facility"), acronyms that sounded like a foreign language when spoken aloud ("SBA loans" became almost French: "zee espeeeayy loan"), and numerous tongue twisters (such as "federally guaranteed," which became "federally guarantweed" during Mr. Geithner's recitation).

The result: The stock market reacted negatively even as the speech was being delivered, with the Dow Jones industrial average falling 382 points by the end of the day.[ii] This one simple act of public speaking caused a real-world loss of value to the stock market, and missed an opportunity to unify the country.

Effective oral advocacy (or its absence) has profoundly affected our history. But the need for oral proficiency extends beyond politics. It matters in nearly every setting. We focus here chiefly upon oral communications—but we also treat rhetoric in a broader sense, as any effort to persuade, no matter the setting, everything from the formal to the conversational. From workplace interactions to discussions with family to any kind of social setting, we are constantly judged by how we speak. Yet the subject is rarely taught in American schools. Therein lies one impetus for this book (as well as for the eight classes we teach each year at the University of Virginia School of Law).

Our central message is positive. Anyone can master basic oral advocacy. As we see every term in our classes, improvement in oral presentation skills usually comes rapidly—and is exhilarating. A combination of heeding the teaching of the masters in the field of rhetoric and regular practice yields a rich payoff for an insignificant down payment.

Four central themes run through these pages:

1. Distinguished advocacy is usually balanced, positive, factual, calm, clear, measured, and with evident logical force.

2. Know what you are talking about. Credibility matters in huge measure. Listeners value experience and authority, as well as common sense, demonstrations of judgment, and a sense of fair play.

3. Bitter, overstated, angry, sarcastic, biting, emotion-dominated rhetoric usually backfires, particularly in the long term. It can stir up the vitriol of those already predisposed to agree with a position, but it is tiresome to most everyone else. Beware the overuse and misuse of passion.

4. Wordsmithing, effective delivery, and colorful uses of stories or imagery transform the forgettable into the memorable. Cadence, tone, gestures, and a well-crafted script are essential tools for a distinguished advocate.

Part One

Essentials of Persuasion

We start with an examination of why verbal persuasion is a skill that is essential for everyone to master. We then look at the time-honored lessons of classical rhetoric. Part One explains how great speakers in ages past have persuaded audiences, applying their teachings to our modern-day world.

Chapter 1

Our Case: The Abiding Importance of Speech

"[A]t a funeral, most people would rather be the guy in the coffin than have to stand up and give a eulogy."

JERRY SEINFELD[1]

A. Why It Matters

Oral advocacy—the ability to verbalize ideas to persuade others—plays an essential role in a healthy democracy. Government "by the people" requires that the people possess some basic understanding of how to speak to one another. The Framers of the Constitution so prized free speech and robust debate that they protected it via the First Amendment.[2] The ability to articulate ideas orally becomes even more significant today as television and YouTube supersede print media as the mechanism through which debate occurs. The fate of the country can rise and fall on how well a candidate—or his supporters—can speak.

Lawyers also recognize the need to hone their verbal skills. Trial and appellate lawyers must be comfortable arguing a case if they hope to have any clients. And non-litigators—corporate attorneys, tax lawyers, and the like—know that they must be able to speak persuasively to counsel clients or impress their colleagues.

But public speaking is not exclusively the province of lawyers and politicians. We all must achieve some basic competency in verbal communications in order to succeed in the world. Anyone can benefit from instruction in oral communications because the ability to express ideas can empower us in so many situations.

WORKPLACE SUCCESS. Rare is the workplace where oral excellence is unrewarded or ineptitude in verbal discourse disregarded. The ability to speak well makes an impact every step of the way, from interviewing for the job to impressing a client to earning high marks in an annual employee review. In almost all work settings, oral skills are important.

FAMILY WELL-BEING. Psychologists counsel that "failure of communication" is the leading cause of marital distress and parent-child dysfunction. They clearly are not talking about written discourse. The communications failures, or successes, to which they refer are the interactions of day-to-day existence: fights over money, working out a better way to deal with in-laws, educating the children about the perils of the world. Each of these conversations offers occasions for effective, thoughtful talk and, sometimes, distinguished advocacy.

SOCIAL INTERACTION. The way other people speak implicitly affects our decision to befriend them, or our desire to speak about serious matters with them, or our choice to do business with them. The value of speech knows no bounds when it comes to social interaction.

SPECIAL-OCCASION SPEECH. We all will face an audience at some point in our lives, and ought to do it well: at the funeral of a mentor, the bridal dinner of a best friend, the 50th anniversary of our parents, when the boss orders us to make a presentation, when protesting some misguided school policy. The list is infinite; the need to be at your best, incontestable.

AN EMPOWERING SKILL. Once you have learned to express yourself aloud, you will find that people pay attention. You will enjoy increased confidence in the classroom, in the workplace, at social engagements—in short, in every aspect of your life. The thought of speaking before a crowd may seem terrifying to you now. Learn how to do it. It will open countless doors for you in the future and help you make your mark on the world.

B. Why Isn't It Taught?: The Educational Black Hole

It is possible to graduate from a good high school, college, even law school, without ever having been taught basic rules of oral communication. Rarely, in most schools, will there even be much opportunity to present orally, much less be critiqued and graded on it. That is not to say *no* high schools or colleges offer instruction in oral discourse. But it remains true that most students can excel at fine institutions without having to say much.

Why are we not making more of an effort to teach oral advocacy? The reasons are several:

1. An Ancient Feud

Rhetoric first became an educational stepchild eons ago during a feud between Aristotle and Plato in ancient Greece. Aristotle advocated the teaching of rhetoric, organizing an Academy to train students in the art and writing at length about the subject. Plato saw the entire enterprise as akin to snake-oil salesmanship: "[R]hetoric is part of a practice created not by art but by the habit of a bold and clever mind, which knows how to act in the eyes of the world. I would call it flattery."[3] Plato succeeded in crushing Aristotle's Academy, and the teaching of oral advocacy foundered for a thousand years. Even today, one can see reflections of Plato's skepticism about rhetoric's legitimacy in modern-day critics of the craft.

2. The Harvard Paradox

The fate of rhetoric at Harvard serves as a proxy for what has befallen the teaching of oral persuasion in the American educational system. In 1806, John Quincy Adams became the first "Boylston Professor of Rhetoric and Oratory," promoting oral persuasion as a skill essential to the health of the fledgling democracy. Adams, like Aristotle before him, believed that truth would emerge from the clash of persuasive advocates grappling with public issues. But as time went on, Harvard repeatedly prized the teaching of written advocacy over public speaking, and the Boylston post slowly morphed into a poetry chair.[4] As recently as 2005, Harvard required every student to study writing but offered no public speaking courses, despite student and alumni demand. If this is the story at Harvard, is it any wonder that the teaching of oral advocacy was either largely ignored at other institutions, or worse, held in disdain? (Note that the Harvard story has a happy ending: Recognizing the value in learning through speaking about a subject, Harvard has recently established an oral persuasion curriculum through its Derek Bok Center for Teaching and Learning.[5])

3. The Odd History of Legal Education

During the early years of legal education in America, in the early- to mid-nineteenth century, students were assessed through frequent oral examinations—a practice that makes sense, when one considers that a major part of an attorney's professional life will be spent speaking to clients, to courts, and to colleagues. In the late 1800s, however, law schools began to adopt the case study method created by Dean Christopher Langdell of Harvard, which coupled in-class Socratic questioning with a single, written exam through which the student would be evaluated. This method of teaching allowed one professor to teach large groups of students—a beneficial economic model for law schools. Today, most law students are graded solely on the basis of a single, written, final exam. Many receive little oral advocacy training, except perhaps a few, humiliating "cold calls" in class that often do not affect the student's grade.[6] In 2007, the Carnegie Foundation issued a report evaluating the American system of legal education, and urging law schools to incorporate training in oral advocacy into the curriculum.[7] It remains to be seen how law schools will respond.

4. Expensive to Teach

The Langdellian model of legal education permits one professor to teach hundreds of students at once. Instruction in oral advocacy requires the opposite: a low student–faculty ratio. To be effective, an oral advocacy class must have (1) a teacher schooled in the substance and mechanics of effective advocacy; (2) hands on, one-on-one attention, including videotaping of speeches, and detailed critiquing of performances; and (3) the chance for repetition. At the University of Virginia School of Law, where the authors teach, for example, each of our classes has a 20-student limit so each student can speak and be critiqued in every class. The instruction is time-intensive for both student and professor. A savvy student will seek out any class with an oral advocacy component (which you may find in trial practice classes, seminars, and clinical offerings) because the offerings may be limited at many universities due to the expense of the program. Schools that commit to offering a public speaking program will find that the investment reaps dividends, however, as students in these classes generally have positive experiences and fond memories of their alma maters. An oral advocacy curriculum can help a school recruit stellar admissions candidates and cement ties to satisfied alumni.

5. Who Is to Teach It?

In some institutions, oral advocacy might be taught by "skills" instructors, unschooled in persuasive advocacy, who offer poor counsel. They erroneously contend that quantity of words is the goal; that if the other side makes 31 points, you should make 32. They may inadvertently scar a student by heaping criticism upon criticism with little regard to how quickly a student can progress and improve.

If you are designing a course in oral advocacy, use this book as a guide to help you see what might be improved in a presentation. Try to offer your critique succinctly and kindly. Choose only one or two things to ask the student to improve at each performance. A suggested curriculum can be found at the end of this book in Appendix A.

C. Who Can Learn It?: Excellence Is Within Reach

Students who take the study of rhetoric seriously improve by leaps and bounds in short order. A combination of some tutoring about the building blocks of persuasion and the mechanics of effective delivery pays off quickly, especially for the student who is willing to get back up and try it again. Anyone can learn how to do this. *Anyone.*

We will start with a quick rhetorical education: a primer on what leading scholars through the ages have taught about effective advocacy.

Chapter 2

The Canons
of Persuasion

A. Time-Honored Pillars
of Classical Rhetoric

What do the leading scholars of rhetoric—the masters from ancient Greece and Rome through the present day—teach about effective oral presentation? Despite all the back-and-forth over the centuries about the importance and quality of good rhetoric, much of classical learning has survived intact to inform good presenters today—as it has for centuries. We offer here a modern list of the greatest hits of time-honored rhetoric scholarship. (If you are interested in a brief history of rhetoric, you can find that in Appendix B at the end of the book.)

1. Aristotelian Basics

We start with Aristotle, who emphasized the importance of the following: *Ethos*, *Pathos*, and *Logos*.

Aristotle. Imagno/Hulton Archive/Getty Images

ETHOS. Ethos is about earning trust from listeners.[8] It has three components:

1. I am a good person with values, not a charlatan or snake-oil salesman; therefore, trust me and my cause. Audiences instinctively detect cheap shots, overstatements, and the opposite. So trust me, or even better, like me.

2. I am credible. I know whereof I speak. Therefore, trust my position.

3. I care, but I have not lost my objectivity.

PATHOS. Pathos involves the ability to engage the emotions.[9] Fine speakers know how and when to invoke Pathos. Wonderful refrains like "I have a dream" and "The only thing we have to fear is fear itself," as well as moving stories and anecdotes, demonstrate how Pathos can persuade the audience by stirring emotion.

But the classicists warned against the misuse or overreliance on Pathos. When a speaker relies too heavily on Pathos, or attempts to rip at heartstrings (to the exclusion of minds), the audience may resent it—poof goes the Ethos appeal. That is, the trust between speaker and audience is broken.

If the speaker appears to be driven by emotion, rather than reason, the audience may doubt the speaker's balance and judgment. The speaker's arguments and conclusions are weakened, and the relationship between speaker and audience is compromised. Howard Dean illustrated this point vividly following defeat in the 2004 Iowa Democratic Caucus through a now-famous outburst:

> Not only are we going to New Hampshire . . . we're going to South Carolina and Oklahoma and Arizona and North Dakota and New Mexico, and we're going to California and Texas and New York. And we're going to South Dakota and Oregon and Washington and Michigan. And then we're going to Washington, D.C. to take back the White House. Yeah![10]

By daybreak commentators were afire with the question, "Do you want this finger on the nuclear button? Is he unbalanced?"[11]

Logos. This is the ability to excite the mind with reason.[12] Aristotle believed in the persuasive power of clear, concise presentation of facts and logical arguments.[13] Trial lawyers continue to echo this theme.

While most audiences tune out or become confused by an avalanche of facts or by unintuitive leaps of logic, they respond well to clear logic and a thoughtful presentation of facts. Listeners react positively when a speaker can clearly show why conclusions follow from facts, and what inferences can be made by applying common sense.

The key here is *simplicity* and *clarity*. Aristotle wrote about the force of the **syllogism**,[14] which is simply a major premise ("all dogs are friendly"), then a minor one ("Hugo is a dog"), that leads toward an inevitable conclusion ("Hugo is friendly"). The even simpler **enthymeme**[15] is a syllogism that is so obvious that the speaker need not recite the major and minor premises in order to state the conclusion ("all bald men are handsome").

Rhetoric 101

- Ethos: Inspiring trust

- Pathos: Effective use of emotion

- Logos: Persuading through facts and logic

2. Other Classical Truisms

In addition to Aristotle's famous Ethos/Pathos/Logos trilogy, classical rhetoricians also prized the following:

DELIVERY. Much of the mechanics of distinguished delivery are covered in the following chapters. Suffice it to say that the classicists saw excellent delivery (also known as *pronuntiatio*) as critical to persuasion.[16] Demosthenes spent hours practicing with a mouth full of pebbles to develop vocal power to better project his arguments. Cicero, the great orator, practiced delivery of his orations for hours on end. Aristotle's Academy, the Lyceum, devoted much training to enhancing the effective presentation of the spoken word, distinguishing it from that of written text.

WORDSMITHING. The classicists placed high value on the writing of that which would later, in some form, be delivered orally.[17] While they warned against memorizing or reciting text by rote, they spoke of the importance of concise, powerful writing as an essential part of preparing to deliver an oral argument. The wonderfully crafted sentences, the refrain, the first and last paragraph—these would often be memorized, but then, after much practice, be delivered as if spontaneous.

RESTRAINT. Classicists like Thucydides also warned against ranging too far in presenting propositions for acceptance.[18] The notion here was to ascertain the narrowest set of propositions that must be established to prove a point, to develop those facts fully, and then stop. When speakers wander out on a limb, the audience is likely to react as follows:

- She must need me to accept this dubious new proposition to persuade me, or else she would not have mentioned it;

- I agreed with the initial essence of her point, but I disagree with where she has now taken it; and

- Therefore, I have lost some confidence in both the speaker and her cause, failings of both Ethos and Logos.

The first oral argument in *Roe v. Wade*, the seminal case legalizing abortion, offers a telling illustration of a "bridge too far," the extreme but unnecessary argument. Before a Supreme Court composed of nine male grandfathers, Sarah Weddington opened by arguing that pregnancy was a pretty disturbing matter to a woman. It disrupted her body and her career. It could affect her emotional well-being . . . and so forth.[19]

Weddington needed five votes from elderly men, none of whom, of course, had ever been pregnant themselves, and all of whom had likely experienced the idea of a baby's arrival as a joyous event. It was at the very least a gamble for Weddington to assume that a majority of Justices would accept an argument that pregnancy was a bit distasteful. Ms. Weddington abandoned her initial approach when she argued before the Justices the second time, and prevailed.

3. The Cicero Commandments

Romans, too, were deeply involved in the development of classical rhetoric. Cicero, the greatest orator of his era, claimed that compelling rhetoric relied on five principles:[20]

Cicero. Hulton Archive/Hulton Archive/Getty Images

1. *Invention* (originality, creativity);

2. *Arrangement* (structuring points logically);

3. *Style* (wordsmithing, providing interesting illustrations, using anecdotes);

4. *Memorization* (but delivered as if extemporaneous rather than word-for-word); and

5. *Delivery* (including cadence, pitch, volume, some showmanship).

Most surprising about this surpassingly florid and apparently confident presenter, Cicero was "always very nervous" when speaking. He acknowledged: "I am afraid of seeming either to promise more than I can perform...or to perform less than I can, which suggests bad faith and indifference."[21] He often so panicked that he cancelled speeches or retroactively revised the published text because he did not like what he actually said. His chief legacies were three:

1. Fanatical preparation involving the creation of draft after draft, paying particular attention to structure to get to the point right away, building by thoughtful "arrangement" to a hard-to-resist forceful conclusion;

2. The adroit use of stories, anecdotes, themes, and refrains, all of which helped him to develop a compelling narrative built around the stuff of everyday life and principles; and

3. Elegant, confident delivery.[22]

Cicero was the "story guy." He was famous for his compelling narratives. But he chose his stories carefully to fit his theme. He knew that the thesis would fail if shoehorned into an inapt example.

❖

Many of the most gifted modern-day speakers seem to have studied closely the venerated lessons of classic scholars, or else have rediscovered the truths in these lessons through their own trial and error. Franklin Delano Roosevelt, John F. Kennedy, Martin Luther King, Jr., Ronald Reagan, Bill Clinton, and Barack Obama all on occasion have sounded as if they sprang forth from the classical Academies.

The Cicero Commandments

■ Invention—Creativity

■ Arrangement—Clear, simple structure

■ Style—Memorable

■ Memorization—Only in part

■ Delivery—Cadence and stories

B. The Contribution of Behavioral Psychology

The lessons of psychology have played a central role in modern-day writings about rhetoric and are much imbued in the consciousness of modern practitioners of oral advocacy. These lessons can be distilled into four canons.

THE CANON OF PRIMACY. We are influenced most by first impressions.[23] Is the speaker someone you want to follow for the next 45 minutes? How do you size up the cut of the speaker's jib? Does she seem smug, fast and loose, or arrogant, or does she come across as likable and credible? The first five minutes are critical to a successful speech. It is possible, though a challenge, to retrieve attention after a mediocre start, but nigh impossible after a wretched one.

THE CANON OF FREQUENCY. Most listeners need help to retain your central points. In order to follow and absorb your message, audiences need to hear it more than once, in a non-repetitive fashion.[24] Try reiterating your point at a different juncture in the speech or in a different context, so your audience's eyes do not glaze over.

THE CANON OF VIVIDNESS. We are much more impressed by, and apt to remember, that which we have seen, as well as heard. Three days after a presentation, audiences remember perhaps 10 percent of what they have heard. That same audience will recall approximately one-third of information if it has been presented visually. But if the information is presented both visually and aurally—that is, if the audience sees it as well as hears it—the audience is likely to retain an impressive *two-thirds* of the data.[25] That is why visual aids—PowerPoint, concise notes on an easel, elegant picture boards, animated presentations of actual airplane crash scenes, or the like—are so useful.

But the visual aid must be done well. *Nothing* is more mind-numbing than a 100-slide PowerPoint presentation, delivered with the speaker standing, her back to the audience, regurgitating text.

THE CANON OF RECENCY. Although we are influenced most by what we hear first, we *remember* best what we hear last.[26]

The Canons of Psychology

- Primacy—Start strong.

- Frequency—Make important points twice without sounding repetitive.

- Vividness—65% recall a point that is both seen and heard.

- Recency—What is remembered best.

The first and fourth canons (primacy and recency) are of paramount importance to all speakers: Make a positive first and last impression. Let us have your theme and get a fix on you early. Then end big: Bring it to a close with more powerful prose and an unforgettable conclusion. The end is the time for clarity and power.

❖

Psychologists also focus on four other positive features of memorable oral persuasion, and one word of caution.

PREEMPTION.[27] Preemption means dealing early with opposing points. Especially at trial, but in many other settings as well, you often advocate positions contested by the other side. (For example, does the Second Amendment really include protection for assault weapons?) There is some instinct here to play the ostrich, to avoid the most persuasive aspect of the opposing position, or to unfairly and inaccurately describe it ("Only crazies holed up in compounds or criminals bent on hurting people want assault weapons!"), so that the speaker can lampoon the mischaracterized argument. That would be a mistake for two reasons: First, the audience will mark you down in evaluating your Ethos. Second, you would miss the chance to meet the point head-on and dissuade the audience from accepting the opposing position with the best you have to offer. For inevitably, they will hear the other side, and it may matter to them. So deal with it head-on.

Use Positive Arguments. We usually react more favorably to positive arguments than negative attacks. We tire quickly of the negative; it does not wear well. Positive arguments, taking a fair position, the common sense of favorable public policy implications, get more traction.

Intense Audience Focus. Audiences are challenging animals. They have short attention spans, three or four minutes at a pop. When their minds wander, you have to recapture their lost attention. And most people are "single-path-processors," unable to grasp more than one thought simultaneously.

Pay close attention to the body language of your audience. Exactly what are you asking them to accept? Do you want some immediate action, such as a vote at the ballot box or in the jury room? Are you speaking to celebrate, to inspire, to entertain? How is the audience reacting? Does it seem bored or confused? Pay attention to what you are observing in your audience and be responsive.

Finally, be certain you do not antagonize anyone by taking an extreme position, relying on profanity, resorting to inappropriate jokes, and the like.

Memorable Repetition. As mentioned before, Cicero was the master of telling on-point stories. He made these memorable by choosing an apt theme, perhaps repeating it in a pithy refrain. The psychologists teach the same lesson as Cicero: Repetition works.[28] We see echoes of this in the rhetoric of effective political campaigns—repeated themes and refrains like "Change You Can Believe In," "Yes, We Can," and "Blood, Toil, Tears and Sweat" all spurred people to action.

Beware Danger Zones. Psychologists teach that people communicate as much through body language and tone as through their words. Make sure you are not indirectly communicating something that you do not intend. Anger, sarcasm, arrogance, woodenness, delivering a text by rote, and language tics ("you know," "like," "ahh," "umm") betray lack of confidence and force, not just in the speaker but also in whether the speaker believes in her cause.

C. A Potpourri of the Best of the Rest

Here are other tips of a more "micro" character, all of which are discussed at greater length in subsequent chapters:

PRACTICE. Regular practice in the age-old techniques of effective delivery will make a speaker and his thesis more believable. Practice to find appropriate gestures. Practice to add vocal variety. Practice maintaining good eye contact with your audience. All of these techniques will become second-nature with practice. See Chapter 5 for more about the importance of rehearsal.

SIMPLICITY. Human beings generally have short attention spans and can digest only a single point at a time. Do not ask your audience to process multiple points at the same time. Instead, design your presentation with a simple, clear structure.

ENGAGING PERSONA. We tend to be influenced in our views of people and their causes by whether we like them or not.[29] Would we like to go to dinner with the speaker? Does she sound mind-numbingly boring? Even the speaker who knows full well what she is going to say, owing to rigorous preparation and knowledge of the subject, is more likely to be persuasive if the speaker is also engaging, warm, conversational, trustworthy, even funny. But be careful about misguided attempts at humor. A story that does not fit or is off-color can spell disaster. What do you do when no one laughs at your joke? Self-deprecating humor usually engages, but too much can be grating.

VISUAL AIDS. Good visual aids command attention. They offer your audience a chance to look at something else or (in the case of video clips) hear a different voice. Graphics can revive interest and, if done well, can be persuasive. (More about this appears in Chapter 7.)

POWER. In analyzing drafts of oral presentations, it is essential to focus intently on the *locus of the power of your thesis*. Where do points of real persuasion come in? Where does the speech "pop"? Are you certain the beginning and end will both command attention and move toward acceptance of your position?

Find an occasion to walk away from the podium to punctuate important points in your speech. Use the dramatic pause to set up an important point or topic sentence. Know when to use so-called "power gestures"—for example, reaching both hands toward the audience for emphasis, perhaps at the conclusion of the presentation. It may be that the single factor elevating the distinguished over the pedestrian speech is that the former has punch, maybe even a "wow" factor, and the latter, a reaction of "so...who speaks next?," as you review the program. (See Chapter 5 for more ideas.)

VARIETY. Almost all distinguished speakers use a *variety* of rhetorical devices to capture the audience's attention or regain it if it flags. Sometimes they use humor; sometimes gravitas; at other times, a variety of physical gestures; and of course cadence and volume. Be aware of your cadence; vary it to add power to a presentation. Modulate the speed of your delivery (which for most speakers means slow down). Use gestures to communicate. The speaker needs to offer variety in order to keep our interest.

BEWARE THE PODIUM AND THE WRITTEN-OUT TEXT. These are tempting, yet ineffective, security blankets. Hands clinging to the podium rarely gesture. Eyes cast down repeatedly at a text detract from the audience's confidence in the speaker and the speaker's points. It can also make the speech harder for the audience to understand. The exercise of turning the written piece into the spoken word is a critical step in the process of finally delivering a compelling speech. Bullet points to prompt memory should be enough at the platform. (See Chapter 5 for a fuller discussion.)

Chapter 3

The Rainbow of Rhetorical Formats

"This is going to be prose, and not poetry."

PRESIDENT BARACK OBAMA'S REMARKS ON THE ECONOMY,
GEORGETOWN UNIVERSITY, APRIL 14, 2009[30]

While the fundamentals of effective advocacy that we have just covered remain true no matter the type of speech, there is yet more that a speaker must take into account when preparing a *particular* speech for a *particular* audience. The speaker must consider the following questions:

- What exactly is my *goal* for the speech as a whole and for each segment of it? Is it supposed to inspire, or to thoughtfully persuade by clear logic and facts? Does it lay out a roadmap for action? If I intend to achieve more than one of these goals, in what order should I make my appeals, and how much emphasis do I give each one?

- How do I devote enough time to maximizing audience attention, while at the same time establishing certain chief points?

- Given the makeup of this particular audience, should the tone and structure of my talk be formal, or is it more important to project warmth and a relaxed demeanor?

27

- Should the points I make be almost exclusively positive, or does my cause require some clear and firm rebuttal?

The point is that oral advocacy comes in a variety of flavors. A State of the Union speech and a family discussion of a problem are different enterprises in fundamental ways. They differ, for instance, in their goals, style, strategy, tone, and length. The ultimate challenge facing the great speaker is to be flexible and comfortable enough to adjust to each setting and audience. That asks a lot of an oral advocate but, as we have discussed, it is achievable with practice, thought, and guidance.

A. Prepared Speeches

Aristotle divided the essential purpose of prepared presentations into three types: the *epideictic* speech, the *deliberative* speech, and the *forensic* speech, each of which is described more fully below.[31] The goals, strategies, and styles of these three types of speech differ one from the other. In other words, the three categories of speech do different work, and the able advocate will recognize this. These are not airtight containers. An advocate might mix and match the categories, perhaps beginning with one style of speech and then moving into another. The skilled speaker will keep in mind his exact goal and select the best way to achieve it in each point of each speech.

The Three Types of Prepared Speeches

- Epideictic—to inspire

- Deliberative—to teach systematically

- Forensic—to convince

1. The Epideictic or Inspirational Speech

This is what the President meant by "poetry" in the quote that begins this chapter. The epideictic address is designed to inspire. Examples of this speech include celebratory occasions, like the Fourth of July, ceremonies, and other occasions of this sort. The goal of this class of rhetoric is to unify listeners, to bring them together; it is less concerned with changing people's minds.[32]

Most memorable speeches contain an epideictic element:

- Lincoln's Gettysburg Address ("Four Score and Seven Years Ago")[33] and his Second Inaugural Address[34] were aimed at reuniting the country. They were calm, reflective, and lyrical. See Part Four for more on the Second Inaugural.

Abraham Lincoln. Hulton Archive/Hulton Archive/Getty Images

- Obama's "Yes, We Can" speech, inspiring faith in the future, reverberated throughout the land during campaign season.[35] It was a masterpiece featuring superb cadence, gestures, and the powerful theme of hope. This speech is discussed more fully in Chapter 5.

- Reagan's Normandy speech[36] and other speeches (as well as his ads)[37] projected calm. They employed memorable phrases and effective pauses. The Normandy speech is dealt with in detail in Part Four.

■ Churchill's many speeches before we entered World War II ("Blood, Toil, Tears, and Sweat"[38] and the like) were designed to boost morale. As Edward R. Murrow memorably said: "He mobilized the English language and sent it into battle [against the Nazis]."[39] Churchill's speeches were marked by unforgettable phrasing and calm, but powerful, delivery. See Part Four for a fuller discussion.

Winston Churchill. Popperfoto/Popperfoto/Getty Images

■ Martin Luther King, Jr.'s "I Have a Dream" speech[40] had the obvious goal of achieving racial justice. It was a classic case of cadence and refrains, as was his "I've Been to the Mountain-top" speech, discussed in Part Four.

In classic rhetorical terms, the epideictic speech has these characteristics:

■ It relies very heavily on careful *wordsmithing* and superb *delivery.*

■ *Ethos* is a central component.

■ It is the most *rehearsed* of the forms of prepared presentation.

So *when* do we use epideictic advocacy?

■ We often use it at the beginning and end of speeches.

■ We use it when we tell stories, tell anecdotes, talk to our family. See "The Cicero Commandments," in Chapter 2.

■ We use it at inherently emotional times such as at funerals or at a couple's 50th Anniversary celebration.

■ We use it for emphasis, in an attempt to inspire *adherence* to, rather than mere *acceptance* of, a point.[41]

■ We use it when we reach out to make amends—when we are being conciliatory.

The epideictic is a necessary part of any fine advocate's rhetorical arsenal, but some words of warning here. Epideictic advocacy can backfire:

■ If it is overused.

■ If people think that the speaker is being phony.

■ If it conveys the impression that the speaker has lost emotional control (such as Howard Dean's outburst after losing the Iowa Caucus[42]).

■ If thought to be designed to incite mischief (as Plato cautioned, discussed more fully in Chapter 15).

Ironically, the more powerful and moving the use of the epideictic, the more it can backfire by incensing opponents. Probably nothing infuriated conservative radio personalities more than Obama's "Yes, We Can" speech. But that does *not* mean you should never use it—after all, most commentators concluded that "Yes, We Can" was a signal success. Just watch out for using it too much. To continue the example, Obama has been extremely careful in subsequent speeches not to rely on his epideictic skills too frequently, lest he erode his credibility.

2. Deliberative Advocacy

"Deliberative" or "prose" speeches are principally designed to assess policy issues to guide future action, to teach, or to lay out a case. If epideictic advocacy is meant to *inspire*, deliberative advocacy is meant to *persuade* by facts and by logic. Presentations by great college professors, such as W.H. Auden's famous lectures about Shakespeare, are examples of deliberative advocacy.

At its essence, the deliberative speech should be

■ Clear;

■ As "simple as possible, but not simpler," as Einstein once said;[43]

■ Calm and unhurried;

■ Balanced and objective in tone, dealing thoroughly and fairly with opposing views;

■ Focused on Ethos to demonstrate the speaker's lack of bias, his knowledge of the subject, and his conviction; and

■ Long on Logos; often fact- and statistics-laden for credibility and clarity.

There are at least three warnings for the deliberative presentation:

1. Avoid the boring. The authors recently attended an address by a highly decorated professor who read every word of his deliberative effort and literally put five people to sleep.

2. Beware of long or complicated speeches.

3. Do not slant facts or arguments.

3. Forensic/Legal Advocacy

"Forensic" or "legal" speeches are sometimes backward-looking speeches designed to ascertain what happened and what we should do about it. Other forensic advocacy looks to future action: What do all of your points add up to and where do we go from here? In general, forensic or legal advocacy is the *resolution* segment of a speech. The best example of the forensic or legal speech is found in a trial, in which an attorney will speak about whether to convict or acquit a defendant.

A forensic speech involves a fairly equal mix of Logos, Ethos, and Pathos. The speaker's credibility (or Ethos) is of paramount significance, particularly in a long trial. So is the speaker's ability to project the Pathos of fair play, justice, the sought result, and the force of his logic.

The danger zones in a forensic speech are

- It can rely on overly complicated logic.
- It can project the values of the snake-oil salesman.
- It tends toward overstatement and misstatement.

❖

While different, each of the types of speech described above requires intense preparation, clarity, and effective delivery. You need to be clear about what style to use in order to fulfill the goals of your speech, and when you need to shift from one kind of speech to the other. In other words, the style of speech you choose should support your goals—as they change, so should your speech.

Barack Obama and his head speechwriter, Jon Favreau, are masters at matching their goals to the appropriate style of speech. Obama's June 6, 2009, D-Day speech[44] was largely powerful, evocative epideictic. His Philadelphia race speech[45] bore some of the epideictic approach, merging with deliberative persuasion; the Notre Dame abortion presentation[46] was quite deliberative; the Egypt speech[47] was heavy on deliberation and resolution (both sides have shaping up to do, and there *must* be a two-state resolution). His most significant Afghanistan speech[48] was virtually all deliberative. His Nobel Peace Prize acceptance speech[49] displayed mastery of all three.

Although Obama is usually at his best in oral endeavors, even skilled advocates like him sometimes stumble with their choice of rhetorical format. Consider his first Oval Office address on June 15, 2010, dealing with the oil spill by British Petroleum and the country's dependence on foreign sources of energy. Viewers, angered over the recent spill, were eager to hear some ardor from the President, but came away largely disappointed. The speech was lambasted, even by those favorably disposed to Obama and his policies, for being too bland and lacking in specifics.[50] President Obama thus may have strayed too far from the inspirational epideictic and into the pure, colorless, deliberative mode of speech.

B. Speeches That Are a Mixture of Prepared and Quizzed Presentations

Most common here are presentations involving a question-and-answer period, press conferences, presentations to bosses or Boards of Directors, government hearings, and the like. See Chapter 11 for a discussion of this sort of presentation in court.

There is often an up-front prepared statement, usually short. The tricky part is answering questions that follow, whether they emanate from hostile or friendly quarters. To succeed in this, keep in mind the following:

1. Answer the question head-on first, then explain. The speaker should never say, "I'll get to that later."

2. Be brief—If the questioner wants more, he will say so.

3. Keep it simple—A straightforward speech is easier for a speaker to deliver, and also easier for a listener to digest. Simplicity also helps to minimize the force of interruptions, compelling discipline in one's responses to audience questions. A simple speech also saves time—no longer does an advocate have to constantly check the clock out of fear that she has gone on for too long.

4. Candor—Don't fight the obvious. Concede what you must. Then explain why that conceded point is outweighed by other considerations.

5. Anticipate questions—Study lists of most likely questions, and practice with a mock Q&A session with colleagues.

6. Be selective—Prioritize the most important points; pay attention to credibility. It is equally crucial to be selective in *quantity*; otherwise one may induce sleep by rattling on about more than folks want to hear (which diffuses one's main points).

7. Admit when you do not have the answer.

8. Make certain you understand the question, especially the garbled one.

The Three Common Settings

- Prepared—Address to a court; presentation about a cause

- Q&A—Short, prepared remarks followed by responses to questions

- Informal—Relaxed, conversational exchange

C. Informal Presentations

Most of us engage in informal "presentations," such as group discussions, panels, committee meetings, or meetings with friends or family. Such exercises require mastery of two qualities: human relations skills, plus proficiency in oral communication. What follows is a list of the top ten tips for speaking informally:

1. All speech of this nature invites some preparation, usually extensive.

2. Ethos—trust in the speaker—is important. It is necessary to appear genuine.

3. Usually it is more effective when these remarks are "natural," uncanned.

4. Projecting warmth is rewarded.

5. Cooperative tone matters.

6. The ability to compromise—the ability to "disagree without being disagreeable"—is often required.

7. Use of humor, especially self-effacing, sometimes is engaging.

8. Expressions of praise for others is helpful where it is warranted.

9. Modesty is usually engaging and successful.

10. Asking questions shows your interest in others' point of view.

Part Two

Getting from Here to There

The task of speaking well involves more than simply understanding the goals of persuasion as taught by the masters of classical rhetoric. That basic grounding is essential, but an equally vital step is to translate those lessons into action. *How* do you achieve Ethos, Pathos, and Logos? Part Two will take you through the nuts and bolts of writing a persuasive speech and delivering it well.

Chapter 4

Writing the Spoken Word

You sit waiting to hear a speech. The speaker rises nervously, clutching notes, and scurries to the stage, to the safety of the podium. She fixes her gaze firmly upon her papers, and this is what you hear:

The presence of Polonium-210 in tobacco is of particular concern because it is one of the most radioactive isotopes, and even a very small dose can have devastating consequences. An extremely rare metalloid that occurs naturally in Uranium ores, Polonium was discovered in 1898 by Marie and Pierre Curie and named for her homeland of Poland. It has several radioactive isotopes, the most common of which is Polonium-210 (^{210}Po), an alpha emitter, which means that it releases a high-energy Helium ion (^{4}He) in its radioactive decay. Alpha radiation is innocuous so long as it remains outside the body, but internally alpha particles are, generally speaking, the most hazardous form of radiation. Polonium-210 is a product of the natural Uranium-238 decay series; the parent isotopes include Radium-226,

Radon-222, and Lead-210. Polonium-210 itself decays to the stable isotope Lead-206 (plus an alpha particle). The isotope has a half-life of 138 days, which is short when compared to the 4.5 billion–year and 1,600-year half-lives of Uranium-238 and Radium-226, respectively. Its short half-life means that the isotope is very "hot," emitting alpha particles at a rapid rate. And since smokers are exposing themselves to new doses with each cigarette, a constant cycle of exposure and decay is played out in the lung.[51]

This is fine academic writing, but difficult to process if you are hearing rather than reading it. The scientific terminology is tough to understand; the sentences are very long; the words are hard to pronounce. Now imagine the speech again, but this time it proceeds as follows:

Would you brush your teeth with Uranium or drink a glass of the stuff every morning with breakfast? Of course not. But every day, millions of people voluntarily expose themselves to toxic radiation by lighting up a cigarette. Cigarettes contain a radioactive isotope called "Polonium-210." It emits a kind of radiation that is harmless outside the body. But if it gets *into* the body—if you suck it into your lungs by inhaling it through a cigarette—you expose yourself to one of the most deadly forms of radiation out there.

Which speech would you rather hear? Which would you rather say?

Here is the point—a speech is not an essay. Writing for speaking is wholly distinct from writing for reading. If you compose a text that is meant to be read, then you know your reader can take it slowly, reread the part she did not understand, look up an unfamiliar word, take notes, and retrace it until she gets it. But writing meant to be spoken takes a different shape. The listener must get it the first and only time around. A speech has to be sufficiently *interesting* so that we want to expend the energy required to get it in our heads; *clear enough* that we can understand it; and *simple* enough to show how the ideas are connected.

At its most basic level, a speech should have three clear parts—beginning, middle, and end. Each does different work.

A. The Beginning

Your beginning needs to grab the attention of the audience. Its purpose is to orient audience members to the type of speech yours will be and why they should listen to it. Audiences tend to decide during the first 30 seconds of a speech whether they want to continue to listen, so you need to give some thought to why your audience should care about what you are saying.

Listeners need a way into your topic. Give them a reason to want to connect with your words.

Often, the "way in" will be whatever is most interesting about your topic. Ask yourself, *why do I like this topic? What made me want to discuss it?* That should give you some sense of why your audience might like to hear it as well.

Suppose you are speaking to a group of law students. You want to encourage them to clerk for a judge after graduation. If you look at the website of the University of Virginia School of Law and fashion your speech based on what you see there, it might start something like, "During the 2008-2009 court year, 51 members of the Class of 2008 clerked for judges. Fourteen of them clerked for judges on the United States Courts of Appeals; 34 of them clerked for United States District Court judges; and 3 of them clerked for state court judges."

If you lead like that, you will have your audience dozing in no time.

Instead, why not reach for the most interesting aspects of the job, perhaps harkening back to your own days as a judicial law clerk if, in fact, you have been one?

> Imagine a job like this. You are the right-hand man (or woman) to one of the most powerful people in the United States—a federal judge. You are the one the judge consults with when he's puzzling over difficult cases. You spend your time crafting judicial opinions that will have an immediate, direct impact on people's lives. You sit in on trials and oral arguments; you meet prosecutors and police officers (just like in *Law and Order*); partners at law firms butter you up; newspapers call you but you decline to speak with them because there's a media relations office to handle that. And you are only 25 years old. That's what it is like to be a judicial law clerk.

That is an opening more interesting to listen to, and easier to deliver.

Take the time to craft a strong, catchy beginning. It can also help assuage stage fright and improve your performance. If you know your opening is strong—that your talk begins with, for instance, an entertaining anecdote—then you can start off with confidence. Your audience *will* pay attention, and you will think to yourself, "Hey, this is going pretty well!"

Wonderful things can happen after a strong start.

B. The Middle

The middle is where the work is done. It is where you make your argument, support your points, and teach your audience. Here is one thing to keep in mind, however: When your audience does not understand you, it will stop listening. To make it understandable, the middle of your speech must be clear. In order for it to be clear, a complicated idea or process needs to be broken down into its simpler elements.

1. Simplify Your Structure

Your structure needs to be clear and logical for an audience to reasonably and readily hear and digest it. The speech that begins, "I've just got three points" is going to be much more successful than the one that tries to tackle 20.

Remember, the brain can only hold so much—three points are about all we can manage, maybe four, five only on a really good day.

But, you say, "I have a hundred things that I need to cover in this talk!"

Okay, don't panic. Here's what you do:

a. Group your points into themes.

Can you organize your various topics or points into a few main ideas? For example, if you were talking about this section of the book, you might want to say you are going to talk about (1) a speech's beginning; (2) the middle; and (3) the end. Within each of those categories you will aggregate several sub-points, but giving your audience the bigger structure of just three big topics makes an otherwise unwieldy topic more manageable.

b. Delete what you do not need.

You may know everything from soup to nuts about your topic, but if you tell us all that you know, you will either bore us or irritate us. Think of the most dull lecture you ever endured in college. Imagine what that lecture might have been like had the professor cut the minutiae, the digressions that he thought sounded weighty—all of the overwhelming bits of information that no one could possibly be expected to retain.

As a speaker, you must resist the temptation to blather on too much—if that is what you are doing, then you are talking to and for yourself and not for the audience. Instead, think of yourself as a gardener weeding out the bits of superfluous grass in order to clear away the pattern of the garden underneath. Try this: Write a list of the bare minimum of what you need to say in order to prove your point, and then concentrate on saying only that. Leave the rest for the question-and-answer session that is likely to follow any great speech.

Lawyers make the mistake of overloading oral presentations with too much information all the time. A lawyer is likely to have crammed the kitchen sink into his written brief, in an effort to anticipate and rebut every argument the other side might make. The brief is chockablock with footnotes and case citations. The day for oral argument arrives. If that lawyer marches into court and proceeds to slog through all of those footnotes, the judge's eyes will glaze over.

The judge wants to know *who should win the verdict*, not who has the most footnotes in his brief. So what the lawyer needs to do in oral argument is to provide the most streamlined argument in support of his proposition that he possibly can. The judge can read the footnotes on his own time if she chooses.

c. Outline the argument.

Outlining can be a useful way of organizing your speech. It should look something like this:

    I. First point
      A. Support
      B. Support
      C. Support

    II. Second point
      A. Support
      B. Support
      C. Support, etc.

Going through this exercise shows visually whether your thoughts are grouped together logically.

If instead you start one thought, then sort of drift off into a second thought without finishing the first, and then finally ten minutes later get around to finishing the first thought, here is the result: Some will have heard the beginning of the thought but will have tuned out before you finally get to the end, so they will not understand your point. Others will be distracted when you began the thought and will not have heard it. Now they hear the conclusion, unsure how you arrived at it. And yet another group was distracted by the digression in the middle, and is not sure whether that is key or whether it was the original thought that merited most attention. When writing for speaking, you need to start and end your thought in the same passage so there is no confusion. An example:

[The right way]: "Snacks are important for small children. Their stomachs are smaller than adults' stomachs are, so they cannot eat as much food at meals as adults can. That's why they are likely to get hungry in between meals, before an adult might. So it is important for a caregiver to have healthy snacks on hand mid-morning and mid-afternoon in order to tide the children over. If you do not, you may have a tearful toddler on your hands."

[The wrong way]: "Snacks are important for small children. They get hungry between meals—well, really, who doesn't? Haven't we all had the experience of sitting in a class or a meeting and suddenly your stomach is growling and you sort of look around hoping that people will think it is someone else's stomach, not yours? I sometimes will close a notebook with a bang or start typing more frantically on my laptop in order to cover up the noise! So that's why you need to feed kids snacks."

A Suggested Plan for Writing a Speech

- Brainstorm. Write down everything you think you might want to cover in your talk.

- Cluster. Group your ideas into a few "themes" (aim for three).

- Cull. Delete what you don't need.

- Sharpen. Hone your logic through outlining; begin to rehearse aloud to make sure ideas flow logically.

- Tighten language. Use words you can pronounce; eliminate jargon.

- Highlight important points through stories, metaphors, refrains, sensory language, or taking more time to explain the idea.

- Craft the beginning. Orient the audience; grab its attention.

- Craft the ending. Deliver the important point one last time. Often refers back to the beginning.

d. Brainstorming and culling.

Here is a helpful exercise: Write the first draft of your script by dumping thoughts onto the page, without worrying about censoring them or worrying about tight logic. Just get it out so that you have a start, and write it so that it sounds like the way that you speak, or like a letter to a friend.

Next, *cull*—cross out all information unnecessary to make your point. Then wade through it *again* and outline the speech as it stands. Check to see whether any thoughts that ought to be grouped together are not and then reorder them if necessary. Good writing is rewriting—by this time, you have probably written three drafts already. Going through multiple drafts also helps you start to memorize your text.

e. Dwell on the most important points.

We need time to process your most significant points. It is not enough just to race through checklists of three (or four or ten or twelve) points you intend to make—if you said it but we did not get it, it is as if you never said it at all. Instead, heed the old aphorism of public speaking: "Tell them what you're going to say, say it, and then tell them what you said." Scan your outline and pick the top three points that you want to make. Circle them. Now make sure to spend the bulk of your time on these, persuading as to each.

You can do this in various ways. You can start in an introductory section by saying that you are going to tell us these three points, then tell us about them in the middle, and then remind us once again at the end that this is what you have talked about.

Another approach is to take time in the middle of your speech to support/illustrate each of your points with examples. Letting the audience work through your examples bolsters your argument. It also gives your audience time to process your point in a way so that it will stick.

Instead of examples, you might choose to use an analogy, anecdote, metaphor, sensory language (language that evokes the senses, such as "the salty smell of the ocean"), themes, or refrains. (The next subsection says more about each of those devices.)

2. Simplify Your Language

Language must be simple enough to be understandable, but vivid enough to engage and make an impression on the listener. This requires yet more drafts. Here is what to look for:

a. Keep sentences straightforward.

Your audience must be able to follow what you are saying without having to pause to diagram the sentence to figure it out. Forget about all that you learned in high school English class about making sentences complex. Instead, think: subject, verb, object. Vary this pattern only when something requires a more complex treatment in the interest of clarity or precision. It is much easier for audiences to process plain sentences that proceed in a straight line rather than those that twirl around on themselves, so that one loses the head of the thought by the time one reaches the tail.

b. Strive to keep sentences short.

Short sentences are easier to deliver because

- There is a natural place to take a breath (at the end of the sentence);

- It gives you a spot at which to pause (also at the end of the sentence); and

- It suggests a place to vary your pitch, pace, and volume (as you start the next sentence).

There is power in the short, punchy sentence. Try delivering these two paragraphs out loud, the first of which has sentences that go on and on, and the second of which has straightforward, short sentences:

> *[Overly complex sentences]:* Samuel Langhorne Clemens, better known by his pen name of Mark Twain, was a prominent American humorist, writing during the mid-to-late 19th and early 20th centuries. Throughout the early days of his career he wrote newspaper articles and travel logs, which documented his adventures from his travels as a young man to the American west, the western frontier, and Hawaii and about his extensive travel around the world from the salons of Europe to the Dead Sea and beyond. His books, which included *The Adventures of Tom Sawyer, The Adventures of Huckleberry Finn,* and *The Prince and the Pauper,* became wildly popular with many critics as well

as common citizens who ordered his books in droves via a subscription service.

[Simple sentences]: Mark Twain was one of the best loved writers of his day. He started his career by writing newspaper articles about his travels. He wrote about his adventures all over the world, from California to Calcutta. But we love him most for his books. *The Adventures of Huckleberry Finn, The Adventures of Tom Sawyer,* or *The Prince and the Pauper*—these stories made him famous. These are stories to remember.

So this is your fourth draft—look at your script, find sentences that are longer than a line or two and cut them in half. Try confining yourself to one thought per sentence. Do not string sentences together. Let each sentence stand on its own. Your authority and presence rise measurably with this simple adjustment.

c. Use sensory language.

Listeners will remember what they can feel, hear, taste, touch, and smell. If you tell your story using language that evokes these senses in your audience's imagination, they will remember what you have said much longer. Compare these two paragraphs, the second invoking sensory language:

[No sensory language]: Ladies and gentlemen of the jury, we are here today because Mr. Jackson burned down his factory. He did this because he needed money, and he thought he could get it from his fire insurance policy. That policy is a contract between Mr. Jackson and the first insurance company. He hasn't upheld his end of the contract, though, because he agreed in that contract not to burn down his building.

[Sensory language]: Ladies and gentlemen of the jury, let me take you back to the night of November 1 of last year. On that night, the evening was cool, so Allison Hanson decided to take her dog for a walk. As she walked along,

she could smell the crisp, fall air and hear the leaves crunching beneath her feet. But when she turned onto River Road, she noticed something new. She didn't just smell the cool air anymore—she could smell smoke. And she could hear something, too—a crackling, and then a huge, frightening, crashing sound. And then she saw it. Mr. Jackson's factory was burning down. It was swallowed in huge, red and orange flames. The smoke made Allison's eyes itch and burn, but she will tell you that she could see that the fire was huge. She could feel it, and it was hot. It frightened her.

When you are looking for the right place in which to insert sensory language, seek the point that seems most important to you. What is the idea you most want us to remember? That is where to stop and spend some time explaining the point. That is a wise time to insert sensory language, to give us a chance to digest the idea.

d. Use themes and refrains.

"Ask not what your country can do for you; ask what you can do for your country." "I have a dream." "If the glove doesn't fit, you must acquit." "Yes, we can." We remember these themes and refrains because they sound good; they are catchy; they are short; they encapsulate the point. They roll off the tongue.

Martin Luther King, Jr. Consolidated News Pictures/Hulton Archive/Getty Images

If you can think of a vivid, crisp way to articulate your main point in about ten words or less, you have the makings of a fine refrain. A refrain will stick in your audience's memory long after the speech ends.

If you decide to use a theme or refrain, make sure you emphasize it through your delivery. Do not say it like it embarrasses you—have fun with it. In order to deliver a refrain with conviction and confidence, you must feel comfortable with it. It has to feel right to you. You must work from the core of your own experience. For example, in his famous "Yes, We Can" speech, Barack Obama refers to slavery, Martin Luther King, Jr., and John F. Kennedy, and he does so in the cadences of a preacher. President Obama can reference these things because he has a connection to all of those influences in his personal background.

As you write the script, look to personal influences, to your core. Do you have a Southern lilt or Brooklyn-ese in your background? That might help you find the right pattern for your refrain. Use it.

e. Choose the $1 word instead of the $10 word.

Often in academic and legal writing, we feel an urge to choose the most complicated word in order to telegraph intelligence and authority. That is absolutely the wrong call in public speaking. If you choose fancy over a plainly spoken word, you will run into problems.

First, the fancy word is often hard to pronounce. Try it yourself—"He overly utilized barking out multisyllabic words," versus "The guy just never tired of great, big words."

Second, if you reach for the fancy word, you run the risk that people will not follow. Some will not know what the word means, and those people will miss your point. Some might be able to guess the meaning from the context, but they may feel annoyed that you are talking above them, or feel left out of the conversation, like they do not have a right to be there, since they are not sure of the vocabulary. Others will know what the word means but will have to pause to remember the precise definition. In that moment you have lost them. Once you lose attention, even briefly, it is difficult to retrieve it. So why say "exogenously" when you could say "outside of"? Why ever describe something as "discursive" instead of "rambling"?

Also be wary of jargon. Instead of using an acronym, for example, use the full version of the title. Try to replace terms of art with plain English. If you must use jargon—for example, if the whole point of your talk is to teach the audience new terms—consider writing the unfamiliar term on a blackboard with a definition, leaving the visual aid visible throughout your talk. That permits others to glance at the unfamiliar word and understand it without losing the flow of your comments.

f. Use analogies, anecdotes, and metaphors.

A personal story, well told, can bring your speech to life. Audiences care more about stories than they do about dry facts or lifeless theories.

Be careful when using metaphors or telling stories that they are appropriate and support your point. Forgo the interesting story that does not actually belong. Otherwise, the audience will walk away thinking, well, that was a good story, but what did it have to do with global warming (or the price of tea or whatever your topic might be)? The audience might say, *Gee, I really enjoyed that story about his first day in kindergarten,* never realizing that there was a greater significance to your talk. Your cute story must *support* your point, not upstage it.

Also, stick to only *one* story or metaphor. If you have more, the audience will try to unravel the web of analogies and may lose you. For example:

> Ladies and gentlemen this reminds me of a childhood accident. I was running through my house and I broke my mother's favorite plate, which stood on our table in

the front hall. I desperately fumbled with the pieces trying to put them back together, but those pieces would not fit. In this case, the pieces just don't fit together. And just like a house on stilts, when one support leg fails the entire house topples over. This case has lost its support legs and is falling into the sea. And it is your job ladies and gentlemen to see through this house of cards. . . .

What a mess.

Be careful not to overplay the Pathos card. If the subject of your story is parallel to the point of your argument, then you will have us enthralled. But if your tangential story is about a child dying or a similar tragedy, the audience may think and resent that you are trying to manipulate emotions rather than make your case.

So in addition to simplifying logic and sentence structure, you have now learned that you need to make yet another round of edits for *word choice.* Look for spots to add sensory language. Consider adding a theme or refrain. Use plainspoken words. Strip away the jargon. Look for the opportunity to add one perfect story that supports and illustrates your main thesis or strongest point.

C. The End

The finale leaves a lasting impression, and, fairly or not, can make or break your speech. If you end with a bang rather than a whimper, we will disregard that flub in the middle where you forgot your place and became tongue-tied. If you swallow your ending and slink off the stage, seemingly embarrassed about the whole enterprise, then we will think, "Well, *that* didn't go very well, and clearly he didn't know a thing about what he was supposed to be talking about."

The close is your chance to make your chief point one last time. In order to do that, you need to be razor-clear on how to say it. You should be able to distill your most important point into a single sentence, and you should also be able to say *what it has to do with us.*

Is your main point, "Throw that lying, cheating scumbag in jail"? Is it, "Start recycling, now!"? Or is it, "That's why this part of contracts law works the way it does, and now that you understand that, you'll be able to understand something really interesting that we will grapple with next week—stay tuned"?

Whatever you want us to take away from your speech—what we should have learned, or what you want us to do—that should be made abundantly clear to us in this final moment.

We said right off that it is of paramount importance to start your speech with a bang. It is equally important to write a compelling close so that you know how to exit gracefully and with force. Even if it's as simple as, "Look, here's the point. Think about adopting a dog. It'll do you a world of good."—that can be delivered with confidence and conviction. And then we will know that you are finished and it is time for us to applaud.

Chapter 5

Hallmarks of Distinguished Delivery: Bringing a Speech to Life

You have written a dazzling script:

- You have the right topic.
- Your beginning really grabs the listener and your ending delivers a knock-out punch.
- You have edited the text to a few central points.
- Your thoughts are grouped logically.
- You have devoted the right space to important points, taking more time to explain complicated things or things you want the audience to remember.
- Your writing style is straightforward and concise.
- You use short sentences and plain English.
- You have made excellent use of sensory language and anecdotes to make your speech vivid.

What now? *Put the script down.*

You will want to do more with your script than simply bury your face in notes and read them. You risk boring the audience, and you will not have achieved your goal of convincing them. It is not enough to write out even wise thoughts and then recite them into air—if we do not listen and understand, it is the same as a speech never given.

To score points, you must sound like a human being—like yourself. The more relaxed and confident you are, the more confidence your audience will have in you. You will draw them into the story, and they will want to listen to you.

But here is the challenge—public speaking is not a natural act for most of us. It is about as unnatural as it gets. There you are, standing up in front of a crowd that is studying you more intensely than in ordinary conversation (where such intense staring would be rude). The paradox: You must sound conversational, but of course this is not a conversation.

In conversational discourse, you do not think about what to do with your hands and feet. When you give a speech, suddenly your feet take off wandering and your hands feel bigger than garbage can lids and you don't know where to put them.

In normal conversation, the voice has different notes—few people naturally speak in a monotone. You rarely think, in conversation, about meaningful pauses or varying your volume. In contrast, when you give a speech, your voice box can freeze up, and suddenly, there you are, squeaking along on that one note, stuck at one volume level, racing through your speech at a single pace as fast as you possibly can.

So what to do?

Actors confront this problem regularly. The following is a simple method many actors use when trying to determine how to "act" a monologue that can be helpful when trying to perform a speech of your own.

A. Break It into Beats

Imagine an actress tackling a monologue. This actress is auditioning to play a high school student who has just failed an exam. She has been handed the script for an audition and has only 15 minutes to parse it and figure out how to deliver it.

She squirrels herself away in a corner. She takes up her pen and begins to look for "beats," or chunks of action. She is trying to figure out where her character changes course or perceives a new emotion—where the "beats" are. What is the character thinking as she speaks, and how do those emotions differ? A beat is the smallest unit of action in a play, and once the actress knows where the beats are, she begins to understand the structure of the script with which she is working. Here is her script:

> I can't believe I flunked again! Mom is going to kill me! I know—maybe I just won't tell her. No, that'll never work—Mom knows my teacher because they're in the same aerobics class. She'll definitely find out in the end. Well, I guess I'll just bite the bullet and tell her.

The auditioning actress must first decide what is going on with the mood of the character. First she's freaked out—panicked—that is, "I can't believe I flunked again! Mom is going to kill me!" But in the next line, "I know—maybe I just won't tell her," she thinks she has come up with a solution to the problem. That is a new beat. Her intention has shifted—she isn't just panicking; she's going to make the problem disappear.

The next beat is, "No, that'll never work—Mom knows my teacher because of aerobics class. She'll definitely find out in the end." That is distinct from what came before; now she is rejecting the idea that seemed promising a second ago.

And then the final beat, "Well, I guess I'll just bite the bullet and tell her." She decides to fess up. That is yet another beat.

You have beats in the speeches that you deliver as well. Let's return to the script from Chapter 4. Here is the cigarette speech, broken into three beats:

Would you brush your teeth with uranium or drink a glass of radium every morning with breakfast? Of course not.

But every day, millions of people voluntarily expose themselves to toxic radiation by lighting up a cigarette. Cigarettes contain a radioactive isotope called "Polonium-210." It emits a kind of radiation that is harmless outside the body.

But if it gets *into* the body—if you suck it into your lungs by inhaling it through a cigarette, you expose yourself to one of the most deadly forms of radiation out there.

Back to our actress. She has made initial decisions about those beats. Now she is going to literally draw lines on the text to remind herself where the beats are. Her text now looks like this:

I can't believe I flunked again! Mom is going to kill me!

I know–maybe I just won't tell her. No, that'll never work–Mom knows my teacher because they're in the same aerobics class. She'll definitely find out in the end. Well, I guess I'll just bite the bullet and tell her.

Or if the actress had access to an electronic version of the text and could reformat and reprint it, she could make the beats even easier to see:

I can't believe I flunked again! Mom is going to kill me!
I know–maybe I just won't tell her.
No, that'll never work–Mom knows my teacher because they're in the same aerobics class. She'll definitely find out in the end.
Well, I guess I'll just bite the bullet and tell her.

This exercise of visually separating your beats is helpful for several reasons:

1. **This gives the actress a quick visual cue to let her know where her moments of transition are.**

   If the actress now has to perform without any additional preparation, she knows that if she sees a line, something is changing. When we speak in everyday life, we usually somehow signify a new thought—we pause, our voices adjust, or we move our hands a bit. Watch this in your next conversation. Note that it takes a moment for your next thought to emerge, and that it takes a moment to transition to that new thought. That is how your friend knows you are saying something new; that is the ebb and flow of normal conversation. So this actress will incorporate some of these transition markers into her performance. These lines let her know where to do it.[52]

   Breaking your script into beats will help you as well. Once you have finalized a script and you are ready to begin practicing it, draw lines separating beats, and then pay attention to those transition moments as you rehearse.

   The first time through, just pause when you come to a line. A pause is the easiest way to separate one beat from another. Then try it again, and see if there are other needed changes as you switch from one beat to the next. Perhaps you will want to take a step forward at the start of the new beat, or gesture or look at some other part of the room. Even a small shift lets your audience perceive the structure of your speech, and gives it more heft.

2. **Drawing beats is the first step toward memorization.**

   Once the actress has found the beats, she sees the skeleton of the piece. If she is successful in the audition and is cast in the role, the day will come when she will have to rehearse it "off book," without script in hand. Those early rehearsals may be rocky because she will not remember each word just as the playwright wrote it. But if she recalls her beats, she will at least be able to get through the arc of the play.

Knowing the beats, but not having memorized the preceding monologue, it may now turn into something like this:

Holy cow, I flunked this test. Mom is going to kill me!
Ok, I'm just going to hide this. She'll never know.
Wait a minute, that is a stupid idea. She'll know the second the sees Mrs. Smith in aerobics class.
OK. Clearly I am going to have to tell her myself.

Not the same text, but the same gist. It is a start. The actress will then take more time to memorize each line. By opening night she will be letter-perfect.

Similarly, once you break the script into beats, you gain a better picture of the structure of the piece. Then when you stand to perform it, if you find the words of your text have simply flown out of your mind, you will still be able to make it through. You will get from the beginning to the end by paraphrasing your beats.

Knowing your beats well helps if you suffer from stage fright. The clearer you are about what you want to say, the more readily you can handle it if you forget your "lines." Feeling confident about your subject matter provides you more confidence in delivery.

How to "Perform" Your Speech

- Break it into beats. Know the structure.

- Practice, practice, practice.

- Memorize as much as you can.

- Choose some points to deliver "extemporaneously" (paraphrasing your script).

- Separate beats with your delivery. (At the very least, pause.)

- Maintain eye contact.

- Feet: Practice a steady stance; walk to emphasize important points.

- Hands: Practice a neutral resting place, but use some gestures to emphasize important moments.

- Voice: Vary your rhythms, volume, and pitches. Make sure we can hear you.

B. Free Yourself from the Script

Speaking extemporaneously (explaining your point using natural, comfortable words rather than reciting a memorized text) is the best way to connect with the audience and bring life to the speech. The suggestion: Spend days, or even weeks, crafting your script. Create the good beginning and ending. Memorize those. Also memorize themes and refrains and whatever gives you trouble—the exact wording and timing of a joke, for example, or the explanation of a knotty concept. But as for the rest, explain it in the proper order as outlined, but using your own everyday words. Once you have mastered this, you will discover that you are better able to connect with the audience, look them in the eye, sound like yourself, move freely, and even field a question or two as it comes your way.

Almost never should you take the stage with full text in hand. In only the most formal of occasions—an inaugural address, perhaps—should you do so. For most any other occasion, from a wedding toast to a lecture before 200 new first-year law students, we urge you to divide your speech into beats and then transform the beats into bullet-pointed text. These bullet points are the notes that you should carry to the podium (or better yet, nothing at all). A bullet-pointed script looks like this:

- Flunked—Mom!
- Don't tell
- Stupid
- OK, tell her

The advantage of a bullet-pointed page is that you will not be tempted to bury your nose in it and drone on like a robot, because there is not much there to read. Instead, you use it as a crutch for reference if you forget your place. Then look right back at the audience to maintain your connection.

Strive to limit bullet-pointed notes to a single page so that you do not need to flip through pages as you speak. Turning pages is distracting, and the papers can get shuffled.

Each bullet should consist of only a word or two—just enough to impart the gist of the idea. Any more, and you will have a hard time getting the thought with a quick glance, and will be tempted to look down too long.

C. Separate Beats with Delivery

When you work with bullet-pointed notes, rest your notes on a podium. Stand out to the side of the podium so that your whole body is before us. That removes the blocking effect of the podium, which otherwise separates you from the audience. It also lets us see your natural gestures. It is easier to connect with the audience if you are not concealed behind a huge, lumpy barrier.

Practice exactly when you will look down. Ideally, you will put in enough rehearsal time to perform the speech without looking down at all. If you must look down at your notes, be sure to do so *in between* beats. Finish the thought of a complete bullet point, *then* glance down to get to the next. If you glance to the next bullet while your mouth is still moving to finish the first, then you will swallow the ending of the beat. The result will not be as clear and forceful as it would have been if you had maintained your connection with us.

Try it: Practice delivering this old joke and the beat that follows it.

A grasshopper walks into a bar, and the bartender says, "Hey, we've got a drink named after you!"
And the grasshopper says, "Why would anyone name a drink Bob?"
That's a corny one; now let me tell you a joke that's a little more sophisticated.

Try this by looking down in the middle of the joke.

Audience: Boring!

Now try it again, maintaining eye contact throughout, with a nice pause after the punch line. Your joke will work better.

Watch Jon Stewart (or any talented comedian) perform, and notice that he pauses and maintains eye contact at the end of every beat. That timing makes Stewart's comedy crisp and gets him the laughs. If you get into the habit of ending beats cleanly, even if you fumble to get to the next, your tempo will be better because of it.

So you have drawn the lines and come up with bullets. It's time now to check on the internal structure. Is it as tight and coherent as it can be? If you find in rehearsing that you invariably forget a point—for instance, a transition that always takes you by surprise—that tells you that your internal structure needs tweaking. If your thoughts are not flowing one from the other as you practice your speech, you can bet they will not flow for your audience either.

Unlike the actress, who may have reservations about the monologue she has to deliver, you are both actor and playwright. If you do not like the lines, you can change them on the spot.

D. Maintain Eye Contact

Working with beats is also important because it enables you to make eye contact. You must look us in the eye when you are talking to us, or we will doubt your conviction. If you are staring at the floor or out over our heads, we subconsciously read that as a telltale sign that you are fibbing or uncertain. If you look at us as you speak, we are more likely to pay attention because it seems rude to tune you out.

When you watch us, you learn much through our body language. You can tell from audience body reaction when you are speaking too quickly or softly, or have baffled or bored us. For example, if you see people in the audience looking confused, that tells you that you need to explain further. Pay attention to body language signals and adjust what you are doing. Slow down, or speak up, explain it again using an analogy, tell a funny story, or call for a five-minute break. Public speaking, at its best, is a conversation, so do not ignore the audience's end of the dialogue. They are in this even while sitting quietly.

E. The Importance of Rehearsal

Back to our hypothetical actress. She has drawn her lines to separate her beats. Now to start rehearsing.

REHEARSAL IS WILDLY UNDERRATED—AND UNDERDONE. So many failed speechmakers leave scant time to practice; instead, they labor over scriptwriting until the last minute. The first time they say the words aloud may be the day of the speech. This is a huge mistake. The process of rehearsing aloud can bring to light any failures in logic, language, and structure inherent in your speech. Rehearsal reveals tongue-twisters, uncomfortable language, and sentences that are too long to let you breathe. Rehearsal lets you work out the kinks in your speech, so that in actual performance you are relaxed enough to project confidence.

Even with a quasi-extemporaneous speech, you must, must, *must* rehearse—and then rehearse some more. Off-the-cuff delivery is never wise. It may work occasionally for the extreme charmer, but even that lucky impromptu speech is unlikely to be as substantial and memorable as something more crafted. For most of us mere mortals, the wholly impromptu speech is likely to be an exercise in abject humiliation.

Here is what you want to do: Say, for example, that you have a week to pull a speech together. Spend the first three days writing it; then spend the *next four days* rehearsing it. (You most likely will rewrite some as you practice.)

When you practice, you must say it out loud. It is not the same exercise to read words silently to yourself. You need to speak them—to hear them in your own voice—to be able to judge whether they have the impact you intended. It is a good idea to buy an inexpensive audio recorder, record yourself delivering your speech, and listen to it. Then practice it again.

This is the start of memorization. When you rise to deliver your speech, you need to know the message so well that it becomes part of your body, part of your bones. If you have only silently read the page over and over again, then those words have not worked their way into your marrow and you may well forget them when the adrenaline hits. You may instead find yourself staring up at an imaginary page in the air, or worse yet, at the floor. That is a failed delivery. If you have practiced a speech out loud, repeatedly, you will hear the comfortable sound of your own voice saying what you have heard before. Even if stage fright hits, the substance will be there in mind and body. You will be able to get through it.

You should also practice in the room where you will deliver the speech, or in circumstances similar to it. Do not rehearse sitting in a chair at your desk—stand up! Get used to what your hands and feet want to do as you speak. Get the speech into your bones so that you know it in your whole body. Practice with props you plan to use, and in those uncomfortable, dressy shoes that you will have to wear, so you get used to them all and they will not throw you off during the performance.

When rehearsing, the actress will attack the text beat by beat. That is the right rehearsal approach for you. Start by practicing only the first beat. Master it and get comfortable with it. Then move on to the next beat and work on just that one. And now the next beat. This technique again reinforces the structure of your speech and ensures that you will not make the mistake of starting from the beginning at each practice, *never* reaching the end. Many make that blunder and end up with a well-rehearsed beginning, an okay middle, and an end that fizzles.

F. What to Do with Hands and Feet: Gestures and Walking

As the actress practices each beat, she will also make choices about "blocking"—where to stand and whether to move. You should do the same. The choices about how to perform each beat arise from

1. The point of it (the "intention" of the beat); and

2. Your own "core" (the person you are in everyday life, with the mannerisms that come naturally to you when you are relaxed).

Imagine the actress working on beat one (from the script at the start of this chapter):

"I can't believe I flunked again. Mom's gonna kill me!"

The actress must decide the motivation of that beat—what is going on in her character's mind? Panic, perhaps. And then she will draw on her own life and think, *OK, what happens to me when I am panicked?* Perhaps when she is panicked her voice rises in pitch, or she talks more quickly, or she gets agitated and gestures with her hands more frenetically. Maybe she freezes like a deer in the headlights.

The actress's own behavior, were she to find herself in the same situation in real life, is a good place to start when figuring out what to do. The actress is unlikely to decide, "Well, I am going to lift my arm over my head like so to deliver this line." Planning out every gesture is distracting and is likely to result in a presentation that does not feel natural. Instead, she will focus on the motivation: "I am panicked!" and let her body and voice behave as they would if she were in fact experiencing panic.

Perhaps her arms would fly up, or perhaps they would go completely rigid. It doesn't matter which, so long as they reflect the feeling of panic. She will try it a few different ways, decide which one she likes, and then move on to the next beat.

The same technique will work for you. Perhaps the point of the beat in the speech on which you are working is to entertain the audience, which you will accomplish through telling an on-point story or joke. The intention, therefore, is to elicit a smile, and your delivery should come from your core, your ordinary-life self. If you are a low-key sort, perhaps your humor will be a dry, deadpan delivery. If you are full of energy, your delivery may be, too. Practice the beat until you know it well—especially that punch line—and then move on to the next beat.

You then will move your hands and feet when you have the impulse to move based on the substance of what you are saying. At other times, develop a resting place that does not

1.   Inadvertently communicate something that you are not intending to communicate, or

2.   Tie up hands and feet so that you do not use them for the rest of the speech.

Let's start with the hands. You need to have a neutral "resting place" for your hands and arms. The best resting place for your hands is to have them hanging casually by your sides. Don't put them in your pockets. This is too casual and sloppy for most presentations and makes it unlikely that you will extract your hands from those pockets to use them. Then we have a speech devoid of all gestures, which looks quite odd. Arms folded across your chest look uncomfortable or defensive, and inhibit movement. Arms clasped behind look stiff, like a military posture. Arms clasped in front hint that you need to use the restroom. Some speakers cultivate a resting spot with elbows bent and hands at chest level, sometimes clasped together, but beware of two problems with this habit: First, your fingers will probably be touching and might play games; second, your gestures will be constrained, more truncated, because your range of motion is reduced to the horizontal plane of the area just in front of your chest. You are unlikely to raise your arms high or low if this is your resting place.

Your arms should hang loosely by your sides. Do make a point of using your hands several times during your speech. If using your hands to gesture feels odd, work on it like this: First, have one rehearsal in which you go through it all without using your hands, keeping them by your sides. Notice that sometimes holding still feels strange because you really need to move at such moments in order to make your point. Those are the moments when you *should* gesture during your speech.

If you are not sure where such moments are, find a reason to move. Use a visual aid that you must pick up or point to. Or look for the moments when you evoke a sensory detail. Use your hands then. Move when you strike a theme or refrain; or move at the top of each beat.

As you focus on your hands, be aware of any tendency to gesture repetitively. Have a colleague watch your delivery and take notes on what you are doing—playing director to your acting job. Ask her to note when you are using only one hand or gesturing in the same pattern. If you do gesture repetitively, rehearse to break the habit. If you only use your right hand, try a run-through in which you consciously use both. Or give your director a rolled-up newspaper and have him whack you when you start the repetitive gesture so that you become averse to doing it! (Old dogs, you will find, can learn new tricks.)

Once you have mastered the gesture during rehearsal, forget about it when you perform. Think then only about what you are saying. Rehearsal is the time to ditch bad habits. During the performance, you should concentrate on substance, not about what your left hand is doing. A note about holding something as you talk—the usual rule is, don't. If you begin by clutching a pen or your glasses, you are likely either to wag the pen like a schoolteacher or clutch your glasses so you gesture with one hand, not the other. The exception to this rule is the remote control that some use to advance slides in a PowerPoint presentation—if that is the talk you are giving, you have to hold the remote control as you speak. It can be a comforting crutch for one just beginning to master public speaking because clicking the button to advance a slide gives you a task. Just be sure that it does not lead to use of only one hand—use both to gesture. After you have a couple of speeches under your belt, make a point of delivering speeches with nothing in your hand at all so that you are able to master that skill.

Your feet need to be positioned to permit you to move when you need to, but so that you are not tempted to wander, sway, or engage in other distracting movements. Spend time developing a stance that is both relaxed and natural. For most, this means standing with feet hip-width apart, knees slightly bent (not locked). This is akin to the resting place for your hands—it is the resting place for your feet. If your stance is wider, it looks odd. You will be unlikely to walk if you use an overly wide stance, even if you have the impulse to. If your feet are too close, you will weave or sway to maintain your balance. This is also why your knees need to be soft—if you lock them, you are more likely to find yourself off-balance. Some need to adjust their stances because of their own physiognomy, perhaps having one foot slightly in front of the other. Again, a director is helpful here. Rehearse the entire speech, focusing just on your feet and keeping your knees soft. Ask your director to tell you what your body was doing.

Walking here and there during a speech (provided the speech is not so formal that this would be inappropriate) can hold attention and suggest that you are relaxed and "own the stage." But watch that walking does not morph into wandering. If you are aimlessly wandering around the space, or worse yet, pacing like a lion in a den, listeners will be distracted or feel uncomfortable without knowing why. Instead, incorporate walking to emphasize the points you are making.

Try this exercise: Paying attention to beats, take a step (one foot, then the other, then STOP) each time you start a new beat. This use of planned movement to break up beats adds visual interest and can retrieve your audience's attention when it wanders. You can also combine walking with use of a visual aid—you will have to walk over to pick up the visual aid, or turn it on (etc.). You can walk up to it to point out something about it. That adds texture to the talk. (See Chapter 7 for a more detailed discussion.)

As you move about the stage, notice the effect walking in different directions makes. A way to get a feel for this is to watch a stage play. Notice when you are particularly entertained or moved by a scene, and then notice whether and in what direction the performers moved in those moments. Moving toward the audience (downstage) can be powerful, as can stopping— try finding the most dramatic line in your speech and delivering it as you walk toward the audience or as you stop moving. Moving left or right, especially on a diagonal, shifts the tone and is a nice way to separate beats to show that you are changing topics. Moving away from the audience (upstage) is usually awkward because you have to turn your back to them to do it. If you must move away from the audience, either do this in between thoughts when not talking, or try moving on a diagonal so that you are still connected with the audience.

Be careful about coming too close to the audience. A listener has "personal space" that you should not violate. If you come too close to your listener, you make him uncomfortable. You will then have to move away and you may be tempted to turn your back to the audience, thereby breaking your connection with them, to do it.

G. A Tale of Two Speeches: John Kerry and Barack Obama

Lest you think paying attention to beats is only about acting, consider two political speeches, both well crafted, to see how delivery can carry—or crush—the day.

The first is John Kerry's speech accepting his party's nomination at the Democratic National Convention on July 29, 2004.[53] He faced two challenges. First, many in the public were not sure if they liked him. He seemed stiff and uncomfortable, in contrast to George W. Bush, who was cited as the kind of guy one might like to drink a beer with. Second, Kerry was nominated by a party that was said to be dominated by far-left liberals who were weak on family values. Here is the middle of John Kerry's speech:

> You don't value families by kicking kids out of after school programs and taking cops off our streets, so that Enron can get another tax break. We believe in the family value of caring for our children and protecting the neighborhoods where they walk and play.
>
> And that is the choice in this election.
>
> You don't value families by denying real prescription drug coverage to seniors, so big drug companies can get another windfall. We believe in the family value expressed in one of the oldest Commandments: "Honor thy father and thy mother." As President, I will not privatize Social Security. I will not cut benefits. And together, we will make sure that senior citizens never have to cut their pills in half because they can't afford life-saving medicine.
>
> And that is the choice in this election.
>
> You don't value families if you force them to take up a collection to buy body armor for a son or daughter in the service, if you deny veterans health care, or if you tell middle class families to wait for a tax cut, so that the wealthiest among us can get even more. We believe in the value of doing what's right for everyone in the American family.
>
> And that is the choice in this election.

This is fine writing for speaking. You have a theme: a riff on phony "family values." There is a refrain: "And that is the choice in this election." There is a good structure of long paragraphs with sensory details, followed by a short, punchy sentence for emphasis. The speechwriter has made the structure of the beats abundantly clear—each paragraph is a beat. The speaker need not even separate these beats by drawing lines because the white spaces in between the paragraphs do the work for him. The writer has very clearly indicated the beats, which call for pauses and volume adjustments.

Imagine the setting. The attendees were believers, thrilled to be there. They had to pull strings to get tickets and eagerly anticipated hearing from their nominee, buoyed by the energy of a large crowd. They had been worked up by other moving speeches preceding the main event and powerful video clips of the candidate. They were ready to cheer.

John Kerry took the stage. But his delivery turned the fine speech into mush.[54] He raced from beat to beat without pausing for breath, leaving no room for the audience to applaud. They clapped and shouted over his words, and Kerry responded by shouting over them. The audience therefore could not hear the beginning of the beats ("You don't value families") because they were still clapping. In apparent frustration, Kerry shouted the beginning more loudly ("You don't—you don't—you DON'T VALUE FAMILIES!"). The speech turned into a power struggle, with the audience trying to participate through applauding, and Senator Kerry plowing on ahead without waiting for them to catch up. The family values theme was lost, and Kerry did nothing to dispel the impression that he was too stiff to really connect with the American people.

Contrast this with Barack Obama's "Yes, We Can" speech,[55] delivered the night after losing the primary election in New Hampshire on January 8, 2008. The mood must have been somber before he took the stage. The loss was unexpected and could have foreshadowed trouble to come. Some worried that it meant that voters were embarrassed to tell pollsters that they would not vote for a black candidate. But when then-Senator Obama took the stage that night, he offered the voters something surprising—hope.

Barack Obama. Jemal Countess/Getty Images Entertainment/Getty Images

Obama first introduced his theme in an understated way:

> For when we have faced down impossible odds, when we've been told we're not ready or that we shouldn't try or that we can't, generations of Americans have responded with a simple creed that sums up the spirit of a people: Yes, we can. Yes, we can. Yes, we can.

His was a soft, simple, conversational delivery, like he was talking just to you. He repeated it once, twice, and his listeners right away recognized it as a refrain and began to chant it. Then he stepped back, smiled, let the energy build, clearly enjoying himself. He began again:

> It was a creed written into the founding documents that declared the destiny of a nation: Yes, we can.

> It was whispered by slaves and abolitionists as they blazed a trail towards freedom through the darkest of nights: Yes, we can.

> It was sung by immigrants as they struck out from distant shores and pioneers who pushed westward against an unforgiving wilderness: Yes, we can.

> It was the call of workers who organized, women who reached for the ballot, a president who chose the moon

as our new frontier, and a king who took us to the mountaintop and pointed the way to the promised land: Yes, we can, to justice and equality.

Obama began to play with volume. He served up the image of the lone voice—that single slave whispering, "Yes, we can." Soon that voice was joined by others—immigrants, singing this time, and so the delivery was a bit louder—"Yes, we can." As the voices built, his volume grew louder and louder to a crescendo, "Yes, we can, to justice and equality!" He cleverly increased his volume simply by leaning into the microphone, so that he was not shouting. He seemed in control; no danger of Pathos run amok here.

He waited again for the cheers of the audience to die, and silenced them by a simple, confident gesture of leadership—raising one hand. His volume was down again—important because he could not reach the end at a fever pitch. If he had held the high volume, we might have felt like we were being manipulated or bludgeoned. Instead, he chose soft, and we heard,

Yes, we can, to opportunity and prosperity. Yes, we can heal this nation. Yes, we can repair this world. Yes, we can.

And so, tomorrow, as we take the campaign south and west, as we learn that the struggles of the textile workers in Spartanburg are not so different than the plight of the dishwasher in Las Vegas, that the hopes of the little girl who goes to the crumbling school in Dillon are the same as the dreams of the boy who learns on the streets of L.A., we will remember that there is something happening in America, . . .

The muted line, "there is something happening in America," set off goose bumps, inviting you to feel the importance of the moment in history. His delivery evoked an almost "can you believe it; we are all here together" response. Imagine that same line delivered at high decibel—it would not work as well. He continued, but this time he let the force of his oratory rip through the room:

> . . . that we are not as divided as our politics suggest, that we are one people, we are one nation. And, together, we will begin the next great chapter in the American story, with three words that will ring from coast to coast, from sea to shining sea: Yes, we can. Thank you, New Hampshire. Thank you. Thank you.

Listen to that volume, that building in pace, that pleasure in pure oratory. Now that's great public speaking.

Chapter 6

Tools of the Trade: Voice and Breath

There once was a man named Demosthenes who lived in Greece around 350 B.C. When he was 18 he learned that his uncles had cheated him out of his fortune. There were no lawyers in those days to argue your case for you. To recover his property, Demosthenes would have to speak on his own behalf before a Greek court. But he had problems—a lisp and a soft voice. According to Plutarch, he had a "perplexed and indistinct utterance and a shortness of breath, which, by breaking and disjointing his sentences, much obscured the sense and meaning of what he spoke."[56] One simply could not understand him.

So he practiced. He moved to a cave by the Aegean Sea and shaved off half his hair so that he would not be tempted to return to town until he had practiced long and hard. He stayed in that cave, filled his mouth with pebbles and recited verses while running until he could be understood, despite being winded and choking on a mouthful of rocks. Then he stood at the edge of the Aegean Sea, shouting over the roar of the waves, arguing full-bore why the court should return his money. And when he was satisfied, he returned to Athens to become one of the greatest voices of democracy in Greece. People came from miles around to listen to him.[57]

Our point: Your voice is a powerful tool. It can be trained. If you know how to use it well, you can transform a run-of-the-mill speech into something that can make all Athens gather around and take notice. Conversely, it does not matter how brilliant your notions are or how well chosen the words, if your audience cannot understand you.

While the academic components of public speaking are crucial to effective persuasion, public speaking is also a demanding *physical* exercise. The law students we teach are sometimes surprised to hear this. They might spend days crafting a brilliant legal argument, choosing the right cleverly turned phrase to make a telling point, imagining that the words they see on the page will be as impressive to listeners as their written texts have been in the past to law professors who have praised their papers. But when the day of oral argument arrives, they stammer, mutter, whisper, or speed-talk. Their voices fail them, and their attempts at persuasion fall flat.

Singers, actors, and other professional public speakers—like trial lawyers, who sometimes address juries day in and day out for weeks on end—attest that the voice is a delicate instrument. If abused, it can betray you when you most need it. But if treated well, your voice can prove to be a powerful part of your arsenal.

Breath, voice, and speech are among the basic tools at your disposal as a public speaker. It is important to understand how they work and how to care for them in order to get maximum results.

This chapter describes useful vocal exercises for warming up your voice before speaking.[58] Some exercises are also geared toward solving particular vocal problems. If performed regularly, these exercises will improve the voice. You may not notice sharp improvements right off, so be patient. An actor or singer often spends a lifetime trying to perfect the voice—it takes practice. These exercises are a good place to start.

A. The Importance of Warming Up

Just as athletes warm up before competing, you need to spend time warming up before speaking, to ensure that your voice and body are ready. Warming up also helps combat nervousness. Your warm-up routine lets you assess how you are doing that day and provides an opportunity to work out kinks in private, before you take the stage. It is not confidence-inspiring to realize that the throat is dry or to discover a crick in the neck when standing in front of an audience a few minutes into a speech—better to take stock before you start, so that you can grab that last drink of water or do a few neck rolls. You will feel more confident if you know that you are physically ready to go. The comfort of a routine that has worked before provides a tonic of needed self-assurance. Finally, taking time to warm up carves out space for you away from the day's distractions, in order to better focus on what to say and how to say it. Your oral advocacy will be stronger if, as they say in the theater, you are "present in the moment," aware of yourself and your surroundings.

Exercise 1: A Physical Warm-Up

Before you make a speech, spend some time loosening up.

1. Roll your head gently around clockwise a few times, then counter-clockwise a few times. If you feel neck tension, stop; massage that part of your neck.

2. Raise your shoulders up to your ears in an exaggerated shrug, then let them fall. Repeat several times.

3. Stretch your hands out as wide as you can, then give them a good shake to get rid of all the tension. Now do your whole arm; your feet; your legs. Finally, shake out your whole body to get some energy into it.

4. Stretch out your face as wide as you can, stick out your tongue, open your eyes, and make a loud, silly noise. Now squinch up your face and make it as small as you can, with a softer, silly noise. Repeat.

5. Stretch as high as you can. Then flop over at the waist, releasing all the air in your body. Roll up slowly. Try to stack the vertebrae one on top of the other.

6. Roll your shoulders back. Stand up straight. Now you're ready to concentrate on your breathing.

B. How the Voice Works

Four important components come together to make up your voice. The first is the *breath*, which is what gives your voice power. It is like the gasoline in your car—without it, the car will not go. That breath travels across your *vocal cords*, which sit in your throat on top of your windpipe. Those cords vibrate in response to the amount of air pushed through them and create the sound of your voice. They are like your car's engine. Then the sound travels around and vibrates against various *resonators*—nose, throat, chest, mask of the face, and so forth. These resonators add richness and tone to sound, which gives color and life. Think of them as akin to the transmission in your car. Finally, you shape the sound into actual words with your *articulators*—tongue, teeth, roof of the mouth. Those are like the wheels on a car as they start rolling to get you from here to there.

C. Breath

The key to having enough breath support lies in understanding how to breathe from your *diaphragm*. The diaphragm is a band of muscles that rests below your lungs. When you inhale, your diaphragm pulls down, allowing your lungs to fill with air. If you constrict your diaphragm by slouching or standing tensely, lungs will not have room to inflate properly, and breathing will be shallow and unsupported. But if you stand up straight and engage your diaphragm, you have the air necessary to produce a full, rich sound. Diaphragmatic breathing offers the power of volume, it gives you the support to speak long sentences, and it provides protection from damage for the vocal cords.

To breathe from your diaphragm, you must know where your diaphragm is. This next exercise helps you locate and become more aware of it.

Exercise 2: Find Your Diaphragm

Stand up straight; place your hands on your torso at the bottom of your ribcage. Exhale all the air in your lungs. Hold for five seconds. Then take in a big breath. That movement that you felt under your hands was your diaphragm expanding to suck in air. Notice how much space you have between your diaphragm and the top of your chest. Aim to fill all that space when you breathe so that you are using your entire lung capacity.

Maintaining good posture allows the diaphragm to expand, giving you optimal air capacity. Become aware of posture as you practice speaking. Do the vertebrae-stacking exercise (see Exercise 1, Step 5) before you speak. Try a yoga class—yoga is an excellent way to improve posture. Be sure to maintain excellent posture every time you perform vocal warm-ups.

Once you are aware of your diaphragm, you can use it more efficiently to expand your breathing capacity. You will be able to better control your breath so that the end of sentences sound as rich and supported as the beginnings. The following exercises aim to improve your breath support and control.

■■■ ─────────────────── ■■■

Exercise 3: Improve Your Breath Control

1. Take a deep breath while stretching your arms out to the sides. Raise your arms as you inhale at a speed that mirrors your rate at which you are inhaling. When you have inhaled fully, your arms should be straight out at shoulder height. Now slowly exhale, letting the arms float down; once all the air is gone, your arms are hanging straight down. Make the exhale last as long as you can. Don't hold your breath—that's cheating! Now do it again; make it last even longer.

2. Say "ha" out loud six times, all on one breath. Repeat, but this time try 12 "ha"s on one breath. Now 18. Now 24. See how far you can go.

3. Read the following sentence aloud, adding each phrase (demarcated by the / symbol), slowly building up to delivery all on one breath:

    I am now practicing/ a very important exercise/ to improve my breath support/ and breath control/ and through practice I will control my breath/ to the end of this long, long sentence/ so that I can read this entire sentence aloud/ and still have enough breath left at the end/ to say ha!

    It is VERY important when you perform this exercise to not hold your breath while you are speaking. Holding your breath may help you get to the end of the sentence, but it is not diaphragmatic breathing and ultimately can destroy vocal cords.

Breath support problems: The gravelly, breathy, or husky voice. If you run out of air before you reach the end of a sentence yet continue to force sound, you will create a gravelly voice. This occurs when air flow is constricted; the vocal cords begin to rub aggressively and become irritated. Breathy and husky voices (think film noir bombshells) exhibit the opposite problem: excessive air pushing through the vocal cords. All of these habits damage the long-term health of the vocal cords and make audiences cringe. Record yourself speaking and listen for these problems; if they are yours, work on breath support and control. You can also combat a gravelly voice by shortening sentences so that you have space to breathe.

Breath support problems: Volume. A speaker with low volume indicates that his words are not worth listening to. Concentrate on supporting words with your entire lung capacity so that you can be heard.

Pay attention to audience size. People in a room absorb sound, so you need to speak more loudly during an oral presentation than in normal conversation. Focus on the audience. Throw your voice to that back row, and imagine that someone in that row doesn't hear well.

Pretend that an audience member is standing in the hallway outside. Raise your voice to include him in the conversation.

Another neat trick: Practice your speech over the white noise of a fan, a hairdryer, or a radio tuned to static. Find the volume that lets you be heard over the white noise. Then use that volume in performance. (This is the modern-day incarnation of Demosthenes' Aegean Sea exercise.)

D. Vocal Cords

Protecting your vocal cords is as much a matter of "clean living" as performing particular exercises. What follows will keep your vocal cords in good health.

1. Water, water, everywhere. Drink at least eight glasses of water a day, and even more on the day of your presentation. Hydrate vocal cords well in advance of a speaking

engagement. Start drinking lots of water 24 hours before you perform, and sleep with a humidifier in your bedroom the night before a big speech. Try warming up in a steamy bathroom to give your vocal cords an extra boost. If your vocal cords get dry, they will rub against each other until irritated, which may result in "singer's nodes" (a painful condition to be avoided at all costs).

2. No smoking. Well before speaking, limit exposure to secondhand smoke.

3. Do not put strain on your vocal cords. No screaming during the big football game. No yelling over the noise at a bar. No speaking in a breathy whisper. A husky voice, while seductive, will kill your vocal cords.

4. Practice diaphragmatic breathing. Proper breath support helps keep vocal cords in good health.

5. Warm up before any public speaking engagement.

6. Perform daily vocal exercises to keep vocal cords in the best health. As little as ten minutes a day can make a huge difference.

E. Resonators

The sound of the voice is enriched by vibrating against resonators throughout your body (such as your chest and face). As you speak, you can put your hands on these various resonating spots and feel for vibrations—those are your resonators at work. Learning how to use all the resonators makes your voice more interesting to hear.

Exercise 4: Warm Up Your Resonators

1. Hum the following sounds, feeling different parts of your face, head, mouth, and nasal passages vibrate:

    MMMMMMMMMMMMMMM (You should feel this on your lips.)
    NNNNNNNNNNNNNNNNN (You should feel this on the top of your nose.)
    VVVVVVVVVVVVVVVV (This sound should be placed at the front of the lips.)
    ZZZZZZZZZZZZZZZZZZZZ (You will feel this most on your teeth.)
    EEEEEEEEEEEEEEEEEEEE (This sound resonates at the back of the lips.)

2. Hum again, picturing the sound traveling from your head down to your toes and then up again. Try to vibrate the parts of your body with your voice as you imagine the hum passing through them. You can also vary pitch as you pass the hum up and down your body.

Resonator problems: The nasal voice. Some speakers overemphasize their nasal resonators, placing sounds that should reverberate in the mouth (such as "ah" and "mm") in the nose instead. Sometimes this is a result of regional accent; others rely on the nasal resonator for a volume boost to compensate for improper breathing. If you have a nasal voice, practice resonator exercises, focusing on developing all your resonators, especially your lips and chest. Make an "nn" sound and feel it on your nose; then make an "mm" sound and feel it on your lips—literally put your hands on your lips and nose so that you can feel the vibration with your fingers. Work to make those two sounds trigger two separate resonators. Also focus on your breath support exercises so that you can project volume without overemphasizing your nasal resonator.

F. Articulators

Articulators (your tongue, your teeth, your lips, the roof of your mouth) shape sounds into words.

Exercise 5: Warm Up Your Articulators

1. Blow "raspberries" by blowing air through loose lips to make them vibrate. Now add sound. Try varying your pitch, low to high, high to low. If you can make a baby laugh by doing this exercise, you're doing it properly.

2. Repeat these nonsense sounds slowly and clearly at first, and then as quickly as you can:

    > Luh duh tuh luh duh tuh luh duh tuh luh duh tuh
    > Tuh duh luh tuh duh luh tuh duh luh tuh duh luh
    > Buh wuh vuh buh wuh vuh buh wuh vuh buh wuh vuh
    > Wub uh wuh wub uh wuh wub uh wuh wub uh wuh
    > Wippity wippity weet watt watt
    > Wippity wippity weet watt woot
    > Wippity wippity week walk walk
    > Wippity wippity week walk wook
    > Wippity wippity weem wamm wamm

Wippity wippity weem wamm woomm
Wippity wippity weeb wab wab
Wippity wippity weeb wab woob

3. Try tongue-twisters. Start slow, articulating clearly, and then try to increase your speed.

Red leather, yellow leather
Unique New York
The tip of the tongue, the teeth, and the lips
Good blood, bad blood
Rubber baby buggy bumpers
Black bug's blood

4. Now try these longer tongue-twisters. You can also use them to practice diaphragmatic breathing by saying longer sections of the verse on one breath, carefully controlling the volume of air expelled. You can also use these as a quick full-body warm-up as well by marching in place as you say the words, increasing the speed of your march as you increase the pace of your speech.

What a to-do to die today at a minute or two to two,
a thing distinctly hard to say but harder still to do.
for they'll beat a tattoo at twenty to two:
a rat-ta tat-tat ta tat-tat ta to-to.
and the dragon will come when he hears the drum
at a minute or two to two today, at a minute or two to two.[59]

To sit in solemn silence in a dull, dark dock,
In a pestilential prison, with a life-long lock,
Awaiting the sensation of a short, sharp shock,
From a cheap and chippy chopper on a big black block![60]

> I am the very model of a modern Major-General,
> I've information vegetable, animal, and mineral,
> I know the kings of England, and I quote the
> fights historical,
> From Marathon to Waterloo, in order
> categorical. . . . [61]

G. Loosening the Jaw

Watch a room of law students taking an exam, and you will notice a fair number clenching jaws or grinding teeth. The jaw is a visible target of tension that freezes up body language. A clenched jaw also muffles the voice, making it difficult to project.

Exercise 6: Warm Up Your Jaw

Put your hands on the sides of your head, and place your thumbs in front of your ears at the spot where your jaw hinges. Massage the joint to loosen your jaw as you gently open and close your mouth.

Now drag your open palms down the sides of your face, letting your jaw hang open. Imagine your hands dragging all the tension out of your jaw. Repeat until you feel your jaw relax.

H. Adding Some Color: Pitch, Cadence, Speed, and Volume

Varying pitch, cadence, speed, and volume keeps listeners awake, alert, and interested. Reading aloud and singing will expand your vocal range.

Exercise 7: Pitch

1. Sing—in the shower; as you drive the car; as you wash the dishes. Singing encourages you to incorporate more notes into your speaking voice.

2. Play with pitch. Read aloud, making an effort to use as many notes as possible. Or read the following piece aloud, going up the scale one half step and then back down one half step:

> She took a deep breath
> Closed her eyes
> Held her nose
> Bent her knees
> Jumped
> And fell
> And fell
> And fell
> Until she hit the water with a splash

[Here's what you just read written out to suggest the change in pitch:]

```
            (5) Jumped
      (4) Bent her knees      (6) And fell
       (3) Held her nose      (7) And fell
     (2) Closed her eyes       (8) And fell
(1) She took a deep breath        (9) Until she hit
                                      the water with
                                      a splash
```

Pitch problems: The monotone voice. Insecure speakers bore audiences by hiding behind a monotone, using only one or two notes as they speak. Sometimes these speakers offer the excuse that they do not want to seem silly or overly theatrical; that flamboyance is not really their style; that they are more focused on thinking big thoughts than performing. But a monotone speaker will put an audience to sleep. Here is the test: Try your performance on a very small child. If the child crawls away out of boredom, then you are not doing enough to vary pitch. Singing, reading aloud, and practicing pitch exercises can help you become more comfortable with using a variety of notes. This will enhance your speaking style.

Pitch problems: An unhealthy pitch. One of the authors has personal experience with the perils of speaking at an unnatural pitch. The strain of speaking at trial, day after day, at a pitch just a tad too low for his physiognomy resulted in vocal nodes, which meant that he found himself battling chronic voice loss in the middle of important trials. Visits to a speech therapist adjusted his pitch and solved the problem. To find your natural pitch say, "mmm hmmm," as if you are agreeing with something. That note is usually about the middle of your pitch range. If you regularly speak at a pitch much higher or lower than this, try adjusting to see if your voice lasts longer.

You might also adjust your pitch if there is a disconnect between your voice and your physical persona. Think of a big, burly man who speaks in a high-pitched, effeminate voice. This incongruity can make an audience uncomfortable and undercut your oral advocacy. This is an exception to the rule that you should work from your core (discussed in Chapter 5). If you naturally sink into a habit that is distracting, like using an odd pitch, you will want to break it.

Pitch problems: The upward inflection. If you end a sentence with a rising inflection, which sounds as if you are asking a question, you immediately undercut your authority. This "uptick" habit betrays a lack of confidence in your words. If this is your bad habit, practice speaking aloud as you make a conscious effort to end each sentence on a falling rather than a rising note. Or arm a friend with a rolled-up newspaper and encourage him to whack you every time you turn statements into questions. You soon will break the habit.

Exercise 8: Volume

Play with volume. Try saying "hello" as if you are in a library, greeting a friend on a street corner, hailing someone from a mountaintop. Always speak with focus, paying attention to where your audience is. Notice how louder volumes require more breath.

Exercise 9: Pace

Play with pace. Try reading the following sentences aloud, first with a fast pace, then with a slow pace. Notice how the shift in pace alters the tone and impact of the sentence.

What could that mean? I don't understand.

Honey, I did it, just like you asked.

I just don't think that can be right.

He's the one; I just know it.

Pace problems. When the nervous adrenaline hits, many speakers find themselves racing through their scripts, just wanting it to end. If friends have told you that you speak too quickly in everyday life, you can assume you will be a speed-speaker during formal presentations as well. Write a note to yourself at the top of any notes that you use during your presentation: "SLOW DOWN!"

Make it a habit to *look at your audience as you speak* and notice body language. If anyone looks confused or appears to be concentrating hard just to understand you, take that as a cue that you are rushing. You will notice that speed-speaking makes it harder to take a breath. If you find yourself short of breath, or hear yourself tripping over your tongue, slow down. A clever orator can write in lines that must be delivered slowly—an emergency brake for a runaway speech.

If you have the opposite problem and find yourself speaking slowly, you will notice eyes glazing over in boredom. Some audience members will interpret a slow, pedantic pace as patronizing. *He must think I am stupid,* they will imagine, *because he is speaking to me as though I don't understand English.* This may occur when you are not completely at ease with your script and are struggling to remember the next line. Extra rehearsal can help smooth things out, as can reading aloud, paying attention to varying your pace.

Exercise 10: Varying Body Language

1. Focus on your stance. Keep your feet hip width apart; soften your knees. Concentrate on not swaying as you perform the first paragraph from one of your speeches.

2. Play with body language. Recite the following lines, putting the emphasis on a different word each time, and finding a different gesture to go with each line read.

    I can't believe you went there.
    What do you want to do?
    Do you mean it?

■ ■ ■   ■ ■ ■

Exercise 11: Read Aloud

Read children's books or poetry aloud. Use your voice to color the words that you are reading. Use different voices for different characters, incorporating a wide range of notes. Pay attention to the speed at which you are reading—use pace to help you set the scene.

I. Some Final Thoughts: Taking Care of Your Voice

To keep your voice in top condition, follow these simple rules:

1. Take ten minutes to warm up before doing any public speaking.

2. Keep those vocal cords hydrated. Drink lots of water and use a humidifier before an important performance.

3. Don't irritate your vocal cords needlessly. Beware of shouting, whispering, and cigarette smoke.

4. Be careful of caffeine and alcohol, both of which can overload your system and derail your speech.

5. Stay away from dairy products if you are congested.

6. Get enough rest.

Chapter 7

Using Visual Aids

During the 2000 presidential race between Al Gore and George W. Bush, Gore suffered from being seen as a stiff, boring robot. He was unable to connect with voters in human terms. Polling results showed a fair percentage of voters favored Bush because they found him the more likable of the two candidates. When Gore spoke, he seemed like a know-it-all, dry professor. Many did not want to listen.

Al Gore lost that election. Several years passed. And then Al Gore made a movie, *An Inconvenient Truth*. Suddenly, boring Al Gore had the whole world abuzz.[62]

The topic of *An Inconvenient Truth*, global warming, is one that Al Gore had focused on for years. Before this movie his words did not do much to inspire action. After the movie, talk was rife with global warming. Legions were riveted by his presentation. He won the Nobel Prize.

What happened? As you watch the film, you will see that Gore is more relaxed in his presentation, to be sure, but that is not what made the principal difference. The reason you cannot look away is the riveting visual aids.

Visual aids can be extremely helpful to most any presentation. They make subjects dramatic and memorable. You do not have to be naturally gifted to give a bang-up presentation if you are supported by well-designed visual aids. They provide flair. If attention lags, a visual aid can get it back.

Visuals help us understand on a visceral level. A significant portion of any audience will be visual learners—those who need to see, not just hear, in order to understand. When explaining an idea while also providing a vivid picture (or a diagram or some other kind of visual aid), you can capture both auditory learners and visual ones. It is more likely that a greater percentage of them will remember what you have said weeks after the speech is over.

If you already are a skilled speaker, a good visual aid will make you even better. Designed properly, it can help you maintain eye contact with your audience. It forces organization. It can substitute for a sheaf of notes and can become your "cheat sheet." And there are situations—like Al Gore's pictures of the polar ice caps melting—in which a picture is worth a thousand words.

A. Things to Consider in Designing a Visual Aid

There are a number of things that you should keep in mind when you are choosing the visual aids to use.

1. Is It Worth Putting onto a Visual Aid?

When you use a visual aid to make a point, it tends to stick with your audience. Be sure that you are using visual aids for important matters, not for mere digressions. For example, if you are teaching an audience about a statute, do not use a visual aid depicting each word of the statute. Just highlight the section you care about.

2. Text or Picture?

Use text if you need us to see specific language—if, for example, you are explaining the meaning of a statute or analyzing a poem. But if you are dealing with a complicated idea, a picture may be preferable. Pictures help us understand viscerally in a way that words on a page sometimes cannot. It can be helpful to use a metaphor—perhaps that will be the essence of your picture. For example, here is a visual aid similar to one that a trial lawyer at the law firm where we both practiced once used to explain a complicated contractual dispute to a jury:

There Is No Contract Without All the Pieces

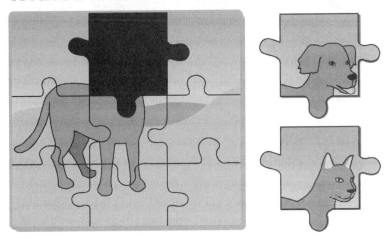

The contract is like a puzzle, and the "missing piece" of the contract the parties have not agreed about is the head of the animal. That missing term determines whether the animal pictured in the puzzle is a dog or a cat. Because the parties have not agreed about the substance of that missing piece, then they have not made a contract that could be enforced in a court. That metaphor—and the nice picture—are a simple way to explain an otherwise difficult-to-understand concept of contract law.

3. Can the Audience See It?

Bring a visual aid into the space where you will speak and look at it from the back row. If you cannot see it clearly, *throw it away* and make another, bigger one. If you have not left yourself enough time to remake the prop, do not use it at all. Better to have no visual aid than one an audience cannot see.

This is especially dangerous territory for Microsoft PowerPoint users. A PowerPoint slide that seems perfectly clear on your computer screen sometimes does not read well from the back of the room. See if adding color will help—it is easier to see white on a dark blue background, for example, than it is to see black on white. Or use animation (a feature in PowerPoint that permits an element of your design to move, which can make it easier to see).

If the size of your visual aid cannot be changed—for example, if you are speaking about how to tune a guitar and want the audience to see the strings—then take charge of your audience and move them around. Ask them to leave their seats and come forward to see what you are doing. Or see if there is technology that will magnify the visual aid and project it onto a screen behind you. You could also pass the visual aid around, although that can be distracting because your audience may focus on it rather than listen to you.

4. How Will You Introduce the Visual Aid Gracefully?

Practice revealing your visual aid until you can do it flawlessly. If you are placing a diagram onto an easel, for example, decide where you are going to locate that easel. Have the diagram *flipped over so that the audience cannot see it until you are ready for them to do so*. Then practice putting it onto the easel until it can be done without knocking things over or fumbling around. You are a magician pulling a rabbit out of a hat—you have to practice the move so that attention stays where you want it to (on you) rather than having it pulled away by that which you do not want them to see (your clumsy hands). This is why many are fond of visual presentation software like PowerPoint—it is easy to introduce your diagram simply by using a remote control to advance to the next slide in your presentation. Done.

5. Once You Have Introduced It, Use It

As soon as you unveil a visual aid, use it right away. If you do not, folks will study the visual aid and stop listening to you. Then the visual aid upstages you. Also make sure that the visual aid is not visible until you want it to be; otherwise, listeners will look at it and wonder, gee, what's that big surfboard got to do with his topic? Then you have lost control of focus. If you employ the visual aid as soon as you introduce it, you have our attention and you have created some drama.

6. Decide How to Interact with It

Say your visual aid is a PowerPoint presentation. Here are some ways you could interact with it:

IT COULD SERVE AS WALLPAPER, SETTING A TONE. If that is what you are up to, then you will face the audience and advance the slides without looking behind you. The slides will probably be big pictures that set some sort of emotional feeling. An example of this: In *An Inconvenient Truth*, Al Gore shows a red line going up, up, up as the carbon dioxide in the earth's atmosphere continues to rise.[63] He lets the red line continue to climb as he talks to the audience about the years passing and often is not looking at the line. But the unremitting climb of that line gives that moment force.

YOU COULD INTERACT WITH IT. Suppose your presentation is made to a jury, and you will argue that there are four independently dispositive reasons why the opposing counsel's position cannot prevail. This is your visual aid:

Four Brick Walls

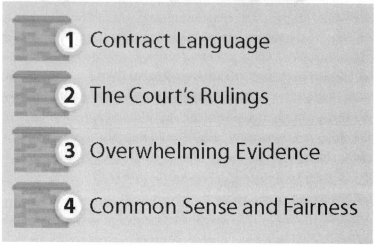

1 Contract Language

2 The Court's Rulings

3 Overwhelming Evidence

4 Common Sense and Fairness

Here is how you could work with this visual aid. You might put that chart up, then literally walk to it and point to the first "brick wall"—"contract language." This gives you a natural gesture—pointing—and a natural time to walk. Just be sure that you do not turn your back to the audience. Keep your feet and torso facing front and gesture with the hand that is closest to the screen. Try to keep your face facing front as well. You can point with a laser pointer, a long stick, or just your hand—whatever best suits the tone of your talk. Then talk about that element. Feel free to walk away from the chart. Then, when you finish that point, return to the chart to tell us that now you are going to examine another "brick wall"—"the court's rulings." Again, the physical chart has given you a reason to move, a natural gesture. And you are using the visual aid to help separate your beats, which will make your speech clearer to your audience.

7. Get Rid of It When You Are Done with It

Do not keep the visual aid in your hand after you have finished with it. You will be tempted to fiddle and distract us with it. You need to permit time in rehearsal to practice how to get the visual aid out of sight gracefully.

Sometimes, though, that is not what you will want to do. Imagine, for example, that you are a lawyer at trial and your visual aid is a list of all the ways the defendant has harmed your client. Perhaps you introduce that visual aid by asking your client to list harms that have befallen him, and you write each one on a board as your client speaks. You might then want to leave that board up and visible for as long as the judge will allow as a powerful reminder to your audience, the jury, about why you are there in court.

B. Choosing the Right Type of Visual Aids

1. Diagrams

A pre-printed diagram can be either low-tech—something printed on a big piece of poster board or drawn on the chalkboard before your audience arrives—or high-tech—such as a diagram that you project via PowerPoint onto a screen. Whichever route you choose, make sure we can see it; practice introducing it; interact with it right away; and then decide if you want to leave it visible or if you should get it off the stage.

2. Pre-Written Road Map

It can assist your audience to know where you are heading with your speech. For example, imagine that you are giving a talk about how to give a great speech. Your talk might have three points: Care about your topic; Speak with conviction; Choose your words carefully. So your visual aid could be a pre-printed list on a whiteboard that looks like this:

Public Speaking Tips

- Care about your topic

- Speak with conviction

- Choose your words carefully

There is your roadmap. We can see where you are in your speech. And the visual aid gives you an easy way to separate your beats—as you transition from one to another ("So you've got a topic that you care about. My next tip is to say it like you mean it—speak with conviction"), you can simply walk up to your visual aid and gesture to the point that you're now making.

3. Chalkboard, Whiteboard, Overhead Transparencies, Flip Chart, Foam Board

If your presentation is more interactive—for example, if you plan to ask the audience for its input—you could construct a visual aid before our very eyes. In that case, you should reach for the chalkboard, whiteboard, overhead transparencies, flip chart, or foam board.

Chalkboards and *whiteboards* are the old-fashioned tools favored by teachers. They can work for you, too. If you use a chalkboard, practice writing on it—you will be surprised how much time it takes to write words out, and you do not want to spend much time in silence, with your back to the audience. You can pre-write some parts, or perhaps ask an audience member to act as a scribe, so that you can continue to speak while the writing is going on. Keep a cloth handy to wipe chalk dust off your hands so you do not end up with handprints on your dark suit. That happens!

Whiteboards work like chalkboards, except that you write with magic markers on a white surface. It is a bit easier to write on the surface of a whiteboard, so you may prefer this to a chalkboard. You can use different colored markers to help compare and contrast your points. As with a chalkboard, you can create in advance some of your presentation in order to minimize time spent writing.

An *overhead transparency* can be a wise interactive choice if your handwriting is bad. You can pre-type some of what you plan to write and put it onto transparency film. You then project this film onto a screen using a transparency machine. You can also write on the film with markers.

A *flip chart* is a giant paper tablet that usually comes with a stiff cardboard back so that it can stand readily on an easel. *Foam board* is a large, stiff sort of light cardboard, easy to move around. You will reach for these instead of a chalkboard if you want to create a visual aid that cannot be erased. For example, if you are an attorney conducting an examination of a very dull witness, a flip chart or foam board can be your best friend. Ask the witness to leave the stand and write whatever is significant about his testimony on the flip chart or foam board. Maybe it is a drawing of an intersection where the witness saw something—you can predraw the intersection and then have the witness mark where he was standing and where the event occurred. Now the witness is more interesting because he is moving, and you have created a nice visual aid that you can introduce into evidence and give to the jury to use during deliberations.

4. Handouts

If your topic is complex, the audience may profit from a handout summarizing key points or providing data or the definitions of unfamiliar terms. Give some thought, though, to how you want to introduce the handout. It is usually a mistake to pass out a handout before a talk begins because the audience will tend to tune you out as they read through it, or may flip to the end to see how much longer you have to go—discouraging to the speaker. Instead, you might want to consider saying, "No need to take notes—there's a handout you'll be able to pick up when the talk is over."

If you need to distribute a handout, figure out how you will control audience attention once they have it. You might say, "I'm giving you a handout, but suggest you keep it face down until we have time to look at it together." Or perhaps you say, "Here's a handout of the text of the statute that we're discussing—I want you to look at paragraph 4, which is about halfway down the first page." You might also use bold or italics to draw attention to particular items in the handout. For example, if your handout is the text of Henry V's speech before the gates of Harfleur and you want to draw attention to Shakespeare's use of alliteration and onomatopoeia, perhaps you use bold and italics like this:

> The **blind and bloody** soldier with foul hand
> Defile the locks of your **shrill-shrieking** daughters;
> Your fathers taken by the silver beards,
> And their most reverend heads **dash'd** to the walls,
> Your **naked infants spitted upon pikes**,
> Whiles the **mad mothers with their howls** confused
> Do break the clouds.... [64]

Now your audience can glance at the handout and quickly see the words that you plan to discuss.

5. Any Three-Dimensional Prop

If you are teaching an audience how to hold a tennis racket, it will be much easier to make them understand you if you have the racket in hand. Bringing along a three-dimensional prop automatically gains attention as soon as you unveil it. Make sure that the audience can see what you need them to, even if it means moving among them or asking them to come closer.

Also explore the potential of using your own body and the room around you as three-dimensional props to enliven and clarify your speech. Al Gore does this in *An Inconvenient Truth* when he inhales and exhales to demonstrate the cyclical nature of the earth's carbon dioxide emissions. It is effective to say to your audience, "See that orange sign on the wall? The distance between me and that sign—that's how far Mrs. Smith was standing from the intersection when she saw the defendant's car run into the truck." Much better than: "Mrs. Smith was 30 feet from the accident." Most people cannot right away conceive of how far a distance of 30 feet actually is. It helps to have them visualize it.

6. Video or Audio Clips

Adding a video or audio clip introduces another voice and reawakens audience interest. Avoid the overly long clip, though—anything over 60 seconds is probably too long. Practice what you will be doing while the clip is playing. You do not want to stand in front of the audience awkwardly, folding and unfolding your arms and shifting from foot to foot. Instead, adjust slightly so that you are facing the screen (in the case of a video clip) so that you put the focus on the screen itself. This is the one time that it is permissible to turn your back to the audience. For an audio clip, keep it short and listen attentively, as you hope your audience will.

7. PowerPoint

PowerPoint is the visual aid of choice for most business presentations, and it is rapidly becoming a favorite of professors and lawyers as well. When PowerPoint is done right, it can be effective—it forces organization of thoughts and frees you from note cards to enhance eye contact. But if done poorly—if you make busy, dull slides and turn your back as you read them aloud—then there is nothing so painful to your audience or detracting from your thesis.

a. Writing your PowerPoint presentation.

You should start writing a PowerPoint presentation the way that you would write any speech—craft your script, check your organization, simplify your structure, sharpen your words, and then distill everything into beats. Those beats become the words on the PowerPoint slides. Do not write the text on the slides in complete sentences; instead, reach for headlines. Keep the slides sparse. Limit yourself to one thought per line, told in maybe four to five words, and only about three to four points per slide. Do not put each word onto a slide—some of the presentation should involve elaboration on your point. The slide merely emphasizes your idea or jogs your memory about the next thing you mean to say. If you go to the trouble to put a thought on the slide, the audience will think it is important. Do not include it unless it merits attention.

Here's the preceding paragraph as a PowerPoint slide:

DRAFTING POWERPOINT

- Write your script
- Then shorten, shorten, shorten
  - Don't put too many words on a slide
  - Use headlines, not sentences
  - 1 thought per line; 3-4 points per slide
- Don't include everything—just the important stuff

Here is the same paragraph as a poorly done PowerPoint slide:

POWERPOINT: DON'T DO THIS

- After preparing a detailed outline, it is really important to pare down your presentation to a few key points on each slide, as opposed to including the exact text of the points you want to make.
- Think of using headlines or sound bites, rather than entire sentences or paragraphs that you would read.
- To keep people's interest, it is better to have only one line for each point, and 3 or 4 points per slide.
- Don't include every single word that you're going to say. We'll stop listening to you and start reading. Also, if you put it into a visual aid, we'll assume it's important, so if you don't want us to get bogged down in dates or something like that, don't include them.

The dangers with the preceding slide are first, that you will be tempted to focus away from us and read it to us, and second, that we will tune you out and read the words on the screen instead. Either way, you have lost our attention.

b. Animation.

PowerPoint has an "animation" feature that allows you to bring in pictures or text or what have you with a big swoop and an interesting sound. Be careful of using too much animation, though. Using it once or twice to highlight a really important point can be effective, but if every new thought is introduced with a lot of movement and sound, it becomes distracting and irritating.

At its simplest form, you can use animation to bring up the words on your PowerPoint slide one line at a time, which helps control the timing through which the audience gets the information you are imparting. (You can do this through the custom animation program—pick the element of the slide you want to animate by putting your cursor next to it, choose "add effect," and then select a simple motion path such as "wipe" or "appear." But be wary of too much motion.)

c. Call-ups.

You can animate a PowerPoint slide to pull out the section of the slide that you most want the audience to examine. Say you are telling your audience about a report from the Department of Justice. Here is the first page of the report:

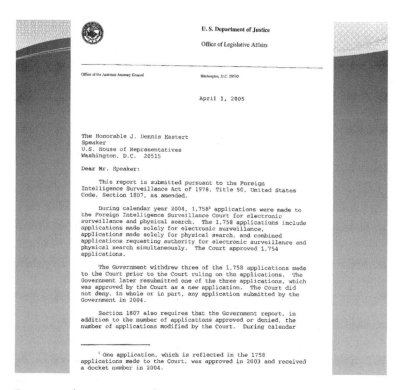

But you do not want them to read the whole thing—just one
sentence. Select that sentence and enlarge it so that the audience's
attention goes to it:

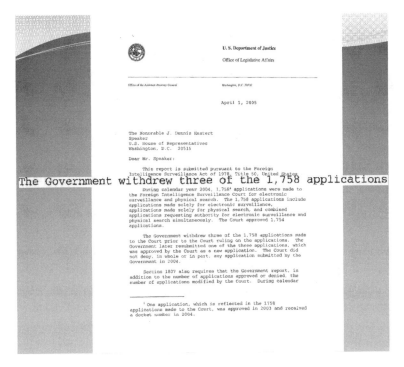

Consider highlighting the text in yellow as well.

C. Rehearsing with Visual Aids

Rehearsal is essential to any speech, but with a visual aid it becomes even more critical. You must live with the visual aid until you can use it seamlessly. Rehearse at least twice in the space where you will speak and with the actual visual aid. No trained actor would willingly go on stage with an unfamiliar prop; likewise, you must rehearse with any visual aid before you perform. Practice how you will introduce it; how you will interact with it; where you will stand in relation to it; and how you will set the visual aid down if you need to. If it is PowerPoint, also practice the timing of advancing from one slide to the next and where you will stand as you do so. When using a visual aid you should be able to set aside notes. PowerPoint gives you this ability, and other visual aids will as well because now you have an organizing principle—to talk about the thing that you are holding and pointing to. Be sure when you use your visual aid you do not upstage yourself—do not turn your back to the audience or allow the visual aid to distract attention. Bring it out when you want us to see it; put it back when you do not.

Finally, prepare for emergencies. It is wise to have an "emergency box" on hand for any presentation. Your box should contain things for physical emergencies—water, tissues, aspirin, a spare tie, or pantyhose—as well as prop emergencies. Bring a duplicate prop if you can. If you have a PowerPoint presentation, bring a backup of it in case your computer dies, and also bring a low-tech paper version in case the worst happens and you find that all the computers around you have died as well. We know of instances where a lawyer has come to court equipped with a fancy computer-driven presentation, only to discover that the computer system has crashed, nothing is working, and the jury is squirming impatiently, waiting for him to proceed. But the well-prepared wisely have on hand printed-out blown-up pictures of all slides so that you can muddle through. Perhaps, with that extra boost of adrenaline brought on by the emergency, your speech will be even better than if all had gone according to plan.

Chapter 8

Gender and Persuasion

Clear logic, the careful use of facts, and a confident delivery matter a great deal in persuading listeners. But the teachers of "New Rhetoric" (discussed more fully in Appendix B) warn that we should be concerned not just with our own attributes, but also with the psychological, sociological, and societal perspectives of our audience. New Rhetoricians point out that audience members have biases, preconceptions, and differences in experience that affect what each of them will find persuasive.

You can see this lesson in action when you consider how audience members may sometimes react differently to a speaker because of the speaker's gender.

This can happen even among the most well-intentioned audience members. As New Rhetoricians will tell you, people are informed by the culture around them. Society imprints ideas about permissible modes of male and female behavior—some of these ideas may be benign, some pernicious. Often these are so ingrained that an audience member may find herself responding viscerally to a speaker for fitting into, or straying from, norms of expected behavior without even realizing the source of the reaction. And some speakers unconsciously engage in gendered behavior, triggering reactions (both positive and negative) that they do not intend.

The fundamental rules of public speaking apply to men and women equally, of course, and have nothing to do with gender. You must know of what you speak. You must decide why you care about the topic and why we should. You should carefully craft your speech, practice it, and show some conviction. Your goal is to persuade your audience, maybe even move them to action. These tenets hold true no matter who you are.

But to be the most effective speaker you can be, you will want to consider whether you do anything unconsciously or habitually to trigger a stereotype because of your gender that might get in your way. Your best defense against the stereotypes is to know that they may lurk in the minds of your audience, so you can navigate around them if you choose to. (These stereotypes are not fair, but the danger they pose is real—even an enlightened listener will pay less attention if you seem to be a caricature of your gender.) Examine any such quality to assess whether it undercuts your authority and adjust accordingly. If you decide that you do not want to change your approach, you at least will be making a conscious decision about it.

A. Pitfalls for Men

Male Advocacy Danger Zones

- Bully: Tiresome, negative
- Patronizing: A turnoff to most
- Wimpy: Projects uncertainty

1. The Bully

Sometimes men are encouraged to perceive power in aggression. Male lawyers frequently adopt an aggressive, Rambo-like persona because of insecurity or even because some law firms cultivate this approach, encouraged by clients who want to see that the lawyer is "man enough" to do battle for them. This attack-dog style leads the male speaker to look at every interaction as a battle and every discussion as an opportunity for bloodshed. The Rambo speaker thinks of advocacy, especially litigation, as war. He exhibits disdain for opposing views and eschews civility and common courtesy because these ill-befit the true warrior.

Examples of this style of approach abound: President Clinton's much-criticized argumentative behavior during his wife's presidential campaign;[65] Rush Limbaugh's antagonistic radio broadcasts; the discourse of many cable news personalities; and finally, the behavior of a disturbing percentage of the trial bar.

Yet, despite its prevalence, many scholars and attorneys have rebutted its efficacy.[66] Among the worst pitfalls of this approach are the following:

- Those in the audience who are not predisposed to accept Rambo's message will be put off because it seems overheated or exaggerated. No jury, for instance, is likely to believe an advocate when he maintains that every single witness for the other side is lying, or to want to listen indefinitely to a lawyer who spends most of his time yelling.

- The overheated approach can lead that advocate to misstate facts. Rambo's opponent will be able to demonstrate where Rambo has played fast and loose with facts, and Rambo's Ethos will suffer.

- The speaker who yells frequently or always resorts to fighting words loses the ability to signal to his audience to listen up and focus on a particular point that he wants to emphasize. He has, by rhetorical excess, deprived himself of any ability to single out—through words, voice, or body language—the argument that really matters. This is the case because all angrily or aggressively stated assertions tend to merge. There is no "atom bomb" held in reserve.

- Even when the advocate does not want to sound aggressive, the habit is contagious and makes him attack regardless. If he tries to use a softer tone, after much bullying, it will ring false.

Potential Rambo speakers should be aware of a number of things:

PHYSICAL PRESENCE. To avoid falling into the Rambo trap, a male speaker should become aware of his own *physical presence*. If you are a large man, realize that standing too close to an audience (like a jury) can intimidate them. You should stand about six feet away from your audience. If necessary, use a tape measure to mark this distance out in a room that closely approximates the space where you will be speaking and tape a line on the floor to let you see how far away you need to be. It can be helpful to have someone watch you practice, to let you know if it feels that you are getting too close.

Notice physical proximity in less formal situations as well. A man may seem overly aggressive when he stands while the rest of the group sits. It will feel to them that he is deliberately towering over them. He may take up a lot of space at a table by spreading out his papers or leaning back in a chair with his legs outstretched, not realizing that the rest of the group understands this as an invasion of their physical space—or an aggressive assertion of his.

GESTURES. Be aware of hand gestures that can seem aggressive to an audience. Pointing or clenching your hands into fists are common mannerisms that can make an audience feel attacked. Practice your handshake to be firm and confident but not bone-crunching. If your handshake causes a wince, your new acquaintance will feel bullied.

VOICE. Pay attention to your voice. The Rambo speaker uses big volume. That can wear thin quickly. Notice if you have a tendency to interrupt others. People will listen more receptively if you have listened courteously to them as well.

TONE. Try to avoid a sarcastic, rude, or angry tone. As William F. Buckley once recounted, "A surgeon doesn't look down on the ruptured appendix and say, 'I'll get you, you son of a bitch.' "[67] Just as we expect calm objectivity from a surgeon, we similarly are more persuaded by it in a speaker. The calm, thoughtful tone of the self-controlled advocate works better, especially over time, than Rambo's tantrums.

This is not to say that there is never a time to be firm. Imagine, though, how much more effective a speaker will be if he has spoken in a calm, level-headed way throughout, and displays anger only rarely, and only when a great injustice has been done.

2. The Patronizing Male

Our second cautionary category is the Megalomaniac. A brother to the Rambo Warrior, the Megalomaniac oozes testosterone and self-satisfaction. All of us have met one—patronizing, arrogant, cocky, with a patent disdain for the views of others. In his megalomania, he believes he is a mental and physical Tarzan. The Megalomaniac may be the professor intimidating you in class, the partner at the law firm where you work, the opposing counsel who calls you "honey."

By putting himself on center stage, rather than the policies or views he hopes to convince us of, the Megalomaniac does not fare so well in his ability to persuade those on the fence. The "Me Tarzan" approach, in which the speaker lectures down to his audience, leaves no room for listeners to form their own opinions. Audiences are more convinced when they feel that they have reached their own conclusions.[68] In fact, many—Presidents Eisenhower, Reagan, and George H.W. Bush, for example—have profited by eschewing the megalomania persona for a more even-handed approach.

The self-importance of the Megalomaniac tends to drown out the understanding of his substantive message. An audience put off by cockiness or condescension will resist persuasion attempted by the Megalomaniac.

If you suspect that you are perceived as condescending or arrogant, try the following:

WORD CHOICE. Make sure to use familiar words rather than jargon. If you must use jargon, define your terms clearly but not in a way that implies the audience is ignorant for not knowing the word.

TONE. Record yourself to see if you unintentionally seem to be speaking down to your listeners. Imagine your presentation as a conversation with friends rather than an occasion in which you are pontificating.

BE CAREFUL OF HUMOR. Sometimes jokes go awry, particularly if the audience does not know you. A joke at the expense of another is not a good idea. An off-color joke is always dangerous. Self-deprecating humor can work, but not if it implies that you think you are smarter than your listeners.

BODY LANGUAGE. Think about how your physical interactions may be perceived. Try not to stand too close to people in a way that might invade their physical space, and be cautious about touching people, especially women—a hand laid casually on a shoulder might seem friendly to you but could be unwelcome to the person you are touching.

EYE CONTACT. When you are in conversation, be sure to maintain eye contact. Do not let your gaze wander, which people may understand as your looking for someone more interesting or important to talk to. And it goes without saying that ogling is unacceptable. Flirting in a professional setting is a no-no.

3. The Wimp

While bullying is not an effective course of action for a male, the opposite tack—wimpiness—also poses problems. Culturally, many expect men to exhibit some modicum of strength and are troubled when they do not. We have seen this play out time and again in our presidential elections. Jimmy Carter suffered from criticism that he was weak and indecisive.[69] John Kerry is another example—he never hit any stride of projecting power and strength, sitting passively for weeks rather than responding to "Swift Boat" attacks about his military career. Michael Dukakis in 1988 similarly could not summon an iota of strength in response to a question about the hypothetical rape and murder of his wife posed to him during the debates. Al Gore as a candidate sometimes seemed like a cardboard cut-out, especially compared to the energized Al Gore of *An Inconvenient Truth*. As discussed in detail in Chapter 14, these men lost presidential elections in part because of perceived weakness.

So what problems face the weak male speaker? When a male speaker is weak, or timid, or speaks with a low volume or with limited body language, an audience is likely to lose confidence in him. In his professional life, he may lose clients or find himself passed over in partnership decisions. In political leaders, the peril of being perceived as weak is that such a perception approaches being fatal—if a politician is not thought to have the strength and the guts to deal with disasters or to defend the country, then he is unlikely to be elected. What to do?

EYE CONTACT. If you struggle with this, be certain to look your audience in the eye. Practice it. Making eye contact is a simple, achievable way of demonstrating confidence. If you practice making eye contact in everyday life, such as when you encounter a colleague in the hallway or in a meeting, you will find that it is easier to meet people's eyes when you are engaged in public speaking as well. Think of your speech as a conversation, and look at a particular person as you make a point. Speak to that person directly. Then look at another person as you say your next sentence. It can be helpful to practice this with a sympathetic listener who can tell you if you are holding her gaze for too long or not long enough.

VOLUME. Make sure that you can be heard. If you speak softly, your audience will not be able to hear you and may become frustrated. The too-soft speaker often is dismissed as inconsequential. Practice speaking at a volume that reaches all your audience, even if it exceeds the volume you naturally use.

GESTURES. Examine your gestures to ensure that they convey confidence. If you clasp your hands together as if you are praying, fidget, or put your hands in your pockets, you unconsciously indicate a lack of strength. Try finding one or two places in your speech when you will use a strong, confident gesture, and practice it so that you feel comfortable doing it. Then strong gestures will begin to flow at other points as well.

B. Pitfalls for Women

Female Advocacy Danger Zones

- The "Little Girl": Lacks authority

- The Whisperer: Shows no confidence; who can hear her?

- The Onlooker: Silencing herself

- The Problem with Emotion (the "Hysterical Woman" versus the "Ice Queen")

1. The "Little Girl"

Women should be aware of vocal and physical mannerisms that unintentionally diminish them, making them seem young, ill-informed, or apologetic. To glimpse the stereotype here, recall the movie *Legally Blonde*. The heroine, Elle Woods, is underestimated because of her vocal and physical mannerisms and her unique style of dress. She surprises everyone with her intellect because her outward appearance makes it hard to take her seriously. It takes time for her to surmount those impressions. If you are worried that you might not be taken seriously, here are some things to watch for:

PITCH. Speaking with the high-pitched tone of a young child suggests that you lack experience and authority. Female voices are naturally higher than men's, and sometimes shoot up when the adrenaline of stage fright hits. If the notes are especially high, the voice can become shrill, which grates on the ears.

A higher pitch is also a cue that you perceive other concerns about the speech that you are making. When you come upon a section that you do not know well, or worse, an argument that you do not fully embrace, the stress may cause you to reach for higher notes in your range. The audience may not know *why* your voice has suddenly gone up a register, but they are likely to grasp that something is amiss. They are less likely to accept your point.

Pay attention to pitch. Record your voice. Listen to what happens when you feel nervous. If you get stuck in your upper register, listen for it and consciously lower your voice a note or two. Be sure to warm up with vocal exercises. Practice reading aloud or singing using the lower notes in your range, to ingrain the habit of reaching for those notes as well, not just the high ones. Every woman's voice includes low notes, even if she is unaccustomed to using them.

Try this exercise: Imagine that your dog is about to grab the dinner and cry out, "No!" Now imagine a child is about to run into traffic and yell, "Get back here now!" Notice how you instinctively use lower notes (and if you don't do so instinctively, try it again with a deeper voice). Note the power and authority that the lower tones give you. Every woman should cultivate her lower notes so she can draw on this authoritative tone when needed. This attracts notice in court and keeps your child out of traffic—both useful abilities.

UPWARD INFLECTION. Elle from *Legally Blonde* routinely uses an upward inflection, turning statements into apparent questions. The effect: We begin to question her, too. Monitor yourself to see if this is a habit. For many, the upward inflection falls mid-sentence (for example, "The reason I like this dress? is because it's blue.").

Again, it's a good idea to record your voice. Listen for upward inflections and notice when it happens. If it happens mid-sentence, try breaking the sentences into shorter ones to see if that solves the problem. Practice speaking aloud, consciously staying at the same pitch mid-sentence and then dropping down at the end. Invite a friend to a rehearsal, arm her with a rolled-up newspaper, and ask her to whack you when you seem to be asking for permission rather than making a compelling point or argument. Break the habit of seeming to question yourself when you know the answer.

Body Language. Many people, when nervous, fidget or adjust their clothes—physical "tells" that let the audience know that nerves are at play. This is distracting no matter what the gender. For women, fidgeting may involve playing with hair or jewelry, tilting the head, or smiling too much, sending unconscious signals that they are non-threatening. This undercuts authority. If you know you launch into "cute-girl" mode when under stress, imagine a "powerful you" to do the talking instead. Visualize it, then practice it over and over.

Remove the temptations that might lead to the fidgets—avoid dangly jewelry or clothes that will not stay still. Beware of the impulse to shrink yourself up or hide. Notice whether you habitually stand with your arms wrapped around yourself or your feet crossed in an effort to make yourself smaller. When you rise to speak, stand tall and proudly. Use your arms to gesture, not to hide. Keep your feet planted, not shifting or rocking. If you know that you tend to retreat or diminish yourself, realize that you have every right to be the one speaking, and take up some space! Smile occasionally, but not so much that you appear to be seeking approval.

Unnecessary Verbiage/Filler Noises. Say it; then stop. Many women will apologize for their words by adding extra phrases to soften their meaning. If you do, it makes you appear weak. Cut out phrases like, "I think," "don't you think so?", "it seems to me," "like," "you know," and "umm." If you routinely use filler words, then you must practice to break the habit. Practice again and again until you perform an entire speech without saying even one filler word.

Notice when you use filler words the most. For many, the habit arises when we search for the perfect word to regain our train of thought. The answer here goes back to Chapter 4, about speech writing. Make sure that your organization is tight. Know the order of your beats. Memorize the tricky parts so you do not reach for words. And then learn to be comfortable with silence. If you need a second to transition to the next thought, take it. The audience will not even notice a pause; periods of silence always seem much longer to the speaker than to the listener.

A related problem particularly dangerous for women is the habit of filling silence with meaningless space-holders. You may resort to this because you feel uncomfortable with silence, and you feel pressured to fill it. Or perhaps you have laid out an idea, but then feel constrained to repeat it or ask for audience agreement because you are uncertain of your power. See if this seems familiar. Instead of saying, "Taking Main Street is the shortest route," recognize whether you would be more likely to say, "I think that Main Street might be the best way for us to get there, because I'm pretty sure that it's shorter than First Street, isn't that right? I'm pretty sure that's right. So do you want to take Main Street?"

If this problem is yours, practice speaking extemporaneously. Try it while you are in the car—look out the window, pick the first thing that you see, and then speak for three minutes about it. Make every sentence short and crisp. Limit yourself to one point per sentence. Connect each sentence to your topic. Then stop.

2. The Whisperer

One of the authors attended a faculty lunchtime workshop and heard a young, female professor present a paper. The listeners included several tenured professors, all male, all elderly, some with hearing impairments. The presenter spoke softly, sometimes compounding the problem by looking down at the table or covering her mouth with her hands. She was competing with exterior noises filtering through an open window, but she did not feel sufficiently confident to take charge of the space and close the window. After the presentation, two of the attendees were overheard discussing the workshop. "Any idea what she said?" said one. "Nope," said the other. "Couldn't hear her."

This young professor had an opportunity to make her fine scholarship known but instead left her listeners with the impression that she was uncertain and too timid to control the workshop, let alone a classroom. This is a problem for any speaker, regardless of gender, but we have noticed over the years of teaching oral advocacy that low volume is much more common in female speakers.

Pay attention to your volume. A soft, melodious female voice is prized in many cultures, so many women are unaccustomed to filling a room with their voices. Other women speak softly because they are uncomfortable when all eyes are on them. Fortunately, low volume is easily corrected.

Know that you have something worth saying and that we would like to be able to hear it. Keep in mind that your volume needs to be a tad louder than you think. You must speak loudly enough so that the last row can hear you without strain. Try the following:

- *Practice raising your voice so that it becomes a habit.* If volume is a problem, conduct at least one rehearsal of every speech with some white noise in the background (a noise machine, a fan, a hairdryer, or the radio tuned to static). Deliver the speech so that it can be heard easily over that noise. Then use that volume in the actual presentation.

- *Speak even more loudly.* Watch the body language of the elderly. Throw your voice to them. If they are nodding and seem to follow, fine. If not, turn up the volume.

- *Include the eavesdropper.* Imagine that someone standing outside the door wants to listen, too. Speak so that he can.

- *Check in with your audience.* If in doubt, ask if they can hear you.

- *Take charge of the physical space.* Acknowledge the problem: "My, it's hard to hear in here!" Then close the window that is letting in noise from the street. Ask people to pull their chairs closer to you. You are the speaker—set up your stage.

3. The Onlooker

Sometimes women do not let themselves speak at all. This is a terrible problem that we see play out every day at the law school where we teach. Despite the fact that bright, talented female students make up half the population at our school, some classes are dominated by male students. When the professor asks a question, confident male hands shoot up into the air. Women are less likely than their male counterparts to volunteer a response (which professors realize, and which many try to remedy by intentionally calling on women to engage them in the discussion).[70] When asked about their reticence, some female students say that they worry about making a mistake, and others express the feeling that they don't know if they have anything useful to say. This is not a new phenomenon. The authors remember this same disparity in action during their own law school days.

The unfortunate result for the woman who sits silently by is that she does not practice answering questions as frequently as her male counterparts do. When she joins a law firm, she may find herself equally reticent in team meetings. This was a topic of discussion very recently at the law firm where both authors once practiced. One extremely smart female lawyer described how women were much less likely to speak up in team meetings. The team loses the benefit of her insight, and the female lawyer finds herself overlooked when plum assignments are handed around.

PRACTICE SPEAKING UP. If you often wish you'd taken the opportunity to speak in group situations, there is a cure. Try consciously making yourself speak in class or at a team meeting. Plan out what you will say so that it (hopefully) goes well. If it doesn't come out exactly as you imagined, *don't worry about it*. Pick yourself up, dust yourself off, and try again. You will find that others are much less critical of how you sound than you probably are of yourself. You will get much better at expressing your ideas the more you practice doing it.

4. The Emotional/Unemotional Woman

Displays of emotion can be problematic for any speaker (see our discussion of Pathos in Chapter 2). But this area is particularly tricky for a woman.

On the one hand, women are expected to exhibit a level of human feeling. Culturally, women are trained to empathize. A woman who does not express "acceptable" emotions—tenderness, compassion, motherliness—when emotion is expected is labeled ice-cold. For whatever reason, our culture distrusts women who do not exhibit caring qualities.

But the woman who cries readily or becomes visibly agitated when angry triggers another pernicious stereotype: the hysterical woman. The prejudice holds that women can be more creatures of emotion than logic. When a woman screams or cries, her anger or tears become the focus of the conversation, rather than the strongly felt message that precipitated the emotion.

An example: Hillary Clinton's emotions became the focus of political analysis during her presidential campaign. When Senator Clinton first announced her candidacy, she was a lightning rod for strong opinions among the electorate—many loved her but many hated her. Those in the latter group spoke of her as an "ice queen."[71]

So Senator Clinton's handlers undertook an effort to loosen her up. They encouraged her to show more of her private self. Senator Clinton began laughing more—but the laugh seemed, to many, unladylike—too big, too loud.[72] It is hard to imagine a similar amount of ink being spilled discussing the volume and quality of a male candidate's guffaw.

She laughs; she cries. On January 7, 2008, hours before the New Hampshire voters went to the polls to vote in the Democratic primary, Senator Clinton fielded a question from an undecided voter: "How did you get out the door every day? I mean, as a woman, I know how hard it is to get out of the house and get ready. Who does your hair?" Her answer was unexpectedly personal as she spoke about how important the campaign was to her and why she forged ahead every day. "Some people think elections are a game: who's up or who's down," she answered, and her voice cracked slightly. "It's about our country. It's about our kids' future. It's about all of us together. Some of us put ourselves out there and do this against some difficult odds." Tears began to well up in her eyes, but just as quickly, Senator Clinton composed herself and offered an articulate, coherent reply:

> This is one of the most important elections we'll ever face. So as tired as I am and as difficult as it is to keep up what I try to do on the road, like occasionally exercise, trying to eat right—it's tough when the easiest thing is pizza—I just believe so strongly in who we are as a nation. I'm going to do everything I can to make my case, and then the voters get to decide.[73]

This genuine display of emotion helped Senator Clinton. She won the New Hampshire primary, to the surprise of pundits and pollsters. The unexpected victory seemed in part to stem from this glimpse of her humanity.[74] That is because the few tears were controlled—just the slightest welling of emotion, quickly managed. She continued on and gave a coherent answer. A woman who shows sincerity and emotion but still retains a grip on logic—audiences love it.

So what to do? The female speaker must walk a fine line between showing too much and too little emotion. The acceptable emotions—conviction, compassion, warmth, humor—are almost always winning bets for women, and many females find it easier to telegraph these emotions than their male counterparts do. But beware the more dangerous emotions—anger, sorrow. If those emotions dot your presentation, set out to lessen them and to prove your grasp of logic so that the emotions do not overshadow the message.

It reduces to this: While you may find yourself measured by a different metric because of your gender, you will find that if you prove that you have something to say, and are under control, your audience will hear you. And then you may put yourself in a position to debunk pernicious stereotypes and replace them with a positive model of your own.

Chapter 9

Generational Issues

"New Rhetoric" posits that an effective speaker can draw on certain *fundamental experiences* to connect with an audience. Universal themes like love, grief, patriotism, or fear resonate across cultures and make audiences listen and believe—think of the themes favored by writers from the past, like Shakespeare, which continue to move audiences today. If a speaker is able to deftly incorporate a universal theme into a speech, she may have a much easier time driving her point home.

But New Rhetoric also teaches that, just as an audience may share certain universal experiences, each audience member also brings with him his own unique perspective. At the same time that a speaker is trying to appeal to certain universal themes, she must also tailor her message to the individual characteristics of the audience. This thoughtful tailoring is one of the most difficult aspects of speech writing.

One of the most commonly overlooked—yet most pervasive—factors that might affect an audience member's attitude toward a speaker (and that might help a speaker find a theme that will resonate) is age. The climate in which a person grew up and spent her productive years has a tremendous impact on her attitudes. In this chapter we discuss strategies for speaking to audiences of different generations. We also discuss communications issues that arise when generations interact with one another. We use the workplace as our primary setting, although the ideas we discuss could apply in any context in which the generations might interact.

Today's adult audiences (those that you will encounter in the jury box or at the workplace) can include four generations, each cohort bringing to the table its own expectations and "language."[75] Members of each generation have lived through their own historical moments that have shaped their perspectives. While people within the same generation may be differently marked by these moments in history, each generation shares certain similar experiences and attitudes informed because its members entered the adult world at around the same time. Of course, these are just general characteristics. Some of us have attributes of several age groups and some of us do not fit comfortably into any one age group. So while you will be able to call to mind people who do not seem to personify their generation, you will also find that most share some bonds with their contemporaries and may respond more favorably to communications that respect those perspectives.

Consider, for example, the mix of generations that you might encounter working at a law firm. Imagine that you have been asked to make a presentation at the law firm where you have been hired to work for the summer. Your audience will include the senior partner, who originally brought the client to the firm; the managing partner, who runs the day-to-day operations of the case; a senior associate who is working her way up to partner status; and a swath of junior attorneys. You will be aware that each holds a different function within the team of people who are working on the particular case. Each of them may also hold a different status at the law firm itself. And each audience member may hail from a different generation. What, then, must you do to connect with this diverse group? We will consider each audience member in turn, beginning with the senior partner, who holds the seat of honor at the meeting.

The Generations

- Traditionalist: Born 1920-1944

- Baby Boomer: Born 1945-1966

- Generation X: Born 1966-1979

- Millennials: Born 1980 or later

A. The Traditionalist Generation

The senior partner is part of the "Traditionalist" generation. Traditionalists were born between 1920 and 1944 and are now in their late 60s, 70s, and 80s. Many came of age in the "Father Knows Best" era of the 1940s and 1950s in families headed by a working father, with a stay-at-home mother as second in command, and children who were sometimes seen more than heard. Traditionalist men often worked for a single employer, expecting that they would remain there indefinitely. If that is true of this senior partner, then he may feel a fierce loyalty to the firm that would mystify his younger colleagues.

The Traditionalists' professional and personal lives were maintained in separate spheres, meaning that many of this generation expected men to be the primary breadwinners, while wives tended to home and family. Rarely did the Traditionalist ask for "work–life balance." Women in this cohort who are now in the workplace often began their careers after their children were grown. Many took on jobs that capitalized on skills honed in familial roles—as support roles to the men in the office (secretaries, administrators); working in industries that center on home, children, and caregiving (such as real estate, teaching, and nursing). To the Traditionalist, work bespeaks duty; it is an obligation undertaken to protect and feed the family.

Influenced perhaps by the hierarchical nature of the families in which they were raised, Traditionalists took that same sense of hierarchy to the workplace. Workplace dress codes in the heyday of the Traditionalists were formal. Language was professional. Success was marked by tangible indicia, such as the corner office.

Even in today's less formal workplace, an employee seeking to impress a Traditionalist would be well advised to dress formally, respect job titles (for example, calling a professor "Professor" or the boss's wife "Mrs." until invited to use a first name), and leave the off-color language at home. Habits of informality might seem natural or comfortable to a younger employee, but to a Traditionalist, they can indicate lack of respect for what this generation accomplished and can offer. The Traditionalists' core values include respect for authority, and because they have worked long years to earn senior status, they will not suffer slights to authority lightly. A younger employee will find it difficult to undo damage if she starts off on the wrong foot with a Traditionalist by addressing him with a "Hey, you" or an off-color joke, or by wearing flip-flops to work. Even though only intending to lighten the mood, her Ethos will suffer and the Traditionalist may question the young employee's judgment.

The Traditionalist learned to communicate at work by dictating (words later transcribed into formal, written memos by helpful secretaries), and also through in-person presentations. When Traditionalist men first became the heads of the office (the 1960s-1980s), there were few computers, no Internet, and no e-mail. Business was conducted face-to-face. Oral presentation skills are particularly prized by this powerful cohort. The written memos produced by this generation were crafted more deliberately than the hastily composed e-mails of today, and so the Traditionalists expect a finished quality to written work.

This is another potential pitfall for the younger employee working for a Traditionalist. The senior partner may have mastered e-mail well enough to hunt-and-peck his way through a short message on his Blackberry, but that message may be full of typos and misspelled words, and exhibit scant attempts at capitalization or punctuation. A younger employee may be lulled into responding in an equally sloppy way. Resist the temptation. While the senior partner will feel fine about sending poorly composed messages (after all, mistakes in spelling in the past were corrected by excellent secretaries, so he rarely fretted about them), if he receives the same from you, he may judge you as sloppy or illiterate. Consider e-mails to be formal business communications and compose them to be business memos. Spell-check them; write a draft, then let it sit and read it over again before pushing "send." Remember, your e-mail sends a message about your professionalism, and the Traditionalist audience member probably will not read it in the same way that a younger recipient might.

Younger employees may be frustrated by the Traditionalists' resistance to technology. Many Traditionalists seem intimidated, stubbornly refusing to master what, to a younger cohort, seems so plain. Some Traditionalists read e-mails only after they have been printed out by their secretaries, and some have no idea even how to turn on computers. Younger co-workers may gripe that the workplace could function more efficiently if the Traditionalists in the room would only make a little effort.

Savvy employees realize that this technology gap offers opportunity for a young worker to forge a connection with a Traditionalist that spawns dividends. The younger employee pausing to think about it will recall that technology like computers and e-mail only recently came into the workplace. To many Traditionalists, learning the new technology is akin to conquering a foreign language late in life. While members of the Millennial generation (born in the 1980s or later) and, to some extent, Generation X (born between 1966-1979), are native speakers of digital technology because they mastered it as youngsters, the older generations may have a more difficult time with it because it came onto the scene later in their lives. A Millennial employee who helps the

Traditionalist use new technology without being patronizing can find that he has a mentor and ally in his corner.

TAKE-HOME MESSAGE: Themes that might appeal to a Traditionalist include duty, loyalty, commitment to the employer, honor, sacrifice, and patriotism. Keep communications formal (no off-color language, no inappropriate jokes, no overly familiar forms of address). Make sure your body language and dress are professional; sloppy clothes, slouching with hands in pockets, and a refusal to observe the niceties of eye contact and a proper handshake may communicate a lack of respect. Manners are important. Traditionalists favor in-person communication over electronic communications. Be respectful of all the contributions Traditionalists have made to the world; sarcasm, eye-rolling, and a know-it-all attitude from a younger speaker will turn off the Traditionalist listener.

B. The Baby Boomers

Baby Boomers were born between 1945 and 1966, and range in age anywhere from their mid-40s to their mid-60s. At many workplaces, Traditionalists have taken senior status; the Baby Boomers are now running the show. They are bringing in work, evaluating your performance, and making hiring and promotion decisions.

The Baby Boomer generation is the largest of the four generations discussed here, and proud of its legacy and contributions to the world. Boomers came of age during the time of "sex, drugs, and rock-n-roll"—many more Boomers claim to have been at Woodstock than could possibly have been there. The nation underwent seismic changes during the youth of the Baby Boomers, and they were at the forefront of bringing those changes about. Boomers rightfully claim credit for the civil rights movement, women's liberation, and putting a man on the moon.

Baby Boomers are also responsible for the 80-hour work-week.[76] Boomers tend to revere career and traditionally have been willing to sacrifice for it, from sleep to family life, in order to excel. Once known as the "Me Generation" for focusing on their own personal development, Boomers later became involved parents who simultaneously sought to continue to climb the corporate ladder. Older Boomers solved this potential conflict by giving their children (Generation X) a measure of autonomy, leading to a generation of "latchkey kids." Younger Boomers, responding to the 24-hour news cycle that makes the world seem so perilous, have scheduled their children's free time to keep them supervised and safe. They are the "helicopter" parents, hovering anxiously over children, hyper-involved in all aspects of their lives.[77]

Junior employees communicating with Baby Boomers need to be mindful of the Boomers' "live to work" ethic. Balance has been difficult for this generation, and many of the cohort will find attempts by younger workers to carve out time for family to be evidence of a lack of commitment to the job. This does not counsel against protecting private time. Instead, it means that you should be sensitive in presenting the issue to a Baby Boomer supervisor. Put in the hours to show your dedication and work ethic before requesting a flexible work schedule, for example. If you want to work remotely, realize that you will need to prove to a Boomer that it will not impact the bottom line.

The Boomer generation ushered in the eras of civil rights and women's liberation, resulting in significant shifts in the workplace. Although this generation is less formal than the Traditionalists, it is still important to pay attention to titles and hierarchy. In particular, if a Baby Boomer supervisor is female or a person of color, he or she may have had to surmount prejudices about ability to be a leader. Do not diminish these achievements by addressing this Boomer less formally or respectfully than you would a white man in the same position.

Baby Boomers are more comfortable with technology than Traditionalists, and make efforts to master it, in order to succeed at work and also to keep up with their children. But they are not the digital natives of the younger generation, and therefore also value memos and in-person communications just as they delivered when they were new to the job. You can impress a Boomer boss by showing adeptness at oral presentations and taking extra time to clean up your e-mails.

TAKE-HOME MESSAGE: Themes that might appeal to Baby Boomers include enthusiasm for work (including a willingness to devote long hours to a task); a belief in the ability to effectuate change; political engagement; and, in the workplace context, a focus on how your idea will generate profits. Show engagement and enthusiasm in your presentations to Baby Boomers; a disaffected, "who cares" approach may turn off a Boomer audience.

In the workplace, build up your Ethos by paying your dues (which may mean demonstrating a willingness to work long hours) before asking for special accommodations. Baby Boomers worked long hours to master the intricacies of the job; if you are a younger employee, your opinion will not carry weight until you, too, have gained some experience.

Get to the point right away; a money-conscious Baby Boomer client will want you to cut to the chase so that you are not running up the bill, and a Baby Boomer on a jury will resent wasted time in the face of all the other demands on his private and professional life.

C. Generation X

The young partner or senior associate probably hails from Generation X. This generation was born between 1966 and 1979 and is in its 30s or early to mid-40s. Gen X is the "baby bust" generation, the cohort that followed Baby Boomers when birth rates declined. As a result, there are far fewer Generation Xers than Baby Boomers.

Gen Xers were born to Traditionalist or Baby Boomer parents, and are more likely than older generations to be children of divorce. They came of age during the 1980s, when the term "latchkey kid" was coined to describe a child who found her own way home from school, entertained herself, got her homework done, and frequently made her own (most likely microwaveable) dinner. As a result, Generation X is independent and brings this do-it-yourself attitude to the workplace.

When Gen Xers entered the workplace, many started companies of their own, such as the Dot-Coms of the 1990s, administered with their own anti-hierarchical instincts and casual dress codes. Many Gen X children grew up to be wealthy Gen X adults by marching to the beats of their own drums. Many others have found they earn less money than their parents because they have intentionally taken jobs paying less but offering more time for family.

Generation X is more likely to be skeptical of hierarchy and of the surrounding world than preceding generations. It is the generation of Jon Stewart and the eye-rolling, shoulder-shrugging "whatever." As the generation has aged, it has become more engaged—Barack Obama and Sarah Palin are both members. Gen Xers watched their grandparents, who may have worked loyally at one company for years, experience layoffs and forced retirements. Many of them were resentful of absent Baby Boomer parents who seemed to give more to employer than family. As a result, Generation X is less likely to be loyal to a single employer. This is the first generation to show willingness to switch jobs every few years in a quest for a better one. Work, to this generation, is often fungible.

Generation X is comfortable with computers and e-mails, although it can recall early days of the rise of technology and wax nostalgic about hours after school dedicated to video games, like Space Invaders on the Atari. It is likely to be open to communication via e-mail, teleconferences, and the like. A chief preoccupation of Generation X is work–life balance—this generation first coined the term. This cohort is at the age of young parenthood, and may be protective of private time. A Gen X boss may be open to flexible work arrangements and nontraditional communications, provided that these help get the job done. If e-mail invites junior associates to pepper Gen X supervisors with questions at all hours that could have been answered with thought, the Gen X boss is likely to be irritated. Generation X has little patience with hand-holding, especially if that erodes its time for holding the hands of its own small children.

TAKE-HOME MESSAGE: Generation X is motivated by themes of self-sufficiency, the world beyond the workplace, family, balance, and independence. If you are speaking to a Gen Xer, you might want to get to the point right away; like the Baby Boomer, a Gen X audience is annoyed by time wasted. Gen X listeners will also be turned off by someone who cannot think for himself. To build up Ethos on the job in the eyes of Generation X, try to be as self-sufficient as you can; constant requests for help and feedback will annoy a Gen X colleague. If you are speaking to a Gen X audience, be mindful of the overuse of Pathos; this generation of skeptics is less likely than previous generations to be swept away by emotional appeals.

D. The Millennial Generation

The youngest generation of workers—the junior associate—is likely to be part of the Millennial Generation. This generation was born sometime after 1979 and is in its 20s. These were parented by young Baby Boomers, the "helicopter parents" who interjected themselves into details of their offspring's lives.[78] Millennial young lawyers are high-achievers who were involved in numerous activities and organizations during their schools days. They are usually driven, with a useful energy and focus. They tend to be closely connected to their families, which instills in them a deep sense of confidence that can lead to rich creativity. Work–life balance is likely to be important, and it gains in importance as Millennials marry and start their own families. They also may have spent hours volunteering and are likely to be motivated by desire to help others or improve the world.[79] As a result, they will respond if you communicate how the task at hand plays a part in a larger, noble goal.

Millennials bear the burden of a negative stereotype of being needy. College admissions officers and law school administrators have written about the shift in academia brought about by the helicopter parents who insist on coming along to campus tours and even job interviews.[80] Professors also have noted that Millennial students are more likely than the preceding ones to demand (often in multiple e-mails) a road map to exactly how to earn an A in a class, and protest if it is not awarded once mapped-out steps are taken.[81] The economic downturn has been hard on Millennials graduating from law school. They are frightened about graduating with huge loans and no job in hand. But they are also disconcerted and depressed that the world does not invariably reward even the most dedicated. It is possible to do it all right and not get what you want and deserve. This is profoundly unsettling to anyone, but even more to a Millennial who, up until now, has known a world of ordered steps and achieved rewards.

The Millennial facing this new reality must tap into her own creativity to forge solutions to the challenges of the new economy. The Traditionalist mentor may offer wisdom if he experienced a surprising layoff of his own late in life, as many did. A Generation X mentor will also have plenty to say, as she did not have faith in an employer's ability to take care of its employees in the first place.

TAKE-HOME MESSAGE: A Millennial audience may be moved by themes of making the world a better place, explanations of how the task at hand plays a role in a greater good, and a demonstration of respect for their ideas and opinions. This group is extremely comfortable with expressing an opinion; a presentation to Millennials may be more effective if the audience is invited to participate and ask questions. Millennials are extremely comfortable with technology and demand visual and aural stimulation, so reach for visual aids when addressing this audience. They can process things quickly and may become bored if your presentation is too labored. Pay attention to your transitions; Millennials are accustomed to fast-moving television, movies, video games, and the Internet, so you may need to jazz up your talk as you move from point to point to keep them engaged.

If you are a Millennial yourself, be mindful of the impression you send because of your cozy tie to technology. Resist overwhelming supervisors from older generations with a slew of e-mails. Traditionalists and Baby Boomers will read disorganization when you ask questions in 20 e-mails that you could have distilled into one. And Generation Xers may muse scornfully that you should have figured out the answer for yourself. You might be accustomed to working anywhere—maybe your favorite study spot in law school was to work at a table at Starbucks with your iPod plugged into your ears—but realize that the older generations in particular expect to see you in the office. (A Generation X supervisor may be more comfortable with you working someplace other than your desk, but you should establish yourself in the office first before you do too much of this so that you have the opportunity to forge personal relationships at work.)

A common complaint by older workers about Millennial co-workers is that they are so plugged into technology (listening to music, constantly texting) that they are not connecting with the team or paying attention to important information about a project. Be mindful of how earphones and Blackberries buzzing might make you appear to older co-workers as if you are distracted or disrespectful. Comfort with technology is an asset, but do not let it distance you from your co-workers. Do not let your ability to multitask lead others to believe that you are not actually listening. If you dispense with the earphones to communicate in person, you can be the standout Millennial—the one others seek to mentor.

Chapter 10

To Sum It Up: Checklists on the Good, the Bad, and the Ugly

A Summary of the Best and Worst of Oral Advocacy

Great advocates carry around mental dos and don'ts lists as they prepare to sally forth. Ours is as follows:

A. The Good

- *Bullet points*—Most good speakers start by writing out important presentations, then editing slavishly, shortening, rearranging, mastering the beginning and the end, and then reducing the text in a last draft to mere bullet points. Following that, they practice and then practice some more. The effective advocate learns his text, hones his structure, and frees himself from his script to connect with his audience.

- *Projecting conviction*—Audiences respond to confidence. There are myriad ways to show confidence: by maintaining good eye contact, utilizing body language, being sensitive to tone, and making effective use of cadence. There is a difficult balance here—over-the-top delivery can backfire, but telegraphing,

"I'm just going through the motions because I get paid to do this" is worse.

- *Power*—The adroit advocate can make his speech more powerful or forceful through the use of pauses, adjustments in volume, and strong gestures.

- *Naturalness*—Reach for a relaxed, conversational tone. Audiences are put off by a memorized, stiff, and halting delivery and straight word-for-word reading that so often masquerades as the stuff of oral presentation.

- *Compelling structure*—The clearly organized speech is easier to follow and more moving. Clear presentation must flow in a simple-to-understand, well-defined order—one that makes sense and leads, ultimately, to the audience's full support of your thesis. Emphasizing transitions to make the structure clear is helpful. Themes are also useful, ones that tie the structure together and can serve as the take-home message.

- *Attention-grabbing*—Be mindful of the short attention span of the audience. When their attention wanders, get it back. The use of effective visual aids, anecdotes, analogies—all of these are likely to be appreciated and enjoyed by your audience, while regaining their attention and making your speech memorable.

- *Clarity*—We understand and are willing to listen to oratory that is precise. Audiences are likely to tune out or grow impatient with needless complexity that sails over their heads.

- *Plain words*—The speaker who can make his point in everyday language is more likely to be effective. Aristotle wrote that strange words should be avoided at all costs. An audience that does not understand your words is likely to either miss the point or be put off by what they interpret as a condescending tone.

- *Connection with the audience*—You must size up the wants, disposition, and possible biases of your listeners. Invoke only those points that ought to be readily acceptable to the "universal audience," for example, common sense and fair play. Note what sets apart your "particular audience." What do you want from the audience? Where do you need to make special appeals to a segment of them? Where are the possible land mines that might alienate some who would otherwise be sympathetic to your position? Better not to take any chances in the direction of potentially offending any segment of your audience. You never know when the occasional swear word, or off-color joke or comment, might seriously offend those who are not expecting it and might block receptivity to your argument.

■ *Rigorous preparation*—Engage in fanatical preparation for your subject matter, because precision and command of a subject inspires confidence and engages your audience. Uncertainty—or worse, inaccuracy—undermines your credibility.

■ *Calm*—In almost all circumstances, a cool, unflappable demeanor enhances Ethos appeal. Flashes of pique and anger suggest that emotions may be overpowering your reasoning.

■ *Preemption*—It is wise to pull the teeth out of the best of an opponent's argument. Deal with your opponent's position accurately, fairly, and head-on.

■ *Visualization*—People remember what they see. Therein lies the overriding importance of effective use of PowerPoint, poster board graphics, computerized reenactments of events— the whole range of graphics. But visual aids must be done well. The truly gifted speaker can sometimes cause an audience to visualize a scene without using graphics, by painting clear pictures through well-chosen words.

■ *Brevity*—Never speak longer than necessary to cover your points effectively.

■ *Positivity*—Audiences tire of negative attacks, particularly those that are personal or mean-spirited. Listeners tend to be more receptive to the affirmative, the justness of a position, its common sense, and the positive force of the arguments and facts flowing in its favor.

B. Unpersuasive Rhetoric: The Bad and Ugly

Here is a checklist of common flaws that can harm oral advocacy:

- *The bridge too far*—There is sometimes an instinct to push a good argument beyond its breaking point or to misstate or overstate your case. As Thucydides said, stick to the essence of what you must show, do it well in order to persuade, and then stop. Argument outside the core of what you need to convince us of is distracting and can result in a lack of confidence in you or your cause.

- *Gambling*—Stick to what you are reasonably sure you can show. Don't play fast and loose with truth or facts. (A room full of people is smarter as a group than virtually any single individual.)

- *Lack of conviction*—Your uncertainty is easily perceived by your audience.

- *Halting beginnings and ends*—This violates core rules of rhetorical teaching. Audiences are most influenced by their first impressions of a speaker and best remember what they hear last. A telling psychological advantage goes to the speaker with the strong start and strong close.

- *The long speech*—If a speech drags on, the audience has difficulty paying attention and grasping the most important points.

- *Misuse of Pathos*—Aristotle taught us that one must, on occasion, be adroit at engaging the emotions of an audience, but sparingly—when called for and when you can convince them that you fully believe in the emotional appeal. Charlatan efforts to rip at the heart strings will surely backfire.

- *The boring*—The audience is unlikely to listen or be susceptible to persuasion if it can't wait to get out of the room.

- *Big words*—You get no oomph from the polysyllabic term if the audience doesn't understand it. They may consider your use of big words an exercise of arrogance.

- *The unstructured*—There is no force to the presentation that wanders all over the map, leaps from conclusion back to premises, and twists up its arguments. We are linear thinkers, single-path processors; sequential reasoning is how we are best persuaded.

- *The canned*—At all costs and in most settings, avoid excessive, even substantial, reading of text or mouthing the apparently memorized. We are accustomed to communicating conversationally, and we come to doubt the earnestness of a speech that is read or delivered by rote.

- *The Rambo approach*—Eschew a mean-spirited or disdainful attitude in advocacy. There are occasions when an advocate needs to get pretty firm, but a constant string of venom about a position or its exponents wears thin quickly.

The "List of Style Failings" can be summarized quickly as:

- *Stiff, cold delivery*—Cast off the security blankets of hanging onto the podium with both hands, defeating gestures, and virtually verbatim reading of written script.

- *Weakness*—We perceive it at once and interpret it as a lack of conviction.

- *Arrogance, cockiness*—These backfire every time.

- *Colorlessness*—If you have only brief three- or four-minute windows of audience attention at a time, you must do something to get it back.

- *Monotone*—The monotone projects boredom with the cause and lack of conviction.

- *The overly theatrical*—Color and interest value are important, but not when it turns into a hand-waving, emotion-laden from-beginning-to-end exercise.

- *Projecting fear*—Practice so that you can think about what you mean to say, not about how nervous you are.

- *Vocal tics*—Audiences are distracted by a bombardment of aahs, umms, likes, and you-knows. They perceive these fillers as a lack of conviction and the exclusive province of the beginner.

- *Misuse of PowerPoint or teleprompter*—PowerPoint, done effectively, can be persuasive and recharge waning attention. Teleprompters are often necessary for politicians, especially when making speech after speech. But used badly, technology can sink your speech.

Part Three

Rhetoric Applied to the Real World

The need for persuasive speaking arises in all sorts of contexts beyond the formal lecture hall. Part Three examines how rhetoric operates in our day-to-day lives, and applies the rules of superior verbal communication to a variety of everyday contexts. Some of the contexts that we examine are specific to attorneys (such as "Rhetoric in Court"); others have a broader reach (like "Rhetoric Gone Haywire," "Oral Communications in the Workplace," and "The Rhetoric of Presidential Campaigns"). Examining rhetoric at work in the real world will help you gain a deeper understanding of the skill of verbal persuasion.

Chapter 11

Rhetoric in Court

Oral advocacy is the bread and butter of being a trial lawyer. You must be able to persuade a jury if you hope to win the case for your client. If a motion is raised in the trial or the case is appealed, you must be able to argue effectively before judges. Any litigator will want to master the fundamental rules of rhetoric because they map perfectly onto the task of persuading judges and juries.

Non-litigators can also benefit from learning about rhetoric in court. The skills required to be a successful trial lawyer have everyday application. At times we all engage in "direct examination" (the questioning of one another for information), "cross-examination" (in which we challenge and test one other), an "opening statement" (an objective overview of a position), and "closing argument" (where we argue our case as persuasively as we know how). "Making an Argument to a Judge," at the end of this chapter, offers tips that will be useful to anyone who must address an audience that might interpose questions during or after the presentation, such as an employer, a board of directors, or a potential client.

> ### "The Essence of Good Trial Advocacy"
>
> ■ Be calm.
>
> ■ Consider the audience's points of view.
>
> ■ Avoid all-nighters.
>
> ■ Project "fair play."
>
> ■ Deal fairly with the opposition.

A. The Trial

Trial lawyers contend that trial is the most difficult advocacy exercise of them all, for the following reasons:

1. The challenge of maintaining credibility for a long period of time;

2. The difficulty of appealing to a diverse audience;

3. Physical exhaustion, if a trial is a long one;

4. The problem of maintaining poise when things go wrong; and

5. The demands placed on a lawyer by the wide range of tasks that he must perform at trial, from opening statements to direct examination and cross-examination to closing arguments to discussions with the judge and opposing counsel.

We discuss each challenge in turn.

1. Credibility

Trial places the maximum strain on a lawyer's credibility. The trial lawyer must be ever mindful of being persuasive without misstating or overstating the facts or hitting the wrong tone.

In daily life, a speaker might pick and choose points on the other side of his position to attack, formulating "straw men" that are easy to knock down. He might misstate facts, exaggerate his case, and conveniently omit evidence that disproves his point.

This approach will backfire at trial. If you play fast and loose with the truth, opposing counsel will seize on what you have done and highlight any misstatement or overstatement for the jury. The jury will remember it. Instead, answer the best points of the opponent's case, deal with them thoroughly and respectfully, and make clear the reasons that your opponent's arguments are outweighed by stronger countervailing ones. Logos, as discussed in Chapter 2, is of paramount importance in a trial.

Credibility also hinges on striking the right tone. The Rambo, tough-guy approach (Chapter 8) is unpersuasive to juries over the course of a long trial. A halting, mumbling delivery (discussed in Chapters 5 and 8) suggests a lack of confidence in your case and erodes attention. Aim instead to project confidence, warmth, and likability. This involves knowing your case well and attacking head-on any fear of public speaking. Relying too heavily on your notes, displaying quivering hands, or having a frozen or muted voice-box can all sever an attorney's connection with the audience, spelling doom for him and his client. It helps here to study great speakers, and to practice, practice, practice.

Finding an experienced mentor to help you can also be useful. At its best, these mentoring sessions involve videotaping of your opening statement, closing argument, and examinations of witnesses (simulated, if necessary), and then line-by-line critiquing until fear erodes and confidence builds.

2. Audience Diversity

At trial, you face an audience with varied interests and roles, such as are discussed in Chapter 9. You must appeal to, and never antagonize, every juror, each having disparate educational and demographic backgrounds. *Voir dire* examination of jurors, jury forms, and other demographic information can help you figure out who are likely to be the leaders of the group and how to persuade them. Pay attention to the body language of the jury. If any juror seems bored or confused, try to explain again (perhaps more clearly or more vividly) the point you are trying to make. Parties in major cases often hire jury consultants, sometimes trained in psychology, to help lawyers deal with the art of persuasion and audience reaction.

You must also be mindful of the point of view of the judge. You must convince your own clients that you have been powerful and persuasive. Finally, you must avoid needlessly antagonizing the opposing party (with whom your client may still want to engage in fruitful settlement negotiations). A hydra-headed audience, indeed.

3. Exhaustion

Many trials now consume weeks or even months. One of the authors was chief trial counsel at an asbestos insurance-coverage case that dragged on for four years in a San Francisco court. The length of a trial is a substantial challenge. It is a physically and mentally taxing exercise: It demands extensive preparation and 9 to 5 "performance" every day at trial. This may be further complicated by the experience of waking up at 3:00 in the morning from an attack of nerves or because you have hit upon some perceived spectacular breakthrough idea that causes you to spend the rest of the night frantically re-working your presentations. The exercises described in Chapter 6 can help keep your voice healthy and calm your nerves before trial.

4. Maintaining Poise and Calm

Especially in a protracted trial, something is likely to go wrong. A key witness may let you down by succumbing to unexpected or superb cross-examination. The judge may rule against you about whether a piece of evidence is admissible or whether a particular line of questioning can continue. A trial is the ultimate test of whether you are able to retain a calm demeanor under stress. It is important to remain calm because the jury will perceive when you have been knocked off your game and react negatively to flashes of anger. Keeping your cool matters in three-day trials; it is even more important in those that last for several months.

5. The Challenge of the Varied Tasks of a Trial

Trial counsel confronts a multitude of tasks, her role constantly adapting to the requirements of the case, making the trial even more challenging. These include pre-trial planning, the opening statement, direct and cross-examination, and closing argument.

a. Pre-trial planning: Choosing a theory of the case.

Before the trial begins, you will want to devise a "theory of the case"—a rational, compelling story that you can tell on behalf of your client. This is much the same as the process discussed in Chapter 4 about finding a reason for the audience to care about your speech. A good theory of the case (for example, "This is a case about police incompetence and a rush to judgment," or "This is a case about a cheater who always takes the easy way out") will help you select the points that are the most important for you to emphasize. It will help you determine where to begin with your opening statement and closing argument, what witnesses to call, and what evidence to present.

The lessons of the psychologists, discussed in Chapter 2, can be helpful as you design your trial strategy. Remember the importance of primacy (the first moment of a presentation) and recency (the last moment) as you decide the order in which to present your case (where to start in your opening statement, which witness to call first, what questions to ask first, where to begin and end in your closing). You will also want to consider before the trial begins how you will preempt the best points that your opponent is likely to make in order to take the sting out of them. This may change what you say in your opening statement or your decision to put a particular witness on the stand, or it may cause you to file a pre-trial motion to exclude something that would be damaging to your case. The structure of a trial must be carefully planned.

It is the trial lawyer's job to keep the jurors interested and engaged throughout the proceeding. As with any audience, jurors need to consider one point at a time, so simplifying your points into themes (discussed in Chapter 4) is key. Helping the jury to visualize your points by using a piece of evidence or a visual aid (see Chapter 7) can be quite effective. Choose your themes and decide what pieces of evidence and visual aids you plan to use before the trial starts. You will want to make sure that all of your pieces of evidence and visual aids are permissible under the rules of evidence and may even want to make a pre-trial motion to make sure that the judge will not prohibit you from using them.

Finally, don't wing it. Preparation is essential to a successful trial.

b. Opening statement.

The trial begins with each side presenting an *opening statement* outlining its version of the case. The opening statement is an exercise in Ethos (Chapter 2)—you must establish that you are credible in order to earn the trust of the jury. The opening statement is also a moment of primacy, or first impression (discussed in Chapter 2). A trial lawyer must project calm in this initial presentation, while at the same time grabbing attention and being clear. Delivery (discussed in Chapter 5) is also crucial. If the jury decides during the opening statement that a lawyer is dull or lacks confidence, the lawyer will find it more difficult to capture and hold the jury's attention.

The Opening Statement

- Simple
- Well-structured
- Non-argumentative
- Extremely important advocacy

The opening statement poses a challenging writing exercise. The law imposes an artificial rule on opening statements: At this point in the trial, the trial lawyer is only permitted to state the facts to be presented in the case and may not yet "argue." This means that appeals to inferences, common sense, fair play, and passion—the stuff of normal conversation—are forbidden.

For example, a lawyer would be permitted to say in an opening statement, "The evidence will show that John Jameson had two affairs, which he kept secret from his wife for years. You will also learn that he told lies to his mistresses about his relationship with his wife during the period of the affairs. Finally, you will learn that Mr. Jameson lied to investigators when questioned about his marriage and these relationships." Those are all facts, and if you are challenged about them, you will be able to tell the judge which witness will testify about them (and why they are admissible statements under the rules of hearsay).

But you are not permitted to draw any inferences from these facts during the opening statement. You could not say, "John Jameson is a liar," although this would be a fair conclusion to draw and certainly a point to imply in questioning and to state explicitly in your closing argument. But in an opening statement, a conclusion like "John Jameson is a liar" is an impermissible argument and will get you into trouble. Careful crafting and wordsmithing are therefore critical to a successful opening statement. You must be careful not to wander into impermissible argument, but at the same time, you will want to be mindful of lining up your facts so that the jury can begin to draw its own conclusions about what those facts mean.

c. Direct examination.

After both sides have delivered opening statements, questioning of the witnesses begins. When a lawyer calls a witness to testify on behalf of his side of the case, he asks her questions in order to elicit facts helpful to his position. This process is called *direct examination.* Then opposing counsel is permitted to ask questions of the witness as well in *cross-examination.*

Direct Examination

- Homework galore—preparation is essential
- Lawyer is not center stage
- Clarify repeatedly
- Short, if possible

Here comes another artificial rule of law: The trial lawyer conducting a direct examination cannot engage in "leading questions" or "a question that suggests its own answer." A proper question on direct examination would be, "Where did you go next?" The question does not suggest an answer; the witness could reply any number of ways ("I went home." "I went to the store." "I went to bed.") A leading question (improper during direct examination) would be, "You went to the store next, didn't you?" because this question suggests the answer ("Yes, I went to the store.").

This is another difficult writing exercise. It is wise to formulate your direct examination questions in advance so that they are asked properly, because this odd way of questioning is not the way we naturally talk to one another in everyday conversation. A simple rule of thumb: Try to start each question on direct examination with "who," "what," "where," "when," "how," or "explain." If you do, you probably will have asked an open-ended question.

Successful direct examination of a witness involves a great deal of strategic thought. You need to carefully plan which witnesses you are going to call and whom to exclude. You need to determine the most effective order in which to present your witnesses (usually putting powerful witnesses at the beginning and end of your case, and burying the weaker ones somewhere in the middle). You must master everything relevant that your witness has written or said in earlier depositions or other testimony so that you know what to ask about and can properly assess whether the witness could give damaging testimony; hone the structure of each examination to keep it simple and easy to follow; prepare the witness for the most effective but truthful answers to the most difficult topics likely to arise on cross-examination.

Direct examination is, therefore, heavy on Logos (Chapter 2) and requires crafting a good structure (Chapter 4). As you make a decision about each witness, ask yourself, what is the theory of my case? How does this witness support the story that I am trying to tell? If several witnesses could tell a particular part of the story, does it make sense to put them all on the stand? (Sometimes it doesn't, if a witness has said or done something damaging that could make him vulnerable on cross-examination.) Just as you would sharpen the structure of a speech, you will also want to sharpen the order of the evidence that you present and the questions that you ask. You will not be able to make a little speech in between witnesses to make it clear to the jury why you have called a particular person to the stand. Instead, you must ask questions of the witness that will elicit the information that the jury needs to draw these connections themselves, until you are able to bring it all together in your closing argument. (More about the closing argument further on.)

Finally, a note about delivery. The trial lawyer must accustom herself, in the course of a trial, to a subordinate role during direct examinations. She does not take center stage; the witness does. The witness is the person who saw the critical events and can tell the jury about them. The jury will believe the evidence more if it comes straight from the witness's mouth, not the lawyer's. Keeping the focus on the witness can be tricky, particularly if you are a better public speaker than the witness is. You can help the witness along by asking clear questions, meeting with the witness numerous times to help him become comfortable with his role, and keeping your own sentences during direct examination short and to the point. Direct examination is the time for evidence from the mouth and writings of the witness, not rhetorical flourishes by the trial lawyer.

d. Cross-examination.

Cross-examination is another question-and-answer exchange between a lawyer and a witness, usually designed to demonstrate flaws in the witness's testimony (for example, "You were 100 yards away from the accident, weren't you? And you weren't wearing your glasses, were you?") or to impeach the witness (that is, "You said the opposite during your deposition, didn't you?"). It is a Logos-laden exercise. To do it well, the trial lawyer should strive to know more about the witness's prior writings and testimony than anyone else, including opposing counsel and even the witness himself. You can learn a great deal by listening to testimony of others and by talking to others who have knowledge of the witness. Watching direct examination gives a lawyer clues about a witness's demeanor, personality, or tendency to anger, misstate, or exaggerate. Like direct, cross-examination should be structured carefully to accentuate the most important points, yet be brief enough to command attention.

During cross-examination, lawyers are permitted to ask leading questions. A leading question (one that suggests its own answer) helps you keep control of the examination so that the witness says only what you want him to say. It is a powerful tool, and you should use it. The focus during a cross-examination rests on the lawyer, who is connecting the dots through his questions, rather than on the witness, who (if the examination is designed well) will probably only say, "yes."

Cross-Examination

- Use leading questions.
- Set hooks for rebuttal and closing argument.
- Use an objective tone.
- Draw out the unbelievable.
- Impeach with facts, not tone of voice.

Cross-examination can and often does backfire. It has been said that "more trial lawyers have committed suicide than homicide" by *gambling*, asking one question too many. Asking questions to which you do not know or cannot prove the answer, or to which you cannot force the witness to agree, is a dangerous game.

For example, imagine that you are examining John Jameson, described above in the opening statement section. You probably will have taken his deposition before the case began, and perhaps during that deposition he will have admitted that he had two affairs, kept them secret from his wife, kept his two mistresses secret from each other, and told the mistresses that he planned to leave his wife when he in fact did not. A safe cross-examination would proceed like this:

> Q: Mr. Jameson, you had an affair with Laura Smith, didn't you?

> Q: And you did not tell your wife that you were having an affair with Ms. Smith, did you?

> Q: In fact, during the period of your affair with Ms. Smith, you kept a credit card that your wife didn't know about, correct?

> Q: And you charged vacations with Ms. Smith to that credit card, didn't you?

> Q: You told Ms. Smith that you would leave your wife for her, true?

> Q: But in fact you did not leave your wife, did you?

If you have a deposition in which John Jameson confirmed that those facts are true, then you should be fine cross-examining him in the manner described above. If he changes his answers, you are permitted by the rules of court to "impeach" him with the deposition; that is, to read his original testimony in order to show that he has changed his story. But resist the temptation to ask that ultimate question ("You're a real jerk, aren't you?" or "So you're a liar, right?") that you know the witness will resist.

It is unlikely that he has admitted to being a jerk or a liar in his deposition, so you will not be able to force him to agree with that statement. He will fight with you, and you will lose control of the examination. Have patience; wait for closing to tie it all together, when the witness is not on the stand to argue with you.

One famous example of a disastrous cross-examination occurred during the prosecution of O.J. Simpson for the murder of Nicole Brown Simpson. The prosecution asked Simpson to try on, in front of the jury and with millions of people watching on television, the leather gloves purportedly used during the murder. But the prosecution could not, and did not, know whether the gloves would fit. The prosecutors had no opportunity to try the gloves on Simpson in advance. By the prosecution's own theory, the gloves had been wet and caked in blood—they might well have shrunk. Nonetheless, they decided to take a chance. When the gloves did not fit, the prosecutors supplied defense counsel Johnnie Cochran with the opportunity to craft a memorable refrain for his closing argument: "If it doesn't fit, you must acquit."[82] This is an excellent illustration of the dangers of gambling.

Another danger in cross-examination: Beware the impulse—through body language, tone, and choice of questions—to beat up on virtually every witness you confront, painting each as either a liar or ignorant. Jurors are often suspicious of highfalutin, high-priced trial counsel, and they are unlikely to believe that witness after witness is incompetent or incapable of telling the truth. They may side with the witnesses.

Even if you are proving a witness to be a liar (for example, when you are impeaching a witness by confronting him with his own prior inconsistent statement), a tone that shows that you are confident and have mastered all the facts works better than a tone that hints that you take pleasure in humiliating the witness. Trial lawyers who bully lose the Ethos battle. The tough stuff should be used pretty rarely and with surgical precision: (1) on the vitally important adverse witness, and (2) when the trial lawyer has solid evidence to prove that a witness is lying; when spins, evasions, or flat-out untruths are unmistakable. For more about bullying, see Chapter 8.

e. Closing argument.

The closing argument is the opportunity at the end of the trial for the lawyer to explain it all to the jury. In a closing, the lawyer goes through the evidence and offers her most persuasive argument about why her side should win. The closing is classic forensic advocacy, as described in Chapter 3, and the lawyer has a whole arsenal of persuasive tools at her disposal. She can use stories, themes, refrains, and humor; she can appeal to common sense, fair play, and the emotions; and more generally, she can project her winning qualities to persuade her audience. To be effective, the closing argument must be clear and logical (Logos); possibly moving (Pathos); and believable (Ethos). The structure must be tight and the delivery full of conviction. The closing argument can be the most fun of all the elements of a trial for a lawyer, but it requires the careful use of all the tools of oral persuasion.

Closing Argument

- Combination of epideictic, deliberative, and forensic speeches

- Explain the unexplained—close the loopholes

- Themes—group into a few big points

- Importance of the "wrap" (the final paragraph)

B. Making an Argument to a Judge

We turn now to the topic of presenting an oral argument to a judge or a panel of judges, either when presenting motions before a trial court or arguing an appeal, and without a jury listening. The tips here are also applicable to any oral presentation in which the speaker must respond to questions, such as presentations to a board of directors, the senior partner in a law firm, or the press. In such an event, you have a cause to advocate and usually will be given a chance at the beginning of the proceeding to state your position. But most of the persuasion will happen in largely extemporaneous fashion, in response to questions or probing. Perhaps you will have submitted a written document in advance to help you make your case, but perhaps not.

Here is how to proceed:[83]

1. Spend Some Time Preparing

You can anticipate many of the questions the judge is likely to ask. Write out the best answers you can give and then reduce your text to bullet points so that you can remember each part of the answer.

2. Practice

Try to arrange a moot court session with a wise colleague who has read the briefs. Practice answering the questions you wrote in Step 1 out of order so that it will not flummox you if the court takes points out of order on the day of the hearing. You might want to write each question on its own index card with a pithy answer on the back, and then shuffle the cards each time you practice.

3. Answer the Question

Answer the question forthrightly and at whatever time it is asked. Never say, "I'll get to that shortly." Answer it now.

4. Be Brief

Brevity sounds more confident than a rambling answer. When the answer does not lend itself to brevity, give the bottom line first and then explain the reason for any caveats or footnotes. Simple answers are easier to deliver and less likely to be interrupted in the middle. They are easier to listen to and they command attention.

5. Respond with Full Candor

Don't ever try to pretend away the obvious strength of the other side or the apparent weakness in your case. Deal fairly and openly with the opponent's best points. Do not risk doing damage to your credibility (Ethos).

6. Be Selective

Be selective, both in the *quantity* of points you make and also in their quality. Get to the main points, prioritize them, and make sure you know when and how to use them. Advancing the unnecessary weak argument rips at Ethos, preventing you from ever getting around to the best that you have to say.

7. Answer the Exact Question That Was Asked

If the judge has asked a question that seems off-point, answer it anyway and then gently steer the conversation back to the main points of discussion.

8. Pay Attention to Delivery

Your tone will be more effective if you focus on the positive aspects of your case rather than ripping at your opponent. Use a calm, confident demeanor and formal body language (no hands in pockets!). Avoid getting defensive. If the judge sounds like he is attacking you, take a deep breath and try to focus on the positive points you want to make. Finally, just relax and do the best you can. None of us ever give the perfect oral argument, but we get better with practice.

A note about the most perplexing feature of this exercise: Some judges are "hot," peppering you with questions from the get-go, while others sit like stone and say very little. (Thankfully most are in the middle.) How do you prepare for everything from vocal tigers to silent sphinxes?

First, run a background check. If you know ahead of time the names of the judges who will be hearing your appeal, try to discover, from a knowledgeable source, what the style of each panel member is like. You sometimes can find videotapes of oral arguments on the Internet, which you could watch to get a sense of the style of the various judges. Prior familiarity with a panel helps an advocate frame his argument and allows him to adeptly interpret a panel member's demeanor while the advocate is speaking.

Second, if in doubt, prepare for a fairly active court. Distill your presentation to your two (possibly three) most important arguments, and formulate succinct, clear answers to the questions you are likely to confront. If instead you are met with silence, take that opportunity to flesh out your most important points, reiterate them, or explain a third affirmative point. Always know your key points, so that you always know how to fill the time.

Chapter 12

Oral Communications in the Workplace

The typical young employee in an office setting may spend much of his first years researching and writing documents for more senior colleagues. He may find himself spending much time alone in his office at his computer. If he uncovers a question about his task, he may fire off an e-mail to his supervisor or perhaps leave a voicemail; simpler, really, than to track the person down and ask the question face-to-face. When finished with the assignment, he may e-mail his product as well, perhaps print it out and leave it on the supervisor's desk. But rarely will he take the time to meet with his boss in person to present his findings orally. This is a mistake.

In a computer-centric world, it is too easy to spend the days communicating in writing rather than in person. Resist that temptation. If you communicate exclusively through the written word, you lose:

1. *The chance to practice.* The more you speak, the better you become at thinking on your feet. (More about this in Chapter 13, "The Effect of Technology on Communications Skills.")

2. *The chance to make a human connection.* If the boss sees you, she is more likely to care about mentoring you and listening to your ideas. We cannot overstate the importance of this.

   To succeed in the workplace, those you work with have to want to keep you there. This will happen only if they actually know who you are and like you. It is not enough to do the work, or even to do it well—you may find that you have checked all the boxes and done everything you have been told to do, but if you lack the informal connections that are essential to succeeding on the job, you will not move ahead. Mentoring is a key to success. No one will mentor you if you are simply an e-mail machine and not a human being.

3. *The chance to charm.* If you hone that skill of looking the other person in the eye and speaking confidently to him, you will be the young employee most likely to be invited to that important dinner with the client.

4. *The chance to read body language and clear up misunderstandings.* When you speak with another person face-to-face, you can tell when the conversation starts to go off the rails. This is harder to notice when an exchange takes place over e-mail. E-mail and other written communication can take on tones that the writer never intended, and you may miss signals of impatience or confusion when your audience is responding in writing rather than conversation.

Here are some thoughts about how to increase the opportunities for making oral presentations in the workplace, and suggestions for how to go about it.

A. When to Speak?

Any time you are given an assignment, seek the opportunity to make an oral presentation, not just a written one. Spend time designing the oral presentation—review Chapter 4 about writing for speaking and be sure to practice out loud. Recognize that you may be interrupted with questions. You need to master the topic so that you can tackle it out of order. Never respond, "I am getting to that." Answer the question as asked. (The techniques described in Chapter 11 about making an argument to a judge apply here as well.)

Be flexible. If there is something that did not strike you as important but your supervisor wants to know about it, then relax and discuss it with him. Do not be concerned if the oral presentation does not proceed as planned. This is a conversation, but one that can show you in a good light if you have prepared in advance and planned out how best to present the most important points. If you have done your homework, your audience/supervisor is sure to be impressed.

Consider using a visual aid. For example, if you are relying on related documents (perhaps a study or a statute) to support your point, bring the most important documents along with relevant sections highlighted and marked with tape flags so that the supervisor can see how you can substantiate the argument.

Seek out opportunities for more formal speaking engagements as well. Does your department need someone to make the presentation to the managers about your recent projects? Raise your hand! The best way to improve your public speaking is to do it as much as possible.

If your employer offers training opportunities to improve public speaking, sign up for them, even if they do not seem directly applicable to your type of work. For example, law firms often will arrange for associates to participate in trial practice workshops. A corporate associate, never in court, still needs to be able to speak well to clients, so sign up to participate if you can. Practicing an opening statement made to a jury will help you hone skills you need even if your only "statement" is going to be made to a board of directors.

Force yourself to attend company social events. Look on these as opportunities to practice improving your speaking skills. Even if cocktail parties make you feel like the shy kid in the junior high school cafeteria, force yourself to walk up to people and introduce yourself. Hold eye contact; speak confidently. These events are intended to enable you to meet others, so it is fine—in fact, encouraged—to approach a stranger with a smile and an outstretched hand to say, "Hi, I'm _____. I don't believe we've met." If you don't know what to say next, try asking what he has been working on lately or talk (in positive terms only, in case you have stumbled upon one of the event organizers) about the food. It gets easier every time, and it offers you yet another way to practice thinking on your feet. You may even make a new friend. Also, you may find that your colleagues are equally uncomfortable in awkward social situations and grateful to find anyone friendly. It is a way to make the connections you need to get interesting assignments at work.

B. How to Speak?

If the situation is informal (a cocktail party, for example), the key is to *listen* intently and to make sure your body language is as relaxed and open as possible. Keep eye contact. Do not let your eyes wander around the room as if you are looking for a better conversation partner. Smile.

For a more formal presentation—a meeting with your supervisor in which you plan to present a project, for example—you need to allow yourself as much time to prepare as you would for a speech with any audience. Organize your thoughts into themes, as discussed in Chapter 4. Practice how you will say them. Practice them out of order as well—perhaps put one point apiece on index cards, shuffle the cards, and then discuss the topics in whatever order they appear.

An important difference between the supervisor and a typical audience is that your boss is a *repeat* audience. She will hear from you today, she has heard from you before, and you hope she will listen to you again. Ethos, or credibility, is important in any presentation, but it is doubly important when you have a captive audience. Resist the temptation to exaggerate facts, to make claims that you cannot support, or to bluff when you do not know something. Ask any lawyer who appears before the same judge again and again—you are much better off by saying, "Your Honor, I do not know, but I will find out," rather than guessing and being proved wrong in the end. Once your credibility has been lost, it is lost forever.

With any audience, body language is important. Good posture bespeaks confidence. Dress professionally in order to project authority. Avoid inappropriate flirtation, the off-color joke, coarse language.

Be aware of time constraints—not your own, but your audience's. In a typical speech, this normally means that you do not exceed the time you have been allotted. In a speech to a supervisor, respect the demands on the supervisor's time. Do not beat around the bush—taking ten minutes to warm up to your topic will only irritate her. Cut to the chase. Give her the answer, and then if she is interested, take whatever time she gives you to present your thoughts, argument, or project.

When you approach your boss with questions that will lead to your final presentation, be sure that you are thoughtful about how you do it. Do not interrupt her every ten minutes with e-mailed questions; instead, wait until you have a critical mass of questions and you cannot make forward progress without consulting her. Ask your questions succinctly and thoughtfully. Take the time to figure out exactly how to ask it so that you do not waste her time with uhs and umms as you struggle to collect yourself.

Respecting the supervisor's time also means respecting deadlines. If you miss a deadline, everything you say thereafter will be colored by the assumption that you are sloppy, lazy, or unreliable. You should assess the pace at which you are working and determine at least 24 hours in advance of a deadline whether you can meet it. If you cannot, go to your audience member/boss and tell her, "I will not be finished with the memo by tomorrow at 5:00, but here is what I can give you" (an oral report, perhaps, or the parts of the memo that deal with x and y). Then tell her when you will be finished and *do not* miss the new deadline, no matter what it takes.

If you meet your deadlines, your audience/supervisor will be more receptive to your ideas about your project. If you cannot meet the deadline but have been professional and responsible about a warning, you should still be able to retain goodwill. But if you blow off a deadline and slink into your boss's office late, that tardy memo will not be well received, and your boss may not want to see you face-to-face at all.

C. Be Canny About E-Mail

In many workplaces, it is possible to spend the entire day on the computer, communicating exclusively through e-mail, with few face-to-face conversations. Don't do it. When chained to e-mail, you are isolated from co-workers and miss the human connections that make your job more worthwhile.

E-mail can also be dangerous because of its informality and the speed with which e-mail messages are composed and sent. You may think you are sending an informal e-mail to a co-worker, but then your co-worker unexpectedly forwards that e-mail to someone more senior, and suddenly your credibility drops because your writing was sloppy.

E-mail messages can also take on an unintended tone. You may think that you are making a funny joke, but the reader of the e-mail may see it otherwise and take offense. Because the communication happens in cyberspace, you are unable to read the facial expressions of the recipient and have no idea when you have done injury to a relationship, whereas in person you could quickly apologize and the incident would soon be forgotten. In e-mail, the offending message sits in the recipient's inbox to be stewed over or very possibly forwarded to others.

It is tempting to shoot off an angry e-mail when tempers are high, a frequent occurrence in a high-stakes profession. Perhaps it feels good at the moment of hitting "send"—you got off a zinger and the person assailed does not have a prompt comeback because that person is not sitting right there. It may seem you have gotten the last word. But you have not. The recipient may respond in kind, and then a relationship capable of salvage has been savaged. People will say things in e-mail that they would not say face-to-face.[84] If you are upset, put the Blackberry down and walk down the hall to work things out. (See Chapter 13 for more thoughts about the effect of technology on communications skills.)

Chapter 13

The Effects of Technology on Communications Skills

In addition to the traditional difficulties that all of us must surmount in order to improve our speaking skills (such as lack of training, fear, haphazard preparation, and the like), there exist new barriers to mastering the art, the likes of which Aristotle or Demosthenes could never have anticipated. How can we hope to master oral communications skills when we speak less and less frequently because of our attachment to a computer or Blackberry? As we evolve toward spending half our communicating hours in silence—twittering, texting, e-mailing, web searching—our verbal skills suffer.

The numbers attesting to the growth of dependence on technology are astonishing. Over the past decade, the number of e-mails that are sent each day has increased twentyfold. Text messages once numbered in the hundreds of thousands; now more than 4 billion are sent each day. Video game revenue has more than tripled. Studies show a sixfold increase over the past decade in time spent online.[85]

William Powers's splendid book, *Hamlet's Blackberry: A Practical Philosophy for Building a Good Life in the Digital Age*, tells of other evidence, both statistical and anecdotal:

- Teenagers surveyed in a Nielsen study averaged more than 2,200 texts sent and received a month.[86]

- Waiting in Manhattan for a stop light to change, Powers noticed a dozen others around him, each immersed in their tiny electronic machines.

We see evidence of this preoccupation with technology in shopping centers, restaurants, offices, universities, and law firms. Rarely do we observe anyone who is not glued to some screen, reading or tapping away. We are all quickly becoming "digital maximalists," the term coined by Mr. Powers to mean the person who cannot escape technology.[87]

There is no disputing that the computer and its offspring do magical things. They connect us to a world of knowledge; they speed up everything (including the writing of this book); they connect us with friends, family, and business; they correct our spelling; they keep our books organized; and they let us buy our clothes at the push of a button. The list grows. Ask anyone how technology improves her life and you are likely to hear her wax rhapsodic with praise.

But concerns also are emerging about the effect of the overuse of gadgetry—what over-dependence on computers can do to an individual's social skills or familial relations, for instance.[88] To those concerns, we would add the following: Does all that silent time spent at the machine erode our verbal competence when it is necessary to once again speak?

It can, unless you are mindful of the role that technology plays in your life. For example, as you work on a presentation, realize that the technology can interfere with your concentration. Allowing a new e-mail pop-up, or the red message-waiting light that blinks on your Blackberry, to disrupt your work momentarily blocks out your preceding thoughts. It takes time to recover your lost train of thought with each interruption.[89] When you are constantly interrupted by various people with messages about different subjects, it is very difficult to do any "big picture" thinking.

The preparation for every fine oral presentation requires periods of quiet, calm, and reflection—a heavy dose of "inward direction." Structuring the order of your presentation is an act of creativity. That is why experienced speakers hole themselves away, far from any distractions, most certainly from the flashing light that signals a new message, to work on their presentation.

Computer mania collides with whatever form of *Walden Pond* experience we crave to achieve—those calm, quiet, contemplative, anxiety-relieving moments. By contrast, a steady diet of computer noise throughout the day is likely to add stress rather than reduce it.[90]

Another danger: When we communicate through e-mail, texts, and the like, we are not speaking, nor are we listening to others speaking. These machines are non-verbal. The tasks they permit are those of silence. (Even a cell phone, which of course can be used as a verbal communications device, is just as likely to be used to e-mail or text nowadays.)

Does this matter? It does, and in central ways. We can improve our speaking skills through verbal interactions with friends, family, and colleagues. These exchanges offer us the ability to practice expressing ourselves verbally, to develop our use of cadence and tone, and to experiment with various substantive forms of argument. We learn what works and what does not work by the myriad conversations we take part in, over and over, every day. If we spend the bulk of our days communicating solely through typing or texting, we miss out on the opportunity to hone our speaking skills.

We also learn by *listening* to those we encounter in daily life. Why do I like that person or why do I not? What did I learn from her? We learn to mimic some of what we admire. Our vocabularies increase in part through reading, but also by *hearing* new words. We decide to use them because they sounded good.

We benefit by listening to wonderful speakers (and we learn what to avoid from bad ones)—but not if we are mentally absent, absorbed in our computers. Many students can remember the spectacular lectures of a favorite professor. But now many professors compete unsuccessfully with the Internet for their students' attention, leading some to ban laptops from their classes.[91] The distractions of technology can rob you of the chance to really observe fine speakers at work.

The case here reduces to an axiomatic, almost syllogistic one. If

1.   verbal interchange is essential to achieving comfort and skill as a speaker, but

2.   we carve out a huge chunk of that experience and forfeit it to silently staring at a screen,

3.   it *has* to follow that our grounding for excellence in speech has been eroded to that precise extent.

The long and the short of the matter is that if we do not take the time to speak or listen, then the quality of our oral skills suffers. Make a point of taking time to call people instead of e-mailing them. Meet friends for coffee and conversation. Put down the Blackberry and go to a colleague's office to discuss an idea face-to-face. Your verbal skills will improve, and you may find that your day is more pleasant as well.

Chapter 14

The Rhetoric of Presidential Campaigns

"Yes, we can."

PRESIDENT OBAMA[92]

"Extremism . . . is no vice."

BARRY GOLDWATER[93]

A crucible on which to test the "why care about public speaking" bias is to study the past 75 years of how, whom, and why we have elected our top leader. Some claim that political campaigns have been reduced to sound bites and sloganeering, or that they lack a nuanced discussion of policy choices. Others hold to the hope that ideological differences, at bottom, explain the results. But neither of those extremes is as certain as another explanation: Winners and losers of all those elections are directly correlated with who best exemplified, and most trampled upon, the classic tenets of rhetoric expounded centuries ago.

A. From the Mouths of the Candidates

1. Franklin Delano Roosevelt (1932, 1936, 1940, 1944)

Roosevelt won four times and guided us through a war and depression. Why did he keep winning? He was a gifted rhetorician: the fireside chats, the comfort he evoked, the Day of Infamy speech after the Japanese attack on Pearl Harbor.[94] (See the Prologue for an example of his excellent speech-making skills.) Despite all the naysayers about the place of rhetoric in recent elections, voters in FDR's day reacted to his persona, his rhetoric, and his advocacy.

2. Harry Truman (1948)

When FDR died, Harry Truman was his Vice President: a lightly regarded, failed haberdasher. Truman was pitted against a formidable foe—Thomas Dewey, an elegant, well-regarded Wall Street lawyer who was extravagantly financed by the Republican elite. Dewey at first had a daunting lead in the polls.

But here came Harry. He fired up his supporters through speeches delivered from the caboose of his train: "Give 'em Hell, Harry," they would shout on his "whistlestop" tour.[95] Dewey, for his part, regurgitated essentially the same wooden speech every time. His supporters implored him to warm up, to show some power, but he did not.

Harry sounded like himself every time because of his plain-spoken style. He started gaining, a point at a time. Even by election night, the famous *Chicago Tribune* news headline barked out "Dewey Defeats Truman." The great radio commentator, H.V. Kaltenborn, as late as midnight after the election votes were dribbling in, claimed that Truman would be swamped by morning's count.[96]

Not so. Truman won the battle of Ethos: People liked the son-of-a-gun. He was long on Pathos (he was a great storyteller and self-deprecating) and comfortable with the logic of his position. His delivery and word choice defied all the conventional wisdom that said he was too unintelligent to be any sort of leader. The classical rhetorician would have predicted a Truman victory and, thus it happened—straight out of Aristotle.

3. Dwight D. Eisenhower (1952, 1956)

The consequences of Truman's victory lived beyond his term of office and reached into the next eight years as well. Had Dewey performed as an adequate advocate (or Truman as ineptly as his meager reputation), Dewey would have won and Eisenhower would never have become President or even sought the office. As David McCullough ably summarizes in his book, *Truman*, Eisenhower had no lust for the job. He was ambivalent about his party affiliation and preferred tranquility to the limelight.[97] He held no ambition to become President, but the Republican Elders prevailed upon him, fearing a second victory by Truman or the man in the wings, Adlai Stevenson. Reluctantly, he let his name be put forward, and he won.

Stevenson was extraordinarily talented and articulate. His command of language and delivery was exquisite—perhaps too eloquent for his own good. He spoke over the heads of his audience, and he was perceived by many to be too highfalutin, too academic, and too intellectual. (For more about the importance of seeking communion with your audience, see Chapters 2, 8, and 9.)

Eisenhower, in contrast, was seen as gentle, calming, and patriotic. He was also considered intelligent (at least, enough to have been a leading architect of World War II victories), sound of judgment, and just plain lovable. The campaign slogan "I Like Ike" captured his appeal. Eisenhower, then, was king of Ethos; his war credits burnished him with Pathos as well. But it goes too far to explain the Eisenhower victory as pure anti-intellectualism, a topic recently recounted in Elvin T. Lim's book, *The Anti-Intellectual Presidency*.[98] Stevenson did not so much lose the office because of widespread antipathy toward his brainpower; rather, Eisenhower won because he was beloved. Voters trusted his judgment. Ethos and Pathos trumped Logos.

Presidential Campaigns in Thumbnail

- FDR: soothing, strong

- Truman: plainspoken

- Dewey: wooden

- Eisenhower: Ethos strong, likable

- Stevenson: highfalutin

- JFK: wordsmith, funny, used refrains well

- Nixon: nervous, sweaty but knowledgeable

- Carter: Ethos strong, perceived as weak

- Reagan: smooth, likable

- Bush I: pleasant but bland

- Dukakis: stiff, poor delivery

- Clinton: warm, powerful, testosterone-driven

- Gore: still, no advocacy "home base"

- Bush II: common man appeal

- Kerry: stiff, cold

- McCain: halting, a reader

- Obama: powerful, evocative

4. John F. Kennedy (1960)

Kennedy's narrow victory over Richard Nixon is yet another triumph for rhetoric over a host of the conventional considerations that hold that he should not have been a candidate for President at that time. Kennedy had no long or distinguished record in the Senate nor was he highly regarded by the Democratic leadership elite. Moreover, his Catholic religion was perceived as a daunting barrier, as his speech writer, Ted Sorensen, lays out in his book, *Counselor*.[99] Nixon, on the other hand, was an old hand, revered by the Republican leadership and well funded.

John F. Kennedy. Verner Reed/TIME & LIFE Images/Getty Images

But then came Camelot. Kennedy was a master of Ethos: He was handsome, elegant, a storyteller, and self-deprecating, and he had a sense of humor (for instance, the phony telegram from his father about the Ohio election: "Don't buy one vote more than is necessary—I'm damned if I'll pay for a landslide,"[100] and his public pretend hurt in response to criticism about the appointment of his brother Bobby Kennedy as Attorney General: "I can't see that it's wrong to give him a little legal experience before he goes out to practice law"[101]). As regards Pathos: He could evoke emotion with the best of them but had the knack of always making it seem heart-felt. And as for Logos: With the help of a powerful staff, he demonstrated a surpassing command of facts and appealing arguments. He understood the power of simplicity, keeping it clear. He was an excellent wordsmith, with the aid of his right-hand speechwriter, Ted Sorensen. With respect to delivery, Kennedy was one of the best ever. His use of cadence, refrains, and themes set him apart from virtually any contemporary speaker. And so rhetoric, again, came to the fore and decided a close election that many experts feel ought to have gone the other way.

5. Lyndon B. Johnson (1964)

Johnson had the advantage of being the Vice President at a time when a grieving nation was ready to elect him because he had served their fallen President. But that would not explain the magnitude of his landslide victory over Barry Goldwater.

As an advocate, Johnson was perceived to be strong, a possessor of good judgment, a centrist, and comforting to many. On Pathos, he was a good storyteller and suffered in Kennedy's assassination. On Logos, he displayed total mastery of everything that had happened in Washington for a good spell. He was not a distinguished wordsmith or deliverer of those words, but adequate.

By contrast, Goldwater came off as an out-of-control cowboy and gunslinger. Goldwater's billboards—"In Your Heart, You Know He's Right"—were trumped by the Johnson campaign's quip: "In Your Guts, You Know He's Nuts."[102] There went Goldwater's chances.

6. Richard Nixon (1968, 1972)

Nixon won no prizes for his advocacy in the race against Kennedy—the visible sweating during the debates, the five o'clock shadow, and the apparent insincerity he could never fully mask. Still, he went on to win two elections, in part because he improved in later years. He delivered clearer speeches, was able by then to demonstrate a vast knowledge of the workings of government, and seemed a tad more comfortable on his feet than before. But his victories over Democratic challengers Hubert Humphrey (in 1968) and George McGovern (in 1972) had less to do with his high marks as an advocate than mistakes in advocacy on the part of his opponents.

The Humphrey election was over the night of the 1968 Democratic Convention in Chicago. Advocacy involves more than the spoken words of an individual speaker; it is also carried by symbols, themes, slogans, and sayings. As Humphrey accepted the Democratic nomination, television cameras showed chaos outside, depicting protesters in a bloody altercation with the police. Some were angry about the Vietnam War and a host of other things, and some relished confrontation for confrontation's sake. Pictures of that melee transfixed Americans.

The Republicans and Nixon were able to seize upon that, to unleash a theme that dominated Republican political advocacy for many years to come. They talked of well-heeled, spoiled-brat kids, irresponsible in their embrace of sex and drugs, the youth of Woodstock. These kids, they said, were architects of anarchy; they pushed everything too far. The rebels that night, the Republicans urged, were proxy for the Democratic Party at large: out of control and undisciplined.

This fit into a broad powerful theme, an Ethos one: While you can trust the Republicans, you cannot trust the Democrats. Its subtext was common sense—if we are the party of common sense, they are not. And that theme mirrored an evolving motif in political rhetoric in general. As Elvin T. Lim points out, while all Presidents through Woodrow Wilson appealed to "common sense" just 11 times in their papers, Presidents since Wilson have done so more than 1,600 times.[103] In 1968, the Republicans grasped it—the blood in the streets sure helped.

McGovern's defeat followed much the same pattern. The rhetoric of the Republicans was that McGovern was out of touch, would do little to protect the country, and would invariably err on the side of the extreme left, the left of irresponsibility, laziness, and protest. Here came another victory for Ethos and Pathos over a strong candidate who possessed Logos, wordsmithing, and delivery, but fell short on the others.

7. Jimmy Carter (1976)

Contesting the incumbent Gerald Ford, Carter started with an advantage—the country wanted change from a badly impaired presidency. Carter also won the rhetoric exercise. He was reasonably strong on Ethos and Pathos, being perceived to be a deeply religious, straight-shooting, honest man. He similarly was good on Logos: He was smart and a good wordsmith. He lacked force in his delivery, but his Ethos and Logos were enough to win this contest.

Ford, on the other hand, faced an Ethos and Logos problem. Many folks saw him as a bumbling, worn-out ex-football player and a weak puppet of whatever the Wall Street insiders wanted. Nor could he surmount those impressions with any flourishes of distinguished oral presentation. Consequently, Carter won.

8. Ronald Reagan (1980, 1984)

But Carter could not stand up to the rhetorical force of Ronald Reagan. The original lukewarm enthusiasm for Carter was diluted by perceived shortcomings during his administration, especially his alleged weakness in dealing with the Iranian hostage crisis. But his larger problem was that he collided with a rhetorical juggernaut. Reagan was a surprising candidate for President: He was widely perceived to be a grade "B" actor, and was not enthusiastically embraced by party leadership, who favored others. Yet he ran and won the nomination, and thereafter, neither Carter nor Walter Mondale could stand up to him.

This would not have surprised Aristotle and his followers. Reagan possessed Ethos in spades—he never bragged and was self-deprecating, warm, and likable. He could tell stories and move folks with his Pathos. He knew to keep points simple, clear, and chock-full of common sense. And his word choice was attractive to many because it was homespun; it was plainspeak. Moreover, he honed his delivery through his acting experience. His speeches were graceful, and full of Cicero stuff—he, the grand exponent of stories, analogies, anecdotes. He was also quick-witted. For example, when he was asked in a debate against Mondale whether he was too old to run for a second term, he cleverly replied: "I will not make age an issue of this campaign. I am not going to exploit, for political purposes, my opponent's youth and inexperience."[104] Reagan's rhetorical skill went a long way toward getting him elected.

9. George H. W. Bush (1988)

The Bush-Dukakis race is the most telling example of butchered rhetoric dictating a result. Massachusetts Governor Michael Dukakis was said to be ahead by as many as 20 points in the polls early on, and by the second debate, he was still in good shape. To be sure, strong advertising attacks against him seemed to resonate with voters—the ads about Willie Horton and his prison furlough policy, the slam on his patriotism because he vetoed a bill requiring all students in public schools to pledge allegiance every morning. Still, he led in the polls.

He was dogged by two problems. One was a Pathos deficiency: His speeches left the impression that he had no heart; that he was a very smart fellow but could not convey conviction, much less emotion, about much of anything. Second, he opposed the death penalty in all cases, which was an unpopular view among voters.

During the second debate between Dukakis and Bush, Bernard Shaw of CNN asked: "Governor, if Kitty Dukakis [Dukakis's wife of 35 years] were raped and murdered, would you favor an irrevocable death penalty for the killer?"[105] The answer helped doom Dukakis's candidacy and probably cleared the way for both Bushes to serve as our Presidents. He mumbled a few sentences about the death penalty, but then waxed on at great length about the Country's drug problem due, especially, to drugs emanating from South America. He failed to grapple much with the question. Worse yet, Dukakis showed no feeling—faced with the specter of the murder of his wife, he never even mentioned her name. He was cold and largely nonresponsive, violating basic tenets of rhetoric galore.

President Bush did not have an excellent rhetoric scorecard—when he spoke, he gave the impression that he was pretty likable and basically trustworthy, but only adequate as an oral advocate in his delivery and word choice. But he did not need more than that, as Dukakis's poor advocacy would snatch defeat from the jaws of certain victory.

10. Bill Clinton (1992, 1996)

Bill Clinton was another rhetorical star that at first blush did not appear to be a serious candidate for his party's nomination. Four years before, Clinton had given an endless, universally derided nominating speech at the Democratic Convention.[106] He also hailed from a small state with few electoral votes, and the party leadership was dubious about his chances. But Clinton developed into a skilled advocate whom neither George H. W. Bush (in 1992) nor Bob Dole (in 1996) could defeat.

In debates, Clinton exuded Ethos: He was warm, engaging, and full of charm. His Pathos was exemplary: He could tell stories about the plight of the poor in Arkansas (or elsewhere) whom he personally knew, and recount the names of the owners of companies that had gone under. He spoke, while on a roll, with the cadence of a preacher. His Logos was impeccable. He knew about government and made a quick study of detail. His word choice was moving and simple, his delivery (especially when extemporaneous) was among the best. He used themes, had superb cadence, and employed expressive gestures and body language. So these are two more elections that were won by distinguished rhetoric against some odds.

11. George W. Bush (2000, 2004)

Two of the last elections were lost by mediocre advocacy, rather than won by distinguished stuff. George W. Bush was no rhetorical star, nor was he a disaster. He had the sense to stick to who he was, a kind of good ol' boy, who sought to keep it simple. Many found that charming. He constantly garbled complex sentences and big words, so he tried to steer clear of them. Consequently, when writers talk about the "dumbing down" of presidential elections and the effectiveness of doing so in delivering votes, they mention Bush's elections high up on the list.

But both Al Gore in 2000 and John Kerry in 2004 made fatal mistakes of advocacy, leaving the door open for a tie in the first race and a thin-margin loss in the second. Gore had much to commend him: the Vice President of a popular President; an able man and as knowledgeable about the workings of government as any. The election was a very close one, and Gore failed because of difficulties with advocacy. He did not strike his affirmative themes powerfully enough and was too mealymouthed in responding to attacks about his patriotism and the like. Much of this came down to style. He never found a campaign "home base." His persona in his concession speech or in his award-winning film *An Inconvenient Truth* might have won for him, but it was not in attendance during the all-important presidential debates.

In the first debate, his handlers must have persuaded him to be an attack dog. At one point he literally left his podium and marched over to Bush's, and gestured at him with forefinger to nose. You could hear him audibly sighing at some of Bush's answers as if to say "holy cow, there the dummy goes again." In the second debate, he turned 180 degrees into a pussycat. In the end, voters were left scratching their heads.

Kerry also had strong advantages coming into the campaign in 2004. The first Bush presidency had been less than a roaring success, with deficits expanding and no signal accomplishments. Kerry was an attractive candidate: smart, capable of articulate flourishes, and seemingly reasonable. Yet he ran a themeless campaign (like Churchill said of his pudding: "Take it away, it has no theme"). Kerry was slow in responding to cheap shots like the "Swift Boat" attack on his service in the Vietnam War. In Pathos, he was stiff and cold; his Logos was excellent, but a little complex and stilted.

The election probably turned on delivery, where Kerry failed. His acceptance speech at the Democratic Convention was an emotionless performance that left national viewers thinking that he was something of a wooden soldier. He was a very well-informed, thoughtful candidate whose rhetoric tripped him up.

B. Advertising Campaigns

Supplementing the words of candidates, the images, symbols, slogans, and emotion-laden terms invoked by highly paid Madison Avenue advertising consultants underlie the advocacy of recent elections. Many have been unfair, but it is folly to ignore their efficacy. Here are some of the central themes:

1. Patriotism

The focus here has been pervasive and furious: the television ads featuring quadriplegic war hero Max Cleland alongside likenesses of Saddam Hussein and Osama Bin Laden, sponsored by his Georgia draft-dodger Senatorial opponent Saxby Chambliss;[107] the claim by Senate challenger John Thune that North Dakota Senator Tom Daschle was supporting the enemy in comments that he made about Iraq;[108] the Swift Boat volley aimed at John Kerry and his military decorations;[109] the shots at Dukakis for vetoing a bill requiring pledge of allegiance duty every day in public schools (so intense, the Governor resorted to the comical tank photo, bedecked in the ill-fitting helmet);[110] the current hints that President Obama is a Muslim.[111] Pervasive stuff, which often works.

2. Fear

The most recent appeal was an ad by Hillary Clinton that was directed at Barack Obama: "It's 3 a.m. and your children are safe and asleep. Who do you want answering the phone?" Most saw this as playing on fear of a nuclear or terrorist attack, implying that she was more prepared for an emergency situation.[112]

The record setter here is Lyndon B. Johnson's 1964 "Daisy" campaign advertisement: a small girl miscounting the petals of a daisy, cut to a nuclear blast count down, and then, the frontal blast at Barry Goldwater's perceived warmongering—a nuclear explosion followed by the message: "We must either love each other, or we must die."[113] Johnson's was a tough message, but it was effective and scared folks.

3. Racism

In the race against Dukakis, the Bush campaign in 1988 unleashed an aggressive television campaign claiming that Dukakis was soft on crime. Their centerpiece was the Willie Horton ad, which played on a fear of African-American men.[114] In 2006, the African-American Congressman and Senatorial candidate Harold Ford, Jr., was brought down by an ad that featured a scantily clad, young, sexy white woman, saying flirtatiously, "Harold, call me," which quickly elicited charges of race-baiting but nonetheless proved effective.[115]

4. Tranquility

After the stresses of the Vietnam War, Watergate, the energy crisis, and a general feeling of unease in the country, Reagan wanted to project calm, peace. The result was a classic: "It's Morning in America." The ad featured quiet, soothing, gorgeous pastoral photography. It was rhetorically powerful and excellently done.[116]

Ronald Reagan. MPI/Archive Photos/Getty Images

Election advertising can have a powerful effect on voters. This form of rhetoric must be mastered. At its worst, it is the rhetoric Plato feared—and, unchecked, it can be a force for real mischief.

C. Does All This Matter? Rhetorical Lessons from Presidential Campaigns

Rhetoric has altered the course of presidential elections. While it can be argued that factors other than rhetorical skill have been determinative, we offer here a chart of who won each of these elections and who might have won (according to such factors as poll numbers before the debates started) if both candidates had been equally adept oral advocates, that is, if we could take advocacy flaws or superiority out of the races so that they were decided entirely by all other objective factors (such as which was the candidate of the majority party, the candidate's standing within that party, evaluation of prior experience, state of the economy, and so forth).

❖

What might history have looked like?

Year	Actual Victor	Eliminating Disparity in Advocacy Skill: Possible Winners
1948	Truman	Dewey
1952	Eisenhower	Dewey/Taft
1956	Eisenhower	Stevenson
1960	Kennedy	Nixon
1964	LBJ	LBJ/Nixon
1968	Nixon	E. McCarthy
1972	Nixon	Ford
1976	Carter	Carter/Humphrey
1980	Reagan	Carter/Bush 41
1984	Reagan	Mondale/Dole/Bush 41
1988	Bush 41	Dukakis
1992	Clinton	Bush 41
1996	Clinton	Dole
2000	Bush 43	Gore
2004	Bush 43	Kerry
2008	Obama	?

Why is advocacy important in the context of presidential elections? The answer: By often dictating who wins, rhetoric has invariably altered the course of American foreign and domestic policy. Political science and history professors could list myriad ways our history would have differed on everything from the economy, to war, to budget deficits, to welfare policy and all manner of other federal government actions in the years between FDR and the current race. The list would vary. But much would have been altered, from the composition of the Supreme Court to tax and economic policies to foreign affairs priorities.

The story told in these elections is the story the ancient rhetoricians tried to teach and wrote down, but few have read or honored. Although they wanted to leave these teachings for posterity, their accounts have largely been ignored for long periods. In part, that sad tale stems from Plato's antipathy toward the entire rhetoric movement and his success in crushing the academy of rhetoric advocates, and that story, as we have seen from a review of modern presidential elections, continues to this day.

Here is a thumbnail sketch of what the wins and losses of the various candidates illustrate, as viewed through the lessons of the early champions of rhetoric.

1. *Truman*—Plainspeak trumps fancy, stilted speech. Self-deprecating humor works (Aristotle).

2. *Eisenhower*—Ethos and Pathos outsell high-brow rhetoric (Aristotle, Cicero).

3. *Kennedy*—Superb delivery matters. The use of humor, themes, and refrains is engaging (Cicero, Demosthenes).

4. *Johnson*—Pathos; our gut reaction to perceived strength. We fear zealots (Aristotle, Thucydides).

5. *Nixon*—Ethos; we sense the tricky, the slick (Aristotle).

6. *Humphrey*—Pathos; we fear chaos (Aristotle, Thucydides).

7. *Reagan*—Ethos, Pathos, delivery; we respond to evokers of calm, warm feelings; stories are powerful (Cicero, Aristotle).

8. *Dukakis*—Ethos, Pathos, and Logos failure; we resist speakers who do not seem to care (Cicero, Aristotle).

9. *Clinton*—Ethos, Pathos, delivery; charm persuades, evocative delivery resonates (Cicero, Demosthenes).

10. *Gore*—Ethos, Logos; we are put off by inconsistency in manner and weak self-defense (Aristotle, Cicero).

11. *Kerry*—Pathos, Ethos, delivery; lack of theme and cold delivery are fatal (Aristotle, Cicero).

The failure of each unsuccessful candidate in 2008 reduces to the following in classical rhetoric analysis. The primaries eliminated these candidates:

- *Rudy Giuliani*—Mostly an Ethos problem; many knew of his marital problems, fiery temper, and position changes.

- *Mike Huckabee*—An engaging dose of Ethos helped Huckabee, who came from nowhere to be a substantial candidate. But many feared that his intensely religious views did not match up to theirs—a Pathos problem.

- *Fred Thompson*—Ethos, Pathos, and Logos issues. Perceived as lazy for his work in the Senate and his late entry into the race. On delivery, positions never were well developed.

- *Mitt Romney*—Ethos problem for flip-flopping, Pathos concern over religion, and delivery problem as stiff and cold.

- *John Edwards*—On Ethos, too pretty for his own good. On Logos, too much a one-trick pony, invariably corporation bashing.

- *Hillary Clinton*—An Ethos problem, polls showing a substantial percentage did not trust her (for claims that she was met with gunfire in Bosnia and other reasons). Excellent on Logos. But on Pathos, perceived to be cold.

In the general election, John McCain was fairly strong on Ethos—a patriot and war hero and an otherwise friendly and likable guy. He was also strong on Pathos because of his background and his ability to tell stories with emotion. But delivery was a disaster—he was addicted to the teleprompter. He read word-for-word, haltingly and with numerous mistakes.

Barack Obama, in turn, was something of an oratorical wunderkind. His delivery was the most superb since Kennedy, with wonderful cadence, pausing, and body language. He was a master wordsmith with soaring rhetoric tempered with a calming choice of everyday words. His story had great Ethos appeal, although it was chipped at by the Reverend Wright scandal and attacks on his patriotism and political philosophy, as well as his perceived elitism. Yet no one invoked Pathos more effectively, and, notwithstanding his limited background in Washington, he was extremely well versed. So, in line with the teachings of the "Gods of Rhetoric" thousands of years ago, Obama's triumph in 2008 was one of "rhetorical skill."

❖

So all of these reviews of real-world speaking have two common threads: (1) advocacy excellence and failings matter a great deal, and (2) they all teach, in real time, the value of the lessons set out in Parts One and Two of this book.

Chapter 15

Rhetoric Gone Haywire

A. A Formulation of "Ethical" Speech

We have focused thus far on the best aspects of rhetoric: the power of a carefully crafted speech to persuade and inspire audiences. Superior rhetoric—exemplified by many of the speeches included in Part Four—can appeal to the best aspects of our humanity.

But rhetoric also has the power to summon the worst in us: to mislead us, exploit our fears, even persuade us to commit illegal acts. Bullies can use rhetoric, too. Words can and have killed, at least indirectly (as with the example of Nazi Germany, discussed more fully below). Even well-meaning advocates sometimes succumb to the temptation to cheat, relying on an intellectually dishonest argument or misusing Pathos.

Not all speech is equal. The American legal system recognizes broad categories of speech that are unprotected or even illegal: hate speech, incitement to violence, libelous or slanderous speech, false commercial claims, and the like. Illegal speech is a helpful starting place to sort out "good" speech from "bad," but it is not the only dangerous species. In addition to speech that is on its face illegal, there exists speech that, while not legally actionable, is so damaging to national discourse that it reaches the disreputable or unethical and should be scorned by honest speakers. Rhetoric is a powerful tool when wielded maliciously—it can come to mischief; it can succeed. That danger is addressed here.

1. The Historical Debate: Honest Advocacy Versus Deceitful Rhetoric

Tension between the usefulness of intellectually honest oral advocacy and the threat inherent in deceit has been brewing since the art of rhetoric was first developed. Two of the first Greek Rhetoricians, Gorgias of Leontini (fifth century B.C.) and his student Isocrates, were successful rhetoric teachers and themselves men of integrity. Yet the movement they founded—Sophistry—became synonymous with the con men who followed, hucksters who established lucrative schools of oral advocacy teaching students how to convince audiences, in effect, that white was black.[117]

Years later, Plato declared rhetoricians and poets equally suspect in their ability to dazzle and hoodwink audiences by playing fast and loose with facts.[118] He distrusted the competence of the multitude to resist the thrall of a persuasive speaker, questioned the value of free speech, and had scant faith in democracy as a form of government.[119] Euripides also warned of the dangers of "[a] man of loose tongue, intemperate, trusting to tumult, leading the populace to mischief with empty words."[120]

The ancients warned of moral laxness in speakers, a penchant to gloss over or deliberately misstate facts in order to manipulate. Plato and his followers feared the emotional force of the gifted rhetorician and the mob action that could arise from an incited crowd. To them, public speaking, at least with an audience made up of the common man, was just too dangerous, too hard to control.

2. Oral Advocacy and Democracy: Dangerous But Essential

Yet oral advocacy is essential to strong democracy. We cannot just say, "too scary; a pox on it." Government by the people requires that the people be involved and share ideas, "[p]ersuade or perish."[121]

In a democracy, citizens should understand how to communicate their ideas. If they delegate the speaking to others—to lawyers or politicians—they risk being misunderstood or not heard at all. The citizen also must understand how to evaluate the ideas of others so that he can determine the best course of public action. For democracy to flourish, voters need to consider a range of ideas and, through a sometimes messy but essential process of debate, come to rational decisions. We cannot impose our will on others or dismiss the points of view of our neighbors. Democracy requires that we talk to one another. It is no accident, then, that within ten years of the rise of the first democracy, the first book on public speaking appeared (in Syracuse, Italy, 460 B.C.).[122]

The Framers of the Constitution thought that free speech and robust debate were indispensible to the health of democracy, codifying this principle in the First Amendment.[123] As Supreme Court Justice Louis Brandeis famously contended in *Whitney v. California*, democracy thirsts for freedom to think and speak:

> Those who won our independence believed that the final end of the State was to make men free to develop their faculties; and that in its government the deliberative forces should prevail over the arbitrary. They valued liberty both as an end and as a means. They believed liberty to be the secret of happiness and courage to be the secret of liberty. They believed that freedom to think as you will and to speak as you think are means indispensable to the discovery and spread of political truth; that without free speech and assembly discussion would be futile; that with them, discussion affords ordinarily adequate protection against the dissemination of noxious doctrine; that the greatest menace to freedom is an inert people; that public discussion is a political duty; and that this should be a fundamental principle of the American government.[124]

Similarly, Justice Oliver Wendell Holmes described democracy as a marketplace of ideas, in which an exchange of thoughts through free speech points to the "ultimate good."[125] John Stuart Mill urged much the same in his essay "On Liberty." He postulated that society benefits when citizens are able to express opinions— if the opinion is true, society benefits; if false, society gains a fuller grasp of the issue, through the conflict presented when the opinion is challenged.[126] Speech leads to truth and to a stronger democracy, an energized electorate, and an open-minded citizenry.

3. The Effect of Modern Modes of Communication on Democratic Debate

Modern modes of communication like television and the Internet expose the public to a myriad of voices, increasing the number of people engaged in a national discourse. In the past, a speaker might have needed wealth or connections in order to be in a position to even address an audience. Today, anyone with access to an Internet connection can "become a town crier with a voice that resonates farther than it could from any soapbox."[127] More people can participate in the discussion than ever before—a good thing in a democracy.

With this privilege comes responsibility. When we speak, especially since (thanks to modern technology) so many more people may be listening, we must take care to speak fairly. Even Plato acknowledged a spot for rhetoric if the speaker made an effort to learn, and speak, the truth about his subject.[128] Plato's fear was that many rhetoricians disparaged ethics and were disinclined to master the facts before attempting to persuade others of their agenda.[129] Sympathetic to these concerns, Aristotle devoted the first two books of his *On Rhetoric* to logic and argument, maintaining that a speaker cannot be wholly persuasive without *substance*.[130]

It has always been the case that some speakers are not honest or accurate. The danger today is that modern modes of communication like television and the Internet can multiply the damage that an unethical speaker can inflict by broadcasting misinformation far and wide, repeating it on numerous websites or in 24-hour-per-day news reports. Even if the story is ultimately debunked, it may have taken on a life of its own simply by spreading quickly.

Audiences may also be too easily impressed by what they see and hear on the Internet, not realizing that their chosen websites lack the vigilant fact checkers of traditional media services. Traditional television news has also been somewhat supplanted by cable news shows, many of which present an overtly political bias in their reporting. Rather than presenting opinions from all sides, services like Fox News or MSNBC depend for much of their revenue on firing up and polarizing listeners. The result is an echo chamber, in which some hear what they want to hear, reinforcing biases without challenging them. The electorate becomes divided, rather than united in a common goal of solutions.[131]

4. Three Rules for Ethical Advocacy

The dissemination of lies that foment discord and anger is a paramount problem, exactly as Plato feared. A speaker can trumpet with an even louder voice today than in ancient days because television and the Internet enable him to reach audiences of millions in an instant. The medium of television or the Internet may help him to dazzle his listeners. If the speaker plays fast and loose with the truth, his words can cause devastating harm.

What, then, should be the rules governing ethical public speaking? For an answer, we turn to the lessons from history and from the American legal system. We suggest three rules for ethical advocacy: (1) honor the facts; (2) let the other side be heard; and (3) beware the misuse of Pathos (using emotion to cloud reason in the minds of the audience).

a. Honor facts.

The first rule of ethical speech is a simple one: Honor the facts. Tell the truth.

A democratic system depends upon the notion that its citizens are capable of forming their own opinions and sifting through a multitude of others to make a reasonable decision. It is harder, perhaps impossible, for citizens to reach a reasonable conclusion if they are fed inaccurate information. The American legal system consequently encourages accuracy and withholds legal protection for some types of speech that are false or misleading. For example, in the United States, bribery and perjury are unprotected speech, and defamatory words are subject to a lesser form of free speech protection than truthful words.[132] Similarly, attorneys arguing in court are barred from misstating either the law or the facts of the case.[133]

The system frowns on falsity because lying skews the market-place of ideas. When obscuring the truth, one tarnishes the highest goal of oral advocacy: to persuade *fairly*. Aristotle argued that the speaker who misleads ultimately does himself the greatest disservice, because a big lie ultimately collapses under scrutiny, at the cost of the advocate's reputation. Once you forfeit Ethos, there goes the trust of the audience.

b. Let the other side be heard.

Our second tenet of ethical speech holds that one speaker should not try to drown out another. Both sides deserve the chance to be heard. In the United States, the legal system discourages "speech" designed to silence other views. For example, speech aimed at inciting violence obviously can cause physical harm to anyone who is the target of the violence, and such speech does nothing to promote the exchange of ideas. Violent speech like this is unprotected by the Constitution.[134] Obscenity, offensive expressions, racial epithets, and "fighting words" also have little redeeming social value and so enjoy less legal protection.

Winning skirmishes by hurting, killing, or shutting out your opponent does nothing to advance the causes of democracy and ultimately is not a sustainable path toward convincing others.

Even if you prevail on day one, you may lose the war. The people you are silencing likely will struggle to make their voices heard somewhere, and the fence-sitters are more inclined to walk away from you rather than succumb to strong-arming. Instead, the ethical speaker persuades by replacing bad ideas with stronger, better ones.[135] If an idea is worth supporting, it should not depend on bullying or violence to make its point.

c. Beware the misuse of Pathos.

Speech that seeks to churn up the audience by playing on its baser instincts (appealing perhaps to racism, sexism, homophobia, xenophobia, and the like)—in other words, a speech that abuses Pathos—can pack a punch, making it a tempting choice for some speakers. And so long as it falls short of falsity or incitement to violence, mere overheated speech is lawful—often constitutionally protected—in America.[136] Americans are fiercely protective of the right to express ideas, even unsettling ones, because the Founders believed that fostering myriad viewpoints was the surest way to protect democracy.[137] The Supreme Court time and again has affirmed our "profound national commitment to the principle that debate on public issues should be uninhibited, robust, and wide-open, and that it may well include vehement, caustic and sometimes unpleasantly sharp attacks on government and public officials."[138]

It is also true that some of the more unpleasant speech—manipulative media advertisements, inflammatory political ads, rabid commentators on one-sided radio shows—falls squarely within the four corners of propaganda. But this speech is, and will remain, legal. If we cede power to the government to control this speech, we face the very real danger of promoting McCarthyism and censorship—the death knell for a democracy.

Speaking with an overheated tone can prove to be successful. It can rally an audience of like-minded people to action. It is naïve to say that angry, divisive speech affirming noxious beliefs and stereotypes is invariably "unpersuasive." Pathos-driven speech struck fear in the heart of Plato explicitly because he recognized its power to call mobs to action.

So the question arises: Since Pathos-laden speech is perfectly legal, perhaps even effective, why not use it?

Speaking with passion and conviction can be exactly what the occasion demands. But speech that aims at manipulating emotions *in order to cloud judgment* does as much damage to the marketplace of ideas as lying does. If a speaker preys on the fears of an audience, foments hatred of others, or deliberately incites a mob, that speaker does nothing to promote a fair exchange of ideas. Consequently, this sort of manipulative speech is unethical by our calculus because it hinders the progress of democracy and the ultimate purpose of thoughtful oral advocacy—a search for truth.

The abuse of Pathos can also backfire in the long run. Speech pandering only to those in accord does little to persuade the unpersuaded and may shut off conversation with those on the other side. We most trust the speaker who projects reason, is fair, measured. Uncivil speakers may offend or drive away adherents. Beliefs are important to those who hold them; if you jeer or denigrate their opinions, you will rarely be able to persuade those people that your cause is just.

The Bedrocks of Ethical Speech

- Honor facts.
- Let the other side be heard.
- Beware the misuse of Pathos.

B. An Example of Unethical Speech Run Amok: Adolf Hitler and the Nazis

Perhaps the most infamous use of unethical speech was that employed by Adolf Hitler and the Nazi regime, which ruled

Germany from 1933 to 1945. In no other time in history were the rules of ethical advocacy so fiendishly subverted, for so terrifying a purpose. The Nazis obfuscated, rather than honored, facts; they silenced, often literally, any voices of opposition; and they overplayed Pathos to a dramatic degree. In short, the Nazis flouted the rules of ethical advocacy, and, in so doing, they represented one of the most despicable and frighteningly successful uses of unethical rhetoric in history.

Hitler and the Nazis refused to honor facts. Instead, they recognized the power of propaganda to control minds when they established the Ministry of Propaganda and National Enlightenment, headed by Joseph Goebbels, for the purpose of manipulating public opinion. "The essence of propaganda," explained Goebbels, "consists in winning people over to an idea so sincerely, so vitally, that in the end they succumb to it utterly and can never escape from it."[139] Nazi propaganda eschewed Aristotle's tenets of Ethos and Logos, and instead perverted the facts in order to achieve its own ends.

For the Nazis, rhetoric was never about truth. Hitler justified the use of *misinformation* in his manifesto, *Mein Kampf*:

> The function of propaganda . . . is not to make an objective study of the truth, in so far as it favors the enemy, and then set it before the masses with academic fairness; its task is to serve our own right, always and unflinchingly.[140]

Nazi propaganda sought to rewrite history. The Nazi party realized that, if lies were regularly repeated, the public would believe them.[141]

Willingness to lie stemmed from disrespect for the intelligence of the listeners, as Hitler made clear:

> All propaganda must be popular and its intellectual level must be adjusted to the most limited intelligence among those it is addressed to. . . . The broad mass of a nation does not consist of diplomats, or even professors of political law, or even individuals capable of forming a

rational opinion; it consists of plain mortals, wavering and inclined to doubt and uncertainty.... The people in their overwhelming majority are so feminine by nature and attitude that sober reasoning determines their thoughts and actions far less than emotion and feeling.[142]

In addition to suppressing facts, the Nazis violated the second rule of ethical speech—letting the other side be heard. Instead, the regime did everything at its disposal to control the dissemination of information in Germany. Goebbels skewed information by censoring speech, burning books, and controlling literature, films, music, radio, art, and newspapers.[143] Rather than meeting oppositional speech with even more speech, as in a democracy, the Third Reich confronted disagreement and dissension with violence and murder, imprisoning and massacring millions.

Finally, Nazi rhetoric was often characterized by deliberate and constant attempts to appeal to listeners' emotions—a violation of our third tenet of ethical speech. To whip up mass sentiments in this way and to spread its message, the Nazis cultivated skilled oral advocates. The party trained roughly 9,800 orators to promote Nazi beliefs in Germany, and these public speakers were extremely skilled in inciting the mobs to violence against the Jews.[144] Adolph Hitler was chief among these orators, and Goebbels made sure that Hitler's audience was as vast as possible by placing loudspeakers in the streets and making inexpensive radios widely available.[145] Hitler's speeches were orchestrated spectacles designed to stir the public's emotions. His speeches were staged in arenas that could hold crowds of 400,000 people. They were illuminated by searchlights so bright that the light could be seen 100 miles away.[146]

Hitler's texts and speeches rested on manipulating crowds through Pathos. He fomented the crowd's anger about the sufferings that were inflicted upon them by other nations after the First World War; then he redirected this same anger toward Jewish targets. Hitler's misuse of Pathos, although subtle, was perhaps the Nazis' most successful and cunning employment of unethical advocacy. For this reason, we will examine this particular technique more closely.

Take, for instance, Hitler's speech to the Nazi Reichstag on January 30, 1939. There he opened with an apparently logical point about the justifications that other countries advanced for refusing to admit Jewish immigrants:

> [T]hey say: . . . "We," that is the democracies, "are not in a position to take in the Jews." Yet in these empires there are not 10 people to the square kilometer. While Germany, with her 135 inhabitants to the square kilometer, is supposed to have room for them!

Logical, his audience might think. But Hitler is not using logic in an effort to persuade; instead, he is suggesting to his audience that they have not been treated evenhandedly by the rest of the world *in order to spark their outrage*. Once he has made his listeners angry about "the democracies," he employs a rhetorical sleight of hand: He redirects their anger toward the Jews.

> When the German nation was, thanks to the inflation instigated and carried through by Jews, deprived of the entire savings which it had accumulated in years of honest work, when the rest of the world took away the German nation's foreign investments, when we were divested of the whole of our colonial possessions, these philanthropic considerations evidently carried little noticeable weight with democratic statesmen.

Economic depression and unemployment weighed heavily on Germany at the time, so Hitler served up two external enemies to blame for their misery: the democracies and the Jews. The Jews, Hitler says, are as culpable as the democracies in causing the economic suffering of Germany, by robbing "honest" Germans of their savings. The propaganda here works because it scapegoats the Jews for German problems and stereotypes them as money-grubbing financiers who shirk work.

Hitler next rehearses a litany of suffering endured by the German people, which he first attributes to the democracies that defeated Germany in World War I, but which he again morphs into an attack on the Jews:

> Today I can only assure these gentlemen that, thanks to the brutal education with which the democracies favored us for fifteen years, we are completely hardened to all attacks of sentiment. After more than eight hundred thousand children of the nation had died of hunger and undernourishment at the close of the War, we witnessed almost one million head of milking cows being driven away from us.... We witnessed over one and a half million Germans being torn away from all that they possessed...and being whipped out with practically only what they wore on their backs.

This description of suffering by Germans—being deprived of all their worldly possessions, watching their children starve to death— eerily mirrors the suffering the Nazis were inflicting on the Jews in concentration camps at the time this speech was given. The irony is perverse—Hitler bemoans cruelty his people have suffered, then offers this as reason the Germans should be vindicated, while knowingly inflicting the identical malicious treatment on Jews.

He continues to invert facts by claiming that the Jews are about to plunge the world into another world war, painting them as aggressors the Nazis would be justified in fighting:

> The Jewish race will have to adapt itself to sound constructive activity as other nations do, or sooner or later it will succumb to a crisis of an inconceivable magnitude.... If the international Jewish financiers in and outside Europe should succeed in plunging the nations once more into a world war, then the result will not be the bolshevization of the earth, and thus the victory of Jewry, but the annihilation of the Jewish race in Europe![147]

The speech turns facts upside down, painting Jews as aggressors and Germans as persecuted, when in fact Jews were being murdered in concentration camps at the time the speech was given. The speech works by stirring up anger, inflaming hatred, and then focusing that anger onto a dehumanized enemy.[148]

In brief, the Nazis violated all the rules of ethical advocacy. Even more troubling is the fact that they were so successful in persuading many people to accept their worldview. While historians may debate precisely how or why they were so successful,[149] teachers of rhetoric must consider why their students should not employ similar rhetorical techniques. Our response: Speech that debases public dialogue violates the precepts of a democracy. It may be effective for a time, but it is unethical. And we have seen, from the narrative of history, what frightening omens this type of speech can portend.

C. "Paranoid Rhetoric": Another Example of Unethical Speech

Another, perhaps more relevant example of unethical speech in the national discourse today is so-called "paranoid" rhetoric. This type of speech has been around since the days of Plato and was well identified in the context of the United States by two-time Pulitzer Prize–winning historian Richard Hofstadter in his 1964 work, *The Paranoid Style in American Politics*. The term "paranoid" is not a clinical one—it does not, for instance, imply that a speaker has a mental disorder—but rather, it describes "a way of seeing the world and of expressing oneself."[150] Paranoid speech is speech that is

- *Overheated*—that is, seething with anger, bitterness, and resentment, playing on the fears and emotions of listeners (for example, "These policies are anti-American, and will endanger each and every child in this country");

- *Overly suspicious*—implying some sort of conspiracy by historical or political actors (for example, "This is all part of a vast right-wing conspiracy"); and, finally,

- *Apocalyptic*—suggesting that a catastrophic denouement to the plans of the conspirators is imminent (for example, "If we do not put a stop to this now, life as we know it will never be the same").

Because rhetoric of this nature often plays fast and loose with established facts, because it intimidates voices of opposition through browbeating and threats of violence, and because it attempts to manipulate the passions of its audience, paranoid speech violates the rules of ethical advocacy that we have laid out.

But paranoid speech can also be intensely attractive. After all, who among us does not enjoy a little bit of conspiracy now and then? Secretive and powerful plots are entertaining and juicy: The continued popularity of Oliver Stone's film *JFK* and the novels of Dan Brown (*The Da Vinci Code* and *Angels & Demons*) epitomize our collective fascination with conspiracy.[151]

When paranoid speech seeps into our political dialogue, though, it becomes poisonous because it is unethical and harmful to democracy. Thus, we must notice paranoid rhetoric and condemn it when we see it. To aid us in this enterprise, we highlight some historical and contemporary examples of this type of speech.

1. What Does Paranoid Rhetoric Look Like?

We have already noted that paranoid speech is overwrought, angry, and foreboding, but we must also mention that it is not the exclusive province of any particular political ideology or strain of thought. It can be tempting to even the most distinguished advocates, and has come from all sorts of places, as the following examples make clear:

Trademarks of the Paranoid

- Apocalyptic: Exaggeration of dangers

- Angry, mean: So why should we listen?

- Uncompromising: No gray in the paint box

a. Conspiratorial and apocalyptic.

Much of the language of the most virulent anti-communist crusaders in the twentieth century could be characterized as "paranoid" because of the conspiratorial nature of their claims. Many of these speakers believed that communist influences were in "almost complete control" of the government,[152] and that prominent American leaders, to borrow the words of Senator Joseph McCarthy, were involved in "a conspiracy of infamy so black that . . . its principles shall be forever deserving of the maledictions of all honest men."[153] For instance, President Dwight Eisenhower was charged with being "a dedicated, conscious agent of the Communist conspiracy."[154] Claims of this sort often brought with them the implication that a political apocalypse, the communist overthrow of the government, was imminent.

We have also seen conspiratorial, paranoid speech in more recent decades. For instance, in 1998 during the Monica Lewinsky scandal, then-First Lady Hillary Clinton claimed that her husband, President Clinton, was the victim of a "vast right-wing conspiracy."[155] Apocalyptic language is likewise extant, as observed in the belief, held by some, that America is on the verge of moral catastrophe due to the availability of abortion and the legalization of gay marriage.[156]

b. Angry, threatening, and demonizing.

Paranoid rhetoric is also marked by bitterness, threats of violence, and the demonization of individuals. For example, during the Vietnam War, protestors would often shout personal invectives like "Hey, hey, LBJ, how many kids did you kill today?"[157] As is often the case, angry rhetoric during the Vietnam era sometimes spilled over into violence—for instance, the exploits of groups like the Weather Underground Organization.[158]

American political dialogue in the last two decades has been replete with angry, paranoid rhetoric. For example, there have been many claims that Presidents Bush and Obama were authoritarians akin to Adolf Hitler.[159] We have also seen our fair share of ad hominem attacks. Popular author and political pundit Ann Coulter once assailed the widows of the September 11 terrorist attacks as "harpies" who were "enjoying their husbands' deaths."[160] Even more extreme were the 2009 remarks by Pastor Steven L. Anderson praying that President Obama "dies and goes to hell."[161]

c. Unreasonable and uncompromising.

Although more difficult to illustrate by example, paranoid rhetoric is marked by its unreasonable and uncompromising nature. The paranoid speaker does not rest on reason, rigorous logic, or proven facts, but rather on emotion, suspicions, and fear. His case, furthermore, is largely a negative one, describing what he opposes but paying little attention to what he favors and why.[162]

In line with the paranoid speaker's belief that catastrophe is impending and that conspiratorial agents are constantly plotting, he is unyielding to compromise. As Hofstadter explained, the paranoid rhetorician "does not see social conflict as something to be mediated and compromised, in the manner of the working politician. Since what is at stake is always a conflict between absolute good and absolute evil . . . [n]othing but complete victory will do [and] the enemy . . . must be totally eliminated . . . ."[163]

2. Effects of Paranoid Rhetoric

Paranoid rhetoric is a pernicious phenomenon because it is ultimately injurious to democracy, where the free and dispassionate exchange of ideas is at a premium. While talking in this way may be effective (particularly to those audiences already disposed to the message), it infringes on the moral precepts of good advocacy. That is, paranoid rhetoric dishonors facts, it intimidates the other side into silence, and it misuses Pathos by overplaying emotional appeals.

The Mischief of Paranoid Rhetoric

- Dishonors facts—Erodes Ethos, misleads
- Stifles dissent—But dissent is important
- Overuse of Pathos—Troubling to most listeners

---

a. Paranoid rhetoric dishonors facts.

The first reason that speech employing paranoid jargon ought to be condemned on ethical grounds is that it routinely stretches or ignores the truth. This results from thinking rooted in emotion rather than in logic or reasoning. When a speaker's arguments are not based on reality or established facts, he is prone to contemplating ominous, but ultimately unrealistic, "parades of horribles" or "what-if" scenarios typical of paranoid speech. Thus, for the paranoid speaker, facts and logical reasoning take a backseat to emotions, and this renders the speech inaccurate and therefore unethical.

b. Paranoid rhetoric stifles dissent.

Perhaps the most unsettling aspect of paranoid speech is that, through its overplay of anger and threats of violence, it frightens and intimidates opposing viewpoints and speakers. When exposed to paranoid rhetoric, a listener may find himself too intimidated to voice a contrary opinion, and will consequently remain silent. His ideas, no matter how valuable, will not enter our political discourse. It is precisely in this way that paranoid rhetoric harms our democracy. If citizens are prevented from speaking their minds, then some of the best ideas may never be articulated. Paranoid speech thus inhibits the marketplace of ideas.

c. Paranoid rhetoric misuses Pathos.

Last, paranoid rhetoric is unethical because it constantly seeks to evoke the emotions of its audience; it abuses Pathos. Paranoid speech clouds the judgment of its audience by injecting venom and rage. In so doing, it works against democracy and the national interest, which rely on reasoned, objective debate.

D. Defusing the Bomb: Fighting Dangerous, Abusive, or Paranoid Rhetoric

What, then, should one do in the face of overheated rhetoric by an opponent?

If you feel the other side is fighting unfairly by reaching for deliberately divisive language, take a step back. Analyze the concern that has triggered this passion; see if you can address it.

For example, in trying to reform health care in America in 2010, rhetoric boiled over, inflamed by politically incendiary speakers. It was tempting to dismiss voices in opposition by marginalizing them as irrationally angry and therefore unworthy of consideration, and certainly some of the speech that transpired fails our test for ethical speech. The fact that the national tone devolved into incivility worried many, as if it were unprecedented. It is important to recall, though, that unpleasant, sometimes nasty disagreement is not new and always will be around in a representative democracy.[164] It is likely to arise whenever those with strongly felt beliefs clash with others. The fears that undergirded the passions in the example of health care reform were real. The reasonable voices that emerged in the dialogue over health care reform on both sides of the aisle (such as the conversations between David Brooks and Mark Shields on the PBS Newshour) addressed those fears. You will want to follow their example. Look past the tone, if you can, in order to understand the concerns underlying it.

What about erroneous information that you may confront on the Internet and elsewhere? Should baseless propaganda and paranoid speech be illegal? Absolutely not. If we empower our government to shut down speech out of fear that it is noxious, overheated, transgressive, or unsettling, then we lose an important freedom, the ability to say what we think. Instead, you must confront unethical speech with speech that is based on intellectual honesty. Get the facts right. Show that you care about your cause, but resist efforts to manipulate emotions in the hope that you will inhibit reasoning. The solution to unethical speech is more speech—accurate, honest, logical, heartfelt speech.

We must also do a better job of educating our citizenry about how to argue persuasively and fairly. Speakers in a democracy must express points logically; they must support claims with facts and understand that reaching for stereotypes, hyped-up emotion, and the tools of propaganda are antithetical to an ethical dialogue. Speaking fairly—with well-researched facts and honest candor—raises the general level of discourse both ethically and substantively. It makes it more likely that listeners will be able to evaluate rhetoric around them and reject distorted political ads, deliberately incendiary talk-show hosts, and purveyors of hatred and discord. The solution here is not a legal one. It lies in more speech, better speech, well taught and understood.

Part Four

The Best of the Best

While most of us admire but cannot duplicate Maya Angelou's verbal artistry or Martin Luther King's gift for the memorable refrain, all can benefit from studying their example. We all will have occasion to make speeches at some point in our everyday lives, perhaps to eulogize a fallen friend, rally support for a fledgling business, bid farewell to a job or community. Or perhaps we must deliver the closing argument to win the case or the campaign speech to cinch the election. These occasions demand skilled rhetoric: carefully chosen words delivered with aplomb. Great rhetoric can convince a skeptical audience, offer hope in the face of despair, even stop a riot.

The speeches that follow illustrate many of the most common difficulties facing a speaker and provide possible answers. They provide a model upon which you can build if you are asked to deliver a eulogy, celebrate an occasion, or present (and win) an argument. Some deal with challenging situations: overcoming bias, addressing uncomfortable topics, speaking to a crowd during a time of crisis. Each of the speakers herein makes choices in crafting the speech, which we highlight.

We urge you to read these speeches, and then reflect upon the speech you need to write. Is it joyous or somber? Brief or prolonged? Spoken to friends or to skeptics? Think about the points you must make that matter most, the attitude of your audience toward you and your topic, and the proper tone to strike, and then look for an analogous speech here to see if it can spark an idea in you. Examine the text to see how the speaker achieved the desired effect; see if that could be a path for you as well. Remember, though, that you must find your own authentic voice. The task is not to copy another's style; it is to seek out your own style and make it better. There are many paths to the top of the rhetorical mountain, and you will discover yours. These speeches might help light the way:

1. Making the farewell speech: Lou Gehrig
2. Delivering the eulogy: Maya Angelou
3. Winning the argument: Barbara Jordan
4. Overcoming bias, Part 1: Sojourner Truth
5. Overcoming bias, Part 2: Mary Fisher
6. Making a speech in a time of crisis, Part 1: Robert F. Kennedy
7. Making a speech in a time of crisis, Part 2: Winston Churchill
8. Making a speech in a time of crisis, Part 3: Abraham Lincoln
9. Making a speech of hope, Part 1: John F. Kennedy
10. Making a speech of hope, Part 2: Ronald Reagan
11. Using a refrain: Martin Luther King
12. Discussing a difficult topic: Barack Obama

Chapter 16

Rhetoric of the Greatest Speeches

A. Making the Farewell Speech: Lou Gehrig

How do you say a final goodbye?

Lou Gehrig's "Farewell to Baseball" at Yankee Stadium on July 4, 1939, is a signal example of grace in the face of tragedy. He was burdened by a grim prognosis: amyotrophic lateral sclerosis, a disease characterized by rapidly increasing paralysis and certain death. Though his body would slowly shut down, Gehrig could expect that his mind, trapped in that frozen body, would remain fully aware to the end. Life, as he knew it, was over, as was his baseball career.

In the face of such a fate, many might have fumbled for the courage to make it through. Before Gehrig steps to the microphone, he is understandably overcome with emotion. But then he speaks, and his message brims with hope and good cheer.

He begins: "Fans, for the past two weeks you have been reading about the bad break I got. Yet today, I consider myself the luckiest man on the face of this earth." Gehrig's words might take a listener by surprise: How can a man with a terminal illness feel lucky? But as Gehrig lovingly itemizes his reasons for gratitude, the audience can see that Gehrig's is a life well lived. He invokes the support of his family, even singling out his mother-in-law for special praise. He recalls tributes paid by other baseball teams—including the Yankees' bitter rivals, the New York Giants—and in his descriptions demonstrates his fondness for his manager and teammates. Gehrig's words are genuine, displaying grace and good humor despite a hopeless diagnosis, endearing him even more to a crowd that already loves him. Paradoxically, the kindness and hope of Gehrig's speech serve to highlight the tragedy of his diagnosis. That such a fate should befall such a man is heartbreaking. This is Ethos: grace under pressure, the ability to look death in the face and find hope there.

The speech that Gehrig delivers so effortlessly could have misfired in the hands of a less humble speaker. It would have been easy for Gehrig to break down or to misplay the complicated emotions of the day. He could have listed a litany of career accomplishments, outlined the injustice of his illness, or recounted the painful symptoms that accompany his disease. Instead, even on that day billed as "Lou Gehrig Appreciation Day," Gehrig focuses on others.

Gehrig's theme of hope is made memorable by his use of repetition. He echoes his "luckiest man" theme as he speaks of the "grand men" with whom he has worked, punctuating each description with the refrain, "Sure, I'm lucky":

> I consider myself the *luckiest man* on the face of this earth.... Look at these grand men. Which of you wouldn't consider it the highlight of his career just to associate with them for even one day? *Sure, I'm lucky.* Who wouldn't consider it an honor to have known Jacob Ruppert? Also, the builder of baseball's greatest empire, Ed Barrow? To have spent six years with that wonderful little fellow, Miller Huggins? Then to have spent the next nine years with that outstanding leader, that smart student of psychology, the best manager in baseball today, Joe McCarthy? *Sure, I'm lucky.*

He then paints memorable pictures of the everyday kindness of friends and family, and his refrain changes—"that's something"—and crescendos with the description of his wife, "the finest I know."

> When the New York Giants, a team you would give your right arm to beat, and vice versa, sends you a gift—*that's something*. When everybody down to the groundskeepers and those boys in white coats remember you with trophies—*that's something*. When you have a wonderful mother-in-law who takes sides with you in squabbles with her own daughter—*that's something*. When you have a father and a mother who work all their lives so you can have an education and build your body—it's a blessing. When you have a wife who has been a tower of strength and shown more courage than you dreamed existed—*that's the finest I know.*

His refrains of "sure, I'm lucky" and "that's something" are simple and conversational. They are the words he might have used in everyday discourse, and so they seem genuine. He seeks communion with his audience by speaking to them as friends.

Gehrig's conclusion shows that his story does not end with this speech: "I may have been given a bad break . . . but I've got an awful lot to live for." The crowd erupts into sustained applause, moved by Gehrig's gratitude and humility. His strong Ethos triggers an explosion of Pathos in his audience, not because he tries to rip at heartstrings, but because he intentionally resists that impulse. The result is a masterpiece of rhetoric.

Text of Lou Gehrig's July 4, 1939, address at Yankee Stadium

Fans, for the past two weeks you have been reading about the bad break I got. Yet today I consider myself the luckiest man on the face of this earth. I have been

*in ballparks for seventeen years and have never
received anything but kindness and encouragement
from you fans.*

*Look at these grand men. Which of you wouldn't
consider it the highlight of his career just to associate
with them for even one day? Sure, I'm lucky. Who
wouldn't consider it an honor to have known Jacob
Ruppert? Also, the builder of baseball's greatest empire,
Ed Barrow? To have spent six years with that
wonderful little fellow, Miller Huggins? Then to have
spent the next nine years with that outstanding leader,
that smart student of psychology, the best manager in
baseball today, Joe McCarthy? Sure, I'm lucky.*

*When the New York Giants, a team you would give
your right arm to beat, and vice versa, sends you a
gift—that's something. When everybody down to the
groundskeepers and those boys in white coats remember
you with trophies—that's something. When you have a
wonderful mother-in-law who takes sides with you in
squabbles with her own daughter—that's something.
When you have a father and a mother who work all
their lives so you can have an education and build your
body—it's a blessing. When you have a wife who has
been a tower of strength and shown more courage than
you dreamed existed—that's the finest I know.*

*So I close in saying that I may have had a tough break,
but I have an awful lot to live for.*

B. Delivering the Eulogy: Maya Angelou

Sometimes we must find our voices during moments of
profound grief. Many of us will be called upon to memorialize
a friend, family member, or colleague. These addresses are

challenging not simply because of the emotional toll they exact, but also because of the speaker's heavy responsibility. The speaker must comfort the grieving without being overcome herself. She must share intimate or personal stories about the deceased without excluding or alienating those who did not know the deceased in the same way. Finally, the speaker must offer her audience a way forward, a reason to hope. The speaker faces difficult choices: How can I move the audience without falling apart myself, what stories should I tell, and what solace can I offer the listeners?

Maya Angelou's tribute to Coretta Scott King offers a model of a eulogy done well. Angelou addressed a formidable audience—more than 10,000 mourners, including world leaders, five United States Presidents, Senators, Congressmen, and numerous civil rights icons. Previous speakers touched on themes one might expect to hear at this funeral: Mrs. King's leadership during the civil rights movement; her devotion to her husband, Dr. Martin Luther King; her opposition to South African apartheid; and her support for equal rights for gay and lesbian Americans.

Angelou's eulogy takes the audience by surprise. She approaches the podium, pauses, and then begins to sing:

> I open my mouth to the Lord and I won't turn back, noooooo. I will go, I shall go. I'll see what the end is gonna be.

As the final note fades, the church erupts into applause. Angelou smiles, looking confident, enjoying the experience— demonstrating how a strong start can help a speaker manage emotions, both hers and the audience's. Angelou uses her moment of primacy, her first words at the podium, to her full advantage. She grabs the audience's attention. She sets the tone: Her song conveys joy, pain, reverence, anguish, and hope all at once. She lets her audience know that, while she shares their profound grief, she has come to celebrate. From that moment on, the stage is hers as

her voice rings above presidents, parliamentarians, and parish-
ioners alike.

Her formal remarks capture the imagination through well-
chosen words, for the speaker is, of course, a celebrated poet.
Angelou tells us:

> In the midst of national tumult, in the medium of
> international violent uproar, Coretta Scott King's face
> remained a study in serenity. In times of interior violent
> storms she sat, her hands resting in her lap calmly, like
> good children sleeping.... [King] was a quintessential
> African-American woman, born in the small town
> repressive South, born of flesh and destined to become
> iron; born a cornflower and destined to become a steel
> magnolia.

These contrasting images of serenity and strength, patience and
determination, capture the imagination through vivid imagery
and also weave an intimate, inclusive tone that continues throughout the speech. Angelou offers the audience cherished stories of
the time she spent with Mrs. King:

> We called ourselves "chosen sisters" and when we traveled
> to South Africa or to the Caribbean or when she came to
> visit me in North Carolina or in New York, we sat into the
> late evening hours, calling each other "girl." It's a black
> woman thing, you know. And even as we reached well
> into our 70th decade, we still said "girl."

The warmth and affection Angelou feels for King and her family
rings through in her delivery because of her rich voice, her direct
eye contact, and her animated face. As she spins her stories, her
sensory language and intimate delivery bring the audience into
the inner circle of those who knew King best. Even listeners
who did not know King well, who come from a different tradi-
tion and are unfamiliar with the social graces shared amongst
African-American women, feel included because Angelou has
invited them into the scene.

It is a beautiful speech, often blurring the line between poetry and prose, spoken word and song. As she closes, Dr. Angelou sings again, repeating the same words with which she opened. The final notes are proud and joyous, and the church, once again, erupts into applause. Angelou has given the audience a way to express its emotions, the main purpose of eulogy. The speech is a masterpiece of Pathos elevated by tone, cadence, wordsmithing, and elegant delivery. In the end, it is impossible not to revere Coretta Scott King all the more, and to feel grateful to Dr. Angelou as well.

Maya Angelou, February 7, 2006, Eulogy for Coretta Scott King

[Singing: "I open my mouth to the Lord and I won't turn back, no. I will go, I shall go. I'll see what the end is gonna be."]

In the midst of national tumult, in the medium of international violent uproar, Coretta Scott King's face remained a study in serenity. In times of interior violent storms she sat, her hands resting in her lap calmly, like good children sleeping.

Her passion was never spent in public display. She offered her industry and her energies to action, toward righting ancient and current wrongs in this world.

She believed religiously in non-violent protest.

She believed it could heal a nation mired in a history of slavery and all its excesses.

She believed non-violent protest religiously could lift up a nation rife with racial prejudices and racial bias.

She was a quintessential African-American woman,
born in the small town repressive South, born of flesh
and destined to become iron, born—born a cornflower
and destined to become a steel magnolia.

She loved her church fervently. She loved and adored
her husband and her children. She cherished her race.
She cherished women. She cared for the conditions of
human beings, of native Americans and Latin—
Latinos and Asian Americans. She cared for gay and
straight people. She was concerned for the struggles in
Ireland, and she prayed nightly for Palestine and
equally for Israel.

I speak as a—a sister of a sister. Dr. Martin Luther
King was assassinated on my birthday. And for over
30 years, Coretta Scott King and I have telephoned, or
sent cards to each other, or flowers to each other, or met
each other somewhere in the world. We called ourselves
"chosen sisters" and when we traveled to South Africa
or to the Caribbean or when she came to visit me in
North Carolina or in New York, we sat into the late
evening hours, calling each other "girl." It's a black
woman thing, you know. And even as we reached well
into our 70th decade, we still said "girl."

I stand here today for her family—which is my
family—and for my family and all the other families
in the world who would want to be here, but could not
be here. I have beside me up here millions of people
who are living and standing straight and erect, and
knowing something about dignity without being cold
and aloof, knowing something about being contained
without being unapproachable—people who have
learned something from Coretta Scott King.

I stand here for Eleanor Traylor and for Harry Belafonte, and I stand here for Winnie Mandela.

I stand here for women and men who loved her— [Constancia] "Dinky" Romilly. On those late nights when Coretta and I would talk, I would make her laugh. And she said that Martin King used to tell her, "You don't laugh enough." And there's a recent book out about sisters in which she spoke about her blood sister. But at the end of her essay, she said, I did have— "I do have a chosen sister, Maya Angelou, who makes me laugh even when I don't want to." And it's true. I told her some jokes only for no-mixed company.

Many times on those late after—evenings she would say to me, "Sister, it shouldn't be an 'either-or', should it? Peace and justice should belong to all people, everywhere, all the time. Isn't that right?" And I said then and I say now, "Coretta Scott King, you're absolutely right. I do believe that peace and justice should belong to every person, everywhere, all the time."

And those of us who gather here, principalities, presidents, senators, those of us who run great companies, who know something about being parents, who know something about being preachers and teachers—those of us, we owe something from this minute on; so that this gathering is not just another footnote on the pages of history. We owe something.

I pledge to you, my sister, I will never cease. I mean to say I want to see a better world. I mean to say I want to see some peace somewhere. I mean to say I want to see some honesty, some fair play.

*I want to see kindness and justice. This is what I want
to see and I want to see it through my eyes and through
your eyes, Coretta Scott King.*

*[Singing: "I open my mouth to the Lord and I won't
turn back, no. I will go, I shall go. I'll see what the end
is gonna be."]*

Thank you.

C. Winning the Argument: Barbara Jordan

Rhetoric is a set of tools an advocate can use to persuade an audience. An understanding of rhetoric can help to level the playing field for a speaker who would seem to be at a disadvantage. Freshman Congresswoman Barbara Jordan's Statement on the Articles of Impeachment, delivered on July 25, 1974, before the House Judiciary Committee, demonstrates how an understanding of Logos and a confident delivery can be powerful tools in the hands of an advocate.

Barbara Jordan had served in Congress for approximately 18 months when the House Judiciary Committee considered the impeachment of President Richard Nixon. She was a junior member of the Committee, not even through her first term in office. She was also the first African-American woman to be elected to Congress from a Southern state, facing a President who came to power by advocating the so-called "Southern Strategy," designed to exploit racial tensions in formerly segregated states. Despite her relative inexperience with national politics, Jordan wrote and delivered a speech that was instrumental in ending Nixon's Presidency.

Jordan begins her address acknowledging the gravity of the moment: Impeaching a President is a traumatic national event. Jordan places her talk in historical context, noting that for more than a hundred years she was not considered a full person under the law. Now, however, she lives in an America that recognizes her right to be included as one of "We, the People," and she declares her ferocious resolve to protect that country and its Constitution:

> Today I am an inquisitor. An hyperbole would not be fictional and would not overstate the solemnness that I feel right now. My faith in the Constitution is whole; it is complete; it is total. And I am not going to sit here and be an idle spectator to the diminution, the subversion, the destruction, of the Constitution.

The power in her delivery comes from her strong, confident voice, unexpectedly deep for a woman and therefore memorable; the cadence of her speech, which catches the ear through its use of triples ("whole, complete, total"; "diminution, subversion, destruction"); and the deliberate, measured pace with which she speaks. From the outset she commands the attention of her audience because the very fact of her presence at the hearing is remarkable in history, and because the power of her delivery shows that she takes that responsibility very seriously.

Jordan tackles two questions in her address: whether the President committed the alleged acts, and whether those acts constitute impeachable offenses under the Constitution. This is a signal forensic speech, and Jordan rightfully emphasizes Logos to bring her points home. She looks to the Framers of the Constitution to establish a definition of an impeachable offense, and measures Nixon's conduct against that standard. Jordan provides an excellent model for legal analysis—state the rule, and then apply the rule to the facts at hand:

> I would like to juxtapose a few of the impeachment criteria with some of the actions the President has engaged in. Impeachment criteria: James Madison, from the Virginia ratification convention. "If the President be connected in any suspicious manner with any person and there be grounds to believe that he will shelter him, he may be impeached."

We have heard time and time again that the evidence reflects the payment to defendants money. The President had knowledge that these funds were being paid and these were funds collected for the 1972 presidential campaign. We know that the President met with Mr. Henry Petersen 27 times to discuss matters related to Watergate, and immediately thereafter met with the very persons who were implicated in the information Mr. Petersen was receiving. The words are: "If the President is connected in any suspicious manner with any person and there be grounds to believe that he will shelter that person, he may be impeached."

Justice Story: "Impeachment . . . is intended for occasional and extraordinary cases where a superior power acting for the whole people is put into operation to protect their rights and rescue their liberties from violations." We know about the Huston plan. We know about the break-in of the psychiatrist's office. We know that there was absolute complete direction on September 3rd when the President indicated that a surreptitious entry had been made in Dr. Fielding's office, after having met with Mr. Ehrlichman and Mr. Young. "Protect their rights." "Rescue their liberties from violation."

The Carolina ratification convention impeachment criteria: those are impeachable "who behave amiss or betray their public trust." Beginning shortly after the Watergate break-in and continuing to the present time, the President has engaged in a series of public statements and actions designed to thwart the lawful investigation by government prosecutors. Moreover, the President has made public announcements and assertions bearing on the Watergate case, which the evidence will show he knew to be false. These assertions, false assertions, impeachable, those who misbehave. Those who "behave amiss or betray the public trust." . . .

> If the impeachment provision in the Constitution of the
> United States will not reach the offenses charged here, then
> perhaps that 18th-century Constitution should be aban-
> doned to a 20th-century paper shredder.

Jordan's word choice also bears mention. Her language is not conversational. It is erudite, formal, even poetic in places as she weaves foundational texts into her argument. The language is appropriate to the moment and advances Jordan's argument: Her dignity, her respect for the institutions of government as reflected through her formal word choice, highlight the shabbiness of Nixon's obscenity-laced plotting, as revealed in the Watergate tape manuscripts.

At bottom, Jordan's presentation is effective because of its simplicity. She lays out the facts alongside the criteria against which they should be judged so that her logic is transparent. At difficult moments, clear, well-reasoned, and well-presented evidence has the power to carry the day.

Congresswoman Barbara Jordan, Statement on the Articles of Impeachment, delivered July 25, 1974, before the House Judiciary Committee

Thank you, Mr. Chairman.

Mr. Chairman, I join my colleague Mr. Rangel in thanking you for giving the junior members of this committee the glorious opportunity of sharing the pain of this inquiry. Mr. Chairman, you are a strong man, and it has not been easy but we have tried as best we can to give you as much assistance as possible.

Earlier today, we heard the beginning of the Preamble to the Constitution of the United States: "We, the people." It's a very eloquent beginning. But when that

*document was completed on the seventeenth of
September in 1787, I was not included in that "We,
the people." I felt somehow for many years that George
Washington and Alexander Hamilton just left me out
by mistake. But through the process of amendment,
interpretation, and court decision, I have finally been
included in "We, the people."*

*Today I am an inquisitor. An hyperbole would not be
fictional and would not overstate the solemnness that
I feel right now. My faith in the Constitution is whole;
it is complete; it is total. And I am not going to sit here
and be an idle spectator to the diminution, the
subversion, the destruction, of the Constitution.*

*"Who can so properly be the inquisitors for the nation
as the representatives of the nation themselves?" "The
subjects of its jurisdiction are those offenses which
proceed from the misconduct of public men." And
that's what we're talking about. In other words, [the
jurisdiction comes] from the abuse or violation of
some public trust.*

*It is wrong, I suggest, it is a misreading of the
Constitution for any member here to assert that for a
member to vote for an article of impeachment means
that that member must be convinced that the President
should be removed from office. The Constitution
doesn't say that. The powers relating to impeachment
are an essential check in the hands of the body of the
legislature against and upon the encroachments of the
executive. The division between the two branches of
the legislature, the House and the Senate, assigning to
the one the right to accuse and to the other the right to
judge, the framers of this Constitution were very astute.*

They did not make the accusers and the judgers—and the judges the same person.

We know the nature of impeachment. We've been talking about it awhile now. It is chiefly designed for the President and his high ministers to somehow be called into account. It is designed to "bridle" the executive if he engages in excesses. "It is designed as a method of national inquest into the conduct of public men." The framers confided in the Congress the power if need be, to remove the President in order to strike a delicate balance between a President swollen with power and grown tyrannical, and preservation of the independence of the executive.

The nature of impeachment: a narrowly channeled exception to the separation-of-powers maxim. The Federal Convention of 1787 said that. It limited impeachment to high crimes and misdemeanors and discounted and opposed the term "maladministration." "It is to be used only for great misdemeanors," so it was said in the North Carolina ratification convention. And in the Virginia ratification convention: "We do not trust our liberty to a particular branch. We need one branch to check the other."

"No one need be afraid"—the North Carolina ratification convention—"No one need be afraid that officers who commit oppression will pass with immunity." "Prosecutions of impeachments will seldom fail to agitate the passions of the whole community," said Hamilton in the Federalist Papers, number 65. "We divide into parties more or less friendly or inimical to the accused." I do not mean political parties in that sense.

*The drawing of political lines goes to the motivation
behind impeachment; but impeachment must proceed
within the confines of the constitutional term "high
crime[s] and misdemeanors." Of the impeachment
process, it was Woodrow Wilson who said that
"Nothing short of the grossest offenses against the plain
law of the land will suffice to give them speed and
effectiveness. Indignation so great as to overgrow party
interest may secure a conviction; but nothing else can."*

*Common sense would be revolted if we engaged upon
this process for petty reasons. Congress has a lot to do:
Appropriations, Tax Reform, Health Insurance,
Campaign Finance Reform, Housing, Environmental
Protection, Energy Sufficiency, Mass Transportation.
Pettiness cannot be allowed to stand in the face of such
overwhelming problems. So today we are not being
petty. We are trying to be big, because the task we have
before us is a big one.*

*This morning, in a discussion of the evidence, we were
told that the evidence which purports to support the
allegations of misuse of the CIA by the President is
thin. We're told that that evidence is insufficient.
What that recital of the evidence this morning did not
include is what the President did know on June the
23rd, 1972.*

*The President did know that it was Republican
money, that it was money from the Committee for the
Re-Election of the President, which was found in the
possession of one of the burglars arrested on June
the 17th. What the President did know on the 23rd of
June was the prior activities of E. Howard Hunt,
which included his participation in the break-in of*

Daniel Ellsberg's psychiatrist, which included Howard Hunt's participation in the Dita Beard ITT affair, which included Howard Hunt's fabrication of cables designed to discredit the Kennedy Administration.

We were further cautioned today that perhaps these proceedings ought to be delayed because certainly there would be new evidence forthcoming from the President of the United States. There has not even been an obfuscated indication that this committee would receive any additional materials from the President. The committee subpoena is outstanding, and if the President wants to supply that material, the committee sits here. The fact is that on yesterday, the American people waited with great anxiety for eight hours, not knowing whether their President would obey an order of the Supreme Court of the United States.

At this point, I would like to juxtapose a few of the impeachment criteria with some of the actions the President has engaged in. Impeachment criteria: James Madison, from the Virginia ratification convention. "If the President be connected in any suspicious manner with any person and there be grounds to believe that he will shelter him, he may be impeached."

We have heard time and time again that the evidence reflects the payment to defendants money. The President had knowledge that these funds were being paid and these were funds collected for the 1972 presidential campaign. We know that the President met with Mr. Henry Petersen 27 times to discuss matters related to Watergate, and immediately thereafter met with the very persons who were implicated in the information Mr. Petersen was receiving.

The words are: "If the President is connected in any suspicious manner with any person and there be grounds to believe that he will shelter that person, he may be impeached."

Justice Story: "Impeachment" is attended—"is intended for occasional and extraordinary cases where a superior power acting for the whole people is put into operation to protect their rights and rescue their liberties from violations." We know about the Huston plan. We know about the break-in of the psychiatrist's office. We know that there was absolute complete direction on September 3rd when the President indicated that a surreptitious entry had been made in Dr. Fielding's office, after having met with Mr. Ehrlichman and Mr. Young. "Protect their rights." "Rescue their liberties from violation."

The Carolina ratification convention impeachment criteria: those are impeachable "who behave amiss or betray their public trust." Beginning shortly after the Watergate break-in and continuing to the present time, the President has engaged in a series of public statements and actions designed to thwart the lawful investigation by government prosecutors. Moreover, the President has made public announcements and assertions bearing on the Watergate case, which the evidence will show he knew to be false. These assertions, false assertions, impeachable, those who misbehave. Those who "behave amiss or betray the public trust."

James Madison again at the Constitutional Convention: "A President is impeachable if he attempts to subvert the Constitution." The Constitution charges the President with the task of taking care that the laws be faithfully executed, and yet the President has counseled his aides to commit perjury, willfully disregard the secrecy of grand jury proceedings, conceal surreptitious entry, attempt to compromise a federal judge, while publicly displaying his cooperation with the processes of criminal justice. "A President is impeachable if he attempts to subvert the Constitution."

If the impeachment provision in the Constitution of the United States will not reach the offenses charged here, then perhaps that 18th-century Constitution should be abandoned to a 20th-century paper shredder.

Has the President committed offenses, and planned, and directed, and acquiesced in a course of conduct which the Constitution will not tolerate? That's the question. We know that. We know the question. We should now forthwith proceed to answer the question. It is reason, and not passion, which must guide our deliberations, guide our debate, and guide our decision.

D. Overcoming Bias, Part 1: Sojourner Truth

Public speaking students sometimes ask if they should change their speaking style. The reserved student wonders if he should become more theatrical. The emotive speaker asks if he should tone it down. While subtle adjustments to achieve clarity and Ethos are always helpful, our answer is usually the same: Be yourself. Find a speaking style that is authentic to you. Anything else tends to backfire: It is not you; you have no practice at it. Your own authentic voice is the most persuasive. Sojourner Truth's famous "Ain't I a Woman?" speech in Akron, Ohio, illustrates the point.

Truth had two strikes against her before she even opened her mouth: She was black—an emancipated slave—in a world that believed that African-Americans were intellectually inferior to whites, and she was a woman in a time when women, seen as less capable than men, could not vote. Her audience, attendees at the Women's Convention of 1851, might have been sympathetic to women's suffrage, but many would not have dreamed of extending the right to African-American women. According to Frances Gage, an abolitionist who attended the meeting,

> There were very few women in those days who dared to "speak in meeting".... When, slowly from her seat in the corner rose Sojourner Truth, who, till now, had scarcely lifted her head. "Don't let her speak!" gasped half a dozen in my ear.[165]

At a time when rhetoric was dominated by the likes of Henry Clay, Daniel Webster, and Abraham Lincoln, who modeled themselves on the Greeks and Romans, Sojourner Truth addressed the crowd in raw, simple language. She spoke in dialect, using commonplace words. The speakers who preceded her, arguing against women's rights, painted a picture of womanhood as a privileged position, shielded from the working world (and therefore protected from the burdens of public life as well) out of necessity because of her inborn frailty. Truth challenged this position with one basic question, "Ain't I a woman?"

Truth begins by itemizing all the ways she is human: She works, eats, bleeds, suffers, just like a man. As she recounts each grief she has borne, more than many men could tolerate, she asks simply, "Ain't I a woman?" This is her haunting refrain:

> Look at my arm! I have ploughed and planted, and gathered into barns, and no man could head me! And ain't I a woman? I could work as much and eat as much as a man—when I could get it—and bear the lash as well! And ain't I a woman? I have borne thirteen children, and seen most all sold off to slavery, and when I cried out with my mother's grief, none but Jesus heard me! And ain't I a woman?

Like most great refrains, this one builds. It starts simply: Truth has planted and gathered, the everyday work of many men and women at the time. She can work and eat like a man "when I could get it"—a darker reference, for she has gone without food. The misery builds: She says she can endure whipping as well as a man, and we are reminded that she knows the degradation of slavery. She raised a family and cried as these children were ripped away from her and sold to new masters.

She asks again, "Ain't I a woman?" Her point: The fantasy that women are too delicate to participate fully in public life is a fallacy. She stands before her audience a black woman who has been tested in her life in ways that many of her listeners have not. By laying out the simple truth of the facts of her life, in her own voice, she wins over a skeptical audience. Another attendee at the conference writes of the effects of the address:

> One of the most unique and interesting speeches of the convention was made by Sojourner Truth, an emancipated slave. It is impossible to transfer it to paper, or convey any adequate idea of the effect it produced upon the audience. Those only can appreciate it who saw her powerful form, her whole-souled, earnest gesture, and listened to her strong and truthful tones.[166]

Sojourner Truth's address is a model for the power of a genuine, conversational tone; an on-point refrain; and the power of Logos-building from the ordinary example to a powerful crescendo—not by quivering voice or flailing arms, but through a series of ever more wrenching, objective facts.

Sojourner Truth, "Ain't I a Woman?," Delivered 1851, Women's Convention, Akron, Ohio

Well, children, where there is so much racket there must be something out of kilter. I think that 'twixt the negroes of the South and the women at the North, all

*talking about rights, the white men will be in a fix
pretty soon. But what's all this here talking about?*

*That man over there says that women need to be helped
into carriages, and lifted over ditches, and to have the
best place everywhere. Nobody ever helps me into
carriages, or over mud-puddles, or gives me any best
place! And ain't I a woman? Look at me! Look at my
arm! I have ploughed and planted, and gathered into
barns, and no man could head me! And ain't I a
woman? I could work as much and eat as much as a
man—when I could get it—and bear the lash as well!
And ain't I a woman? I have borne thirteen children,
and seen most all sold off to slavery, and when
I cried out with my mother's grief, none but Jesus
heard me! And ain't I a woman?*

*Then they talk about this thing in the head; what's this
they call it? [member of audience whispers, "intellect"]
That's it, honey. What's that got to do with women's
rights or negroes' rights? If my cup won't hold but a
pint, and yours holds a quart, wouldn't you be mean
not to let me have my little half measure full?*

*Then that little man in black there, he says women
can't have as much rights as men, 'cause Christ wasn't
a woman! Where did your Christ come from? Where
did your Christ come from? From God and a woman!
Man had nothing to do with Him.*

*If the first woman God ever made was strong enough to
turn the world upside down all alone, these women
together ought to be able to turn it back, and get it
right side up again! And now they is asking to do it, the
men better let them.*

Obliged to you for hearing me, and now old Sojourner
ain't got nothing more to say.

E. Overcoming Bias, Part 2: Mary Fisher

Like Sojourner Truth more than a century before her, Mary Fisher faced an audience that was likely to dismiss her because she bore a stigma: She was HIV-positive.

At the time of the 1992 Republican National Convention in Houston, the GOP had not adopted a comprehensive policy regarding treatment and prevention of HIV and AIDS. HIV was still considered a disease that affected only the unpopular subcultures of gay men and intravenous drug users.

Two days before Fisher spoke, Pat Buchanan gave what became known as his "Culture War" speech. It was the keynote address for the first day of the convention. He mocked Democrats for political "cross-dressing." He warned that the Democratic presidential and vice presidential candidates would be "the most pro-lesbian and pro-gay ticket in history." He received raucous applause from the crowd.[167]

Fisher, in contrast, was only tepidly applauded as she took the stage. But with careful attention to Logos and her calm, measured tone, she soon moved many to tears.

Fisher is unapologetic in her position: HIV and AIDS are everyone's problem. She derides the stigma and isolation AIDS patients face, pointing out that no group deserves societal isolation:

> We may take refuge in our stereotypes, but we cannot hide there long, because HIV asks only one thing of those it attacks. Are you human? And this is the right question. Are you human? Because people with HIV have not entered some alien state of being. They are human. They have not earned cruelty, and they do not deserve meanness. They don't benefit from being isolated or treated as outcasts. Each of them is exactly what God

> made: a person; not evil, deserving of our judgment; not
> victims, longing for our pity—people, ready for support
> and worthy of compassion.

She is a sympathetic figure—a beautiful, young wife and mother, the daughter of a wealthy, influential Republican family, who contracted AIDS from her dying husband and who is facing her own death with courage and grace. But Fisher declares herself a part of anyone who suffers the ravages of AIDS:

> Tonight, I represent an AIDS community whose members
> have been reluctantly drafted from every segment of
> American society. Though I am white and a mother, I am
> one with a black infant struggling with tubes in a
> Philadelphia hospital. Though I am female and contracted
> this disease in marriage and enjoy the warm support of my
> family, I am one with the lonely gay man sheltering a
> flickering candle from the cold wind of his family's
> rejection.

Hers is a risky statement against the backdrop of Buchanan's intolerance, but the audience listens. By her demonstration of compassion, Fisher galvanizes her entire party to follow her good example.

Fisher demands that the country's reaction to AIDS must change. She takes the GOP to task for its inaction in the face of the AIDS crisis, pointing out that inaction by policy makers has "helped [AIDS] along. We have killed each other with our ignorance, our prejudice, and our silence." Hers is an uncompromising speech, openly challenging and criticizing stereotypes. Fisher's message succeeds in large part because she lays out fact after fact after fact in support of her position; her Logos is strong.

The speech is also a model of Pathos done well. Throughout, Fisher is careful to maintain a reasonable, controlled tone. Her frankness never turns to anger. Her urgency never approaches defiance. She mixes a blunt call for action with vivid descriptions of her own struggle with the disease and the toll it is taking on those dearest to her, including a heartbreaking address to her two young children, who risk growing up without a mother because no cure for AIDS has yet been found. It is a gentle, vulnerable moment and helps to contextualize Fisher's urgent pleas for help on behalf of the AIDS community. But even when bidding farewell to her own children, Fisher herself never loses control. Her eyes remain dry, while throughout the hall, Republican leaders openly weep.[168]

In order to inspire the crowd to action, Fisher must reach the hearts of the unmoved. She does so through her remarkably calm demeanor—measured cadence, a soft tone—as she piles fact upon fact. As classic rhetoricians urged, Fisher reaches her audience through the mind rather than through a frontal assault on emotion. Her remarkable composure and control in the face of so difficult an address makes memorable the Pathos of her appeal.

Excerpts from Mary Fisher's Address to the Republican National Convention, August 19, 1992

Less than three months ago at platform hearings in Salt Lake City, I asked the Republican Party to lift the shroud of silence which has been draped over the issue of HIV and AIDS. I have come tonight to bring our silence to an end. I bear a message of challenge, not self-congratulation. I want your attention, not your applause. . . .

In the context of an election year, I ask you, here in this great hall, or listening in the quiet of your home, to recognize that AIDS virus is not a political creature. It does not care whether you are Democrat or Republican; it does not ask whether you are black or white, male or female, gay or straight, young or old.

Tonight, I represent an AIDS community whose members have been reluctantly drafted from every segment of American society. Though I am white and a mother, I am one with a black infant struggling with tubes in a Philadelphia hospital. Though I am female and contracted this disease in marriage and enjoy the warm support of my family, I am one with the lonely gay man sheltering a flickering candle from the cold wind of his family's rejection.

This is not a distant threat. It is a present danger. The rate of infection is increasing fastest among women and children. Largely unknown a decade ago, AIDS is the third leading killer of young adult Americans today. But it won't be third for long, because unlike other diseases, this one travels. Adolescents don't give each other cancer or heart disease because they believe they are in love, but HIV is different; and we have helped it along. We have killed each other with our ignorance, our prejudice, and our silence.

We may take refuge in our stereotypes, but we cannot hide there long, because HIV asks only one thing of those it attacks. Are you human? And this is the right question. Are you human? Because people with HIV have not entered some alien state of being. They are human. They have not earned cruelty, and they do not deserve meanness. They don't benefit from being isolated or treated as outcasts. Each of them is exactly what God made: a person; not evil, deserving of our judgment; not victims, longing for our pity—people, ready for support and worthy of compassion.

My call to you, my Party, is to take a public stand, no less compassionate than that of the President and Mrs. Bush. They have embraced me and my family in memorable ways. In the place of judgment, they have shown affection. In difficult moments, they have raised our spirits. In the darkest hours, I have seen them reaching not only to me, but also to my parents, armed with that stunning grief and special grace that comes only to parents who have themselves leaned too long over the bedside of a dying child. . . .

My call to the nation is a plea for awareness. If you believe you are safe, you are in danger. Because I was not hemophiliac, I was not at risk. Because I was not gay, I was not at risk. Because I did not inject drugs, I was not at risk.

My father has devoted much of his lifetime guarding against another holocaust. He is part of the generation who heard Pastor Nemoellor come out of the Nazi death camps to say,

"They came after the Jews, and I was not a Jew, so, I did not protest. They came after the trade unionists, and I was not a trade unionist, so, I did not protest. Then they came after the Roman Catholics, and I was not a Roman Catholic, so, I did not protest. Then they came after me, and there was no one left to protest."

The—The lesson history teaches is this: If you believe you are safe, you are at risk. If you do not see this killer stalking your children, look again. There is no family or community, no race or religion, no place left in America that is safe. Until we genuinely embrace this message, we are a nation at risk.

Tonight, HIV marches resolutely toward AIDS in more than a million American homes, littering its pathway with the bodies of the young—young men,

young women, young parents, and young children.
One of the families is mine. If it is true that HIV
inevitably turns to AIDS, then my children will
inevitably turn to orphans. My family has been a
rock of support. . . .

But not all of you—But not all of you have been so
blessed. You are HIV positive, but dare not say it. You
have lost loved ones, but you dare not whisper the word
AIDS. You weep silently. You grieve alone. I have a
message for you. It is not you who should feel shame. It
is we—we who tolerate ignorance and practice
prejudice, we who have taught you to fear. We must
lift our shroud of silence, making it safe for you to reach
out for compassion. It is our task to seek safety for our
children, not in quiet denial, but in effective action.

Someday our children will be grown. My son Max,
now four, will take the measure of his mother. My son
Zachary, now two, will sort through his memories.
I may not be here to hear their judgments, but I know
already what I hope they are. I want my children to
know that their mother was not a victim. She was a
messenger. I do not want them to think, as I once did,
that courage is the absence of fear. I want them to
know that courage is the strength to act wisely when
most we are afraid. I want them to have the courage to
step forward when called by their nation or their Party
and give leadership, no matter what the personal cost.

I ask no more of you than I ask of myself or of my
children. To the millions of you who are grieving, who
are frightened, who have suffered the ravages of AIDS
firsthand: Have courage, and you will find support.
To the millions who are strong, I issue the plea: Set

*aside prejudice and politics to make room for com-
passion and sound policy.*

*To my children, I make this pledge: I will not give in,
Zachary, because I draw my courage from you. Your
silly giggle gives me hope; your gentle prayers give me
strength; and you, my child, give me the reason to say to
America, "You are at risk." And I will not rest, Max,
until I have done all I can to make your world safe.
I will seek a place where intimacy is not the prelude to
suffering. I will not hurry to leave you, my children,
but when I go, I pray that you will not suffer shame on
my account.*

*To all within the sound of my voice, I appeal: Learn
with me the lessons of history and of grace, so my
children will not be afraid to say the word "AIDS"
when I am gone. Then, their children and yours may
not need to whisper it at all.*

God bless the children, and God bless us all.

Good night.

F. Making a Speech in a Time of Crisis, Part 1: Robert F. Kennedy

Robert Kennedy's remarks in Indianapolis following the assassination of Martin Luther King demonstrate the force of the well-chosen word. Kennedy's message, hastily arranged and only minutes long, may well have kept a riot at bay. The setting: a campaign rally for Robert Kennedy, who hoped to secure the Democratic nomination for President. The audience: Kennedy supporters, both white and black, excited to be there, who had no idea of Dr. King's death. The challenge: Kennedy must tell the crowd that Martin Luther King has been shot and killed in

Memphis. The rally is taking place in a part of Indianapolis that the police consider to be a dangerous neighborhood; violence could erupt once the news becomes public.

Kennedy takes the microphone to deliver the tragic news, cancelling the rally and calming the crowd. His speech is an excellent example of grace in a time of crisis.

Kennedy's words are clear and direct. He explains King's death, tells his supporters what will happen next, and asks them to undertake simple action, of which they are capable: Go home. Pray for the King family. Pray for our country. Pray for our people. Kennedy offers his listeners a plan of action to alleviate their feelings of helplessness and despair. In crises, achievable action can offer comfort.

Kennedy's tone is pitch-perfect, offering understanding without patronizing. He is uniquely positioned to empathize with the helplessness and anger that the listeners must feel; after all, as he explains to them:

> For those of you who are black and are tempted to be filled with hatred and mistrust of the injustice of such an act, against all white people, I would only say that I can also feel in my own heart the same kind of feeling. I had a member of my family killed, but he was killed by a white man.

He does not try to control the emotion of the moment. Such a task would be impossible. He acknowledges that one course of action in response to the assassination would be violence and hatred. But he frames the issue as a moment of choice for the audience:

> For those of you who are black . . . you can be filled with bitterness, and with hatred, and a desire for revenge. We can move in that direction as a country, in greater polarization—black people amongst blacks, and white amongst whites, filled with hatred toward one another. Or we can make an effort, as Martin Luther King did, to

> understand and to comprehend, and replace that violence,
> that stain of bloodshed that has spread across our land,
> with an effort to understand, compassion and love.

Kennedy does not impose beliefs or morals on the crowd, but with empathy and authenticity offers an alternative to hatred: unity and love. His act of empowering the audience with a choice lets the audience see that the story does not end with Dr. King's death. Instead, the assassination is an important moment in history, and it is up to them to take the next steps forward into the future. He offers his listeners a cause, a place in history, and a course of action that can help them manage their grief.

Speeches at times of crisis and grief are often not about logic. They are about the use and management of emotion—an appropriate display of emotion by the speaker, to show that he cares and understands the feelings of his listeners; and some emotional relief for listeners, a moment of catharsis. In classical rhetoric terms, this had to be an epideictic event. Speakers showing authenticity and empathy, and then offering a semblance of hope, will often carry the day. Kennedy does this masterfully. His tone is soft. His words are painstakingly chosen. His cadence is gentle and slow. He logically moves through his words and evokes the name of the fallen martyr. He is calm and he conveys that to his shocked audience.

The result: There was no riot.

Text of Robert Kennedy's Address in Indianapolis, 1968

Ladies and Gentlemen—I'm only going to talk to you just for a minute or so this evening. Because . . .

I have some very sad news for all of you, and I think sad news for all of our fellow citizens, and people who love peace all over the world, and that is that Martin

*Luther King was shot and was killed tonight in
Memphis, Tennessee.*

*Martin Luther King dedicated his life to love and to
justice between fellow human beings. He died in the
cause of that effort. In this difficult day, in this difficult
time for the United States, it's perhaps well to ask what
kind of a nation we are and what direction we want to
move in.*

*For those of you who are black—considering the
evidence evidently is that there were white people who
were responsible—you can be filled with bitterness,
and with hatred, and a desire for revenge.*

*We can move in that direction as a country, in greater
polarization—black people amongst blacks, and white
amongst whites, filled with hatred toward one another.
Or we can make an effort, as Martin Luther King did,
to understand and to comprehend, and replace that
violence, that stain of bloodshed that has spread across
our land, with an effort to understand, compassion
and love.*

*For those of you who are black and are tempted to be
filled with hatred and mistrust of the injustice of such
an act, against all white people, I would only say that
I can also feel in my own heart the same kind of feeling.
I had a member of my family killed, but he was killed
by a white man.*

*But we have to make an effort in the United States, we
have to make an effort to understand, to get beyond
these rather difficult times.*

My favorite poet was Aeschylus. He once wrote: "Even in our sleep, pain which cannot forget falls drop by drop upon the heart, until, in our own despair, against our will, comes wisdom through the awful grace of God."

What we need in the United States is not division; what we need in the United States is not hatred; what we need in the United States is not violence and lawlessness, but is love and wisdom, and compassion toward one another, and a feeling of justice toward those who still suffer within our country, whether they be white or whether they be black.

(Interrupted by applause)

So I ask you tonight to return home, to say a prayer for the family of Martin Luther King, yeah that's true, but more importantly to say a prayer for our own country, which all of us love—a prayer for understanding and that compassion of which I spoke. We can do well in this country. We will have difficult times. We've had difficult times in the past. And we will have difficult times in the future. It is not the end of violence; it is not the end of lawlessness; and it's not the end of disorder.

But the vast majority of white people and the vast majority of black people in this country want to live together, want to improve the quality of our life, and want justice for all human beings that abide in our land.

(Interrupted by applause)

Let us dedicate ourselves to what the Greeks wrote so many years ago: to tame the savageness of man and make gentle the life of this world.

Let us dedicate ourselves to that, and say a prayer for our country and for our people. Thank you very much. (Applause)

G. Making a Speech in a Time of Crisis, Part 2: Winston Churchill

June 1940: Britain is at war and fears the worst. Cut off from its ground forces, mired in Dunkirk, shipping lanes compromised by the presence of U-boats, the Island is alone and under threat. German forces have overwhelmed the French and Belgian resistance and are positioned less than 20 miles from British shores. Their arrival means that aerial bombardment of the British mainland is imminent. If Britain cannot evacuate its remaining ground forces from Dunkirk, England will be virtually indefensible and the Nazis could launch an invasion at will. Public anxiety is amplified by political indecisiveness and uncertainty in the face of this threat, particularly under previous Prime Minister Neville Chamberlain.

Winston Churchill has been Prime Minister for less than a month. Under his leadership, the British launch a massive effort to evacuate their troops from Dunkirk before German forces arrive. On June 4, 1940, Churchill delivers an address to the House of Commons in order to inform them of recent military events and bolster the morale of the nation. His address, known for famous lines such as "We shall fight on the beaches," inspired a beleaguered nation and became one of the defining speeches of the time.

Churchill begins by acknowledging the public anxiety. He tells his audience that he feared he would have to address the nation to tell them of a disaster: that British forces had been annihilated by fighting in Dunkirk. Instead, a massive military and civilian rescue effort successfully evacuated virtually all British troops unharmed. Churchill's description of the fighting is riveting in its detail, painting a picture of the enormity of the struggle and the valor displayed by the soldiers. "I will tell you about it," he promises his people, and tell them he does, spinning his tale of a cornered army, enemy fire, magnetic mines, waves of hostile aircrafts, and finally "a miracle of deliverance, achieved by valor, by perseverance, by perfect discipline, by faultless service, by resource, by skill, by unconquerable fidelity." The battle is one for the cinema and the history books. By painting a larger-than-life picture, Churchill elevates the actions of the soldiers, at once praising and inspiring them.

The news is good, but Churchill carefully manages expectations. He must prepare the nation for an extended bombing campaign against the mainland and a possible invasion, a grim task. How do you tell people that the enemy is coming and fighting will be brutal? He warns Britons that they should not confuse the success of the Dunkirk rescue effort with a victory, for "wars are not won by evacuations." He then switches from passive to active voice, empowering his people. He acknowledges the threat of invasion but says that the Island can survive for years if necessary—that if Hitler and his forces attempt to take the mainland the nation and its people will fight:

> Even though large tracts of Europe and many old and famous States have fallen or may fall into the grip of the Gestapo and all the odious apparatus of Nazi rule, we shall not flag or fail. We shall go on to the end. We shall fight in France, we shall fight on the seas and oceans, we shall fight with growing confidence and growing strength in the air, we shall defend our Island, whatever the cost may be. We shall fight on the beaches, we shall fight on the landing grounds, we shall fight in the fields and in the streets, we shall fight in the hills; we shall never surrender.

"We shall fight," goes the refrain. A country that once lacked a clear and defined war strategy is toughened by this rallying cry.

Churchill makes deliberate choices in his text to drive his point home. He catches the ear with subtle alliteration ("grip of the Gestapo"; "odious apparatus"; "flag or fail"). His pace quickens and crescendos with each repetition of his promise, "we shall fight." The refrain grips the imagination; the force of the speech compels the audience toward the fight ahead. His voice is sonorous, thrilling. This is what radio listeners will remember.

Churchill gives his listeners a place in history, elevating their actions and sacrifices to provide meaning for the struggle. He gives them a reason to fight. Most importantly, he bolsters their pride. This speech perfectly illustrates the interplay between skilled writing, Ethos, and Pathos: The deft use of a refrain to bring out emotion, and the power of a credible speaker to inspire courage in an audience, can arm a people to face a grim reality with courage.

Excerpts from Winston Churchill's June 4, 1940, Address to the House of Commons of British Parliament

... When, a week ago today, I asked the House to fix this afternoon as the occasion for a statement, I feared it would be my hard lot to announce the greatest military disaster in our long history. I thought—and some good judges agreed with me—that perhaps 20,000 or 30,000 men might be re-embarked. But it certainly seemed that the whole of the French First Army and the whole of the British Expeditionary Force north of the Amiens-Abbeville gap would be broken up in the open field or else would have to capitulate for lack of food and ammunition. These were the hard and heavy tidings for which I called upon the House and the nation to prepare themselves a week ago. The whole root and core and brain of the British Army, on which and around which we were to build, and are to

build, the great British Armies in the later years of the war, seemed about to perish upon the field or to be led into an ignominious and starving captivity.

That was the prospect a week ago. But another blow which might well have proved final was yet to fall upon us. . . . [A]t the last moment, when Belgium was already invaded, King Leopold called upon us to come to his aid, and even at the last moment we came. He and his brave, efficient Army, nearly half a million strong, guarded our left flank and thus kept open our only line of retreat to the sea. Suddenly, without prior consultation, with the least possible notice, without the advice of his Ministers and upon his own personal act, he sent a plenipotentiary to the German Command, surrendered his Army, and exposed our whole flank and means of retreat. . . .

The enemy attacked on all sides with great strength and fierceness, and their main power, the power of their far more numerous Air Force, was thrown into the battle or else concentrated upon Dunkirk and the beaches. Pressing in upon the narrow exit, both from the east and from the west, the enemy began to fire with cannon upon the beaches by which alone the shipping could approach or depart. They sowed magnetic mines in the channels and seas; they sent repeated waves of hostile aircraft, sometimes more than a hundred strong in one formation, to cast their bombs upon the single pier that remained, and upon the sand dunes upon which the troops had their eyes for shelter. Their U-boats, one of which was sunk, and their motor launches took their toll of the vast traffic which now began. For four or five days an intense struggle reigned. All their armored divisions—or what was left of

*them—together with great masses of infantry and
artillery, hurled themselves in vain upon the
ever-narrowing, ever-contracting appendix within
which the British and French Armies fought. . . .*

*. . . Suddenly the scene has cleared, the crash and
thunder has for the moment—but only for the
moment—died away. A miracle of deliverance,
achieved by valor, by perseverance, by perfect
discipline, by faultless service, by resource, by skill, by
unconquerable fidelity, is manifest to us all. The enemy
was hurled back by the retreating British and French
troops. He was so roughly handled that he did not
hurry their departure seriously. The Royal Air Force
engaged the main strength of the German Air Force,
and inflicted upon them losses of at least four to one;
and the Navy, using nearly 1,000 ships of all kinds,
carried over 335,000 men, French and British, out of
the jaws of death and shame, to their native land
and to the tasks which lie immediately ahead.*

*We must be very careful not to assign to this
deliverance the attributes of a victory. Wars are not
won by evacuations. But there was a victory inside this
deliverance, which should be noted. It was gained by
the Air Force. Many of our soldiers coming back have
not seen the Air Force at work; they saw only the
bombers which escaped its protective attack. They
underrate its achievements. I have heard much talk of
this; that is why I go out of my way to say this. I will
tell you about it. . . .*

*I have, myself, full confidence that if all do their duty,
if nothing is neglected, and if the best arrangements are
made, as they are being made, we shall prove ourselves*

once again able to defend our Island home, to ride out the storm of war, and to outlive the menace of tyranny, if necessary for years, if necessary alone. At any rate, that is what we are going to try to do. That is the resolve of His Majesty's Government—every man of them. That is the will of Parliament and the nation. The British Empire and the French Republic, linked together in their cause and in their need, will defend to the death their native soil, aiding each other like good comrades to the utmost of their strength. Even though large tracts of Europe and many old and famous States have fallen or may fall into the grip of the Gestapo and all the odious apparatus of Nazi rule, we shall not flag or fail. We shall go on to the end, we shall fight in France, we shall fight on the seas and oceans, we shall fight with growing confidence and growing strength in the air, we shall defend our Island, whatever the cost may be, we shall fight on the beaches, we shall fight on the landing grounds, we shall fight in the fields and in the streets, we shall fight in the hills; we shall never surrender, and even if, which I do not for a moment believe, this Island or a large part of it were subjugated and starving, then our Empire beyond the seas, armed and guarded by the British Fleet, would carry on the struggle, until, in God's good time, the New World, with all its power and might, steps forth to the rescue and the liberation of the old.

H. Making a Speech in a Time of Crisis, Part 3: Abraham Lincoln

The challenge confronting Abraham Lincoln at the time of his second inaugural address was staggering: to unite a war-ravaged, bitter nation. The address took place during the closing days of the Civil War, a month before General Robert E. Lee's surrender. Thousands of Americans lay dead; families were shattered; the country remained deeply divided. Lincoln did not wish to deliver a victory speech or an excoriation of the South, as many might have expected. Instead, he sought to usher in peace. Striking the right tone would be tricky. Lincoln could not risk sounding weak or conciliatory to Northern ears without insulting the sacrifices and accomplishments of the Union army; at the same time, he could not demoralize or demonize the South without permanently fracturing the nation.

There existed no obvious symbol of unity around which to rally both sides. Images that could inspire hope to one half of the country would smack of disrespect to the other. The one vestige of commonality that still existed between North and South was a shared belief in God. Though a man guarded about his own religious views, Lincoln recognized that many were reaching for some way to make religious and moral sense of the blood and death they had suffered. Lincoln therefore rooted his address in theology in an attempt to find a middle ground, a way to speak to both North and South.

Lincoln recounts the Civil War not through memorializing the battles or reviewing the political decisions that led to secession, but instead by describing the belief systems of both sides. Both sides appealed to God, believing their cause to be righteous. Both sides believed God favored their cause. Both sides continued to fight in the name of God. "Both read the same Bible, and pray to the same God; and each invokes His aid against the other." And both sides have suffered:

> Both parties deprecated war; but one of them would make war rather than let the nation survive; and the other would accept war rather than let it perish. And the war came.

Both North and South are responsible for ushering in war, Lincoln explains.

Interestingly, Lincoln describes North and South as cut from the same cloth, motivated by similar beliefs, similarly surprised by the outcome, so focused on each other that they do not notice the entrance of a third party—war—until it is too late:

> Neither party expected for the war, the magnitude, or the duration, which it has already attained. Neither anticipated that the cause of the conflict might cease with, or even before, the conflict itself should cease. Each looked for an easier triumph, and a result less fundamental and astounding.

The problem, then, is not North or South; it is the interloper, war, which is equally hated by both. Both sides must work together to banish war from their midst.

Just as North and South are united in their reaction to the war, so are both sides equally hungry for and mystified by God's opinion of the conflict:

> The prayers of both could not be answered; that of neither has been answered fully. The Almighty has his own purposes. "Woe unto the world because of offences! for it must needs be that offences come; but woe to that man by whom the offence cometh!" If we shall suppose that American Slavery is one of those offences which, in the providence of God, must needs come, but which, having continued through His appointed time, He now wills to remove, and that He gives to both North and South, this terrible war, as the woe due to those by whom the offence came, shall we discern therein any departure from those divine attributes which the believers in a Living God always ascribe to Him? Fondly do we hope—fervently do we pray—that this mighty scourge of war may speedily pass away. Yet, if God wills that it continue, until all the wealth piled by the bond-man's two hundred and fifty years of unrequited toil shall be sunk, and until every drop of blood drawn with the lash, shall be paid by another drawn with the sword, as was said three thousand years ago, so still it must be said "the judgments of the Lord, are true and righteous altogether."

By describing both North and South as linked—both responsible for American slavery and both punished for it by this "terrible war"—Lincoln makes it clear that the two sides must work together if they hope to eradicate themselves from a situation that all hate.

Finally, Lincoln proposes a common way forward. Just as both sides pray to the same God, both sides also owe a debt of gratitude to their soldiers, and both North and South have an obligation to care for the families of the war dead:

> With malice toward none; with charity for all; with firmness in the right, as God gives us to see the right, let us strive on to finish the work we are in; to bind up the nation's wounds; to care for him who shall have borne the battle, and for his widow, and his orphan—to do all which may achieve and cherish a just and lasting peace, among ourselves, and with all nations.

Lincoln describes the healing of the nation as the correct moral path in the eyes of God. The tone of this speech is at once tragic, tough, but ultimately soothing. Lincoln's instinct to unify exhibits a strong Ethos, good judgment and calm in the toughest of circumstances.

Abraham Lincoln, Second Inaugural Address, Saturday, March 4, 1865

At this second appearing to take the oath of the presidential office, there is less occasion for an extended address than there was at the first. Then a statement, somewhat in detail, of a course to be pursued, seemed fitting and proper. Now, at the expiration of four years, during which public declarations have been constantly called forth on every point and phase of the great contest which still absorbs the attention, and

*engrosses the energies of the nation, little that is new
could be presented. The progress of our arms, upon
which all else chiefly depends, is as well known to the
public as to myself; and it is, I trust, reasonably satis-
factory and encouraging to all. With high hope for the
future, no prediction in regard to it is ventured.*

*On the occasion corresponding to this four years ago,
all thoughts were anxiously directed to an impending
civil war. All dreaded it—all sought to avert it. While
the inaugural address was being delivered from this
place, devoted altogether to saving the Union without
war, insurgent agents were in the city seeking to destroy
it without war—seeking to dissolve the Union, and
divide effects, by negotiation. Both parties deprecated
war; but one of them would make war rather than let
the nation survive; and the other would accept war
rather than let it perish. And the war came.*

*One eighth of the whole population were colored slaves,
not distributed generally over the Union, but localized
in the Southern part of it. These slaves constituted a
peculiar and powerful interest. All knew that this
interest was, somehow, the cause of the war.
To strengthen, perpetuate, and extend this interest was
the object for which the insurgents would rend the
Union, even by war; while the government claimed no
right to do more than to restrict the territorial
enlargement of it. Neither party expected for the war,
the magnitude, or the duration, which it has already
attained. Neither anticipated that the cause of the
conflict might cease with, or even before, the conflict
itself should cease. Each looked for an easier triumph,
and a result less fundamental and astounding. Both*

*read the same Bible, and pray to the same God; and
each invokes His aid against the other. It may seem
strange that any men should dare to ask a just God's
assistance in wringing their bread from the sweat of
other men's faces; but let us judge not that we be not
judged. The prayers of both could not be answered;
that of neither has been answered fully. The Almighty
has his own purposes. "Woe unto the world because of
offences! for it must needs be that offences come; but
woe to that man by whom the offence cometh!" If we
shall suppose that American Slavery is one of those
offences which, in the providence of God, must needs
come, but which, having continued through His
appointed time, He now wills to remove, and that He
gives to both North and South, this terrible war, as the
woe due to those by whom the offence came, shall we
discern therein any departure from those divine attributes which the believers in a Living God always
ascribe to Him? Fondly do we hope—fervently do we
pray—that this mighty scourge of war may speedily
pass away. Yet, if God wills that it continue, until all
the wealth piled by the bond-man's two hundred and
fifty years of unrequited toil shall be sunk, and until
every drop of blood drawn with the lash, shall be paid
by another drawn with the sword, as was said three
thousand years ago, so still it must be said "the judgments of the Lord, are true and righteous altogether."*

*With malice toward none; with charity for all; with
firmness in the right, as God gives us to see the right, let
us strive on to finish the work we are in; to bind up the
nation's wounds; to care for him who shall have borne
the battle, and for his widow, and his orphan—to do
all which may achieve and cherish a just and lasting
peace, among ourselves, and with all nations.*

I. Making a Speech of Hope, Part 1: John F. Kennedy

Berlin in 1963 was a city under siege, the last outpost of democracy in Soviet-controlled East Germany. A wall separated U.S.- and British-controlled West Berlin from Soviet-run East Berlin, severing friends from friends and family from family. Supplies reached the city primarily via Western government airlifts. President Kennedy came to Berlin on June 26, 1963, to rally a beleaguered populace and stir up support from the international community. He had been seasoned by the lessons of the Bay of Pigs invasion and his successful handling of the Cuban Missile Crisis, early tests for Kennedy's Administration. The time for leadership was at hand, and Kennedy knew that the right words could impact the world. Should his speech be uncompromising or conciliatory, tough or empathetic?

Kennedy's remarks at the Berlin Wall are brief, fewer than 600 words. His speech both reassured Berlin and defined U.S. foreign policy for years to come. It is an address notable for its brevity, its themes and refrains, the communion it achieves with its audience, and the impact it made on the world.

Kennedy begins with a nod to classical rhetoric: "Two thousand years ago the proudest boast was *civis Romanus sum.* Today, in the world of freedom, the proudest boast is *Ich bin ein Berliner.*" The statement assumes that the audience has studied its Latin. As a listener with a classical education would know, a speaker who could claim *civis Romanus sum*, "I am a citizen of Rome," was cloaked with all the rights of Roman citizenship and enjoyed the privileges of living in a free society—a reason to be proud. Kennedy links the famous words, "I am a citizen of Rome," to the modern cry, "I am a Berliner." In two sentences he links more than 2,000 years of struggle for democratic rule. It is an empowering rhetorical move (which perhaps would pack less of a punch with audiences today, as many listeners might not understand the Latin reference). Residents of Berlin may rightfully regard their situation as bleak and terrifying; they inhabit the last outpost of freedom in the area, surrounded on all sides by the Soviet army. Kennedy offers them a place in history, a reason to be proud, not frightened. Berliners now bear the torch of democracy. Their struggle moves freedom forward.

"I am a Berliner" also establishes communion between the speaker and his audience. Kennedy attempts to address the listeners in their language, although he engagingly admits that he has relied upon the assistance of a translator. (Indeed, urban legend has it that some listeners in the audience chuckled because the phrase should have been *Ich bin Berliner*—by including "ein," Kennedy may literally have said, "I am a jelly doughnut." We do not know whether the listeners would have understood him this way, but we can see by looking at videos of the speech that the audience was cheering, not laughing.) Even if the German was imperfect, the audience reacts to it in the spirit with which it was intended—he is one of them. With wild applause, they embrace the speaker and his message.

Kennedy then broadens the circle of the community of Berlin and himself to include all Americans ("I want to say, on behalf of my countrymen, who live many miles away on the other side of the Atlantic, who are far distant from you, that they take the greatest pride that they have been able to share with you, even from a distance, the story of the last 18 years") and finally all free people everywhere: "All free men, wherever they may live, are citizens of Berlin." The citizens of Berlin may suffer from their isolation, but they should know that they are not truly alone. "You live in a defended island of freedom, but your life is part of the main," Kennedy tells them. The entire free world is with them.

In the middle part of the speech, Kennedy adroitly wields a second powerful refrain. To those who extol the values of communism, those who claim reconciliation and understanding are the way to move forward, he says simply, "Let them come to Berlin":

> There are many people in the world who really don't understand, or say they don't, what is the great issue between the free world and the Communist world. Let them come to Berlin. There are some who say that

communism is the wave of the future. Let them come to Berlin. And there are some who say in Europe and elsewhere we can work with the Communists. Let them come to Berlin. And there are even a few who say that it is true that communism is an evil system, but it permits us to make economic progress. *Lass' sie nach Berlin kommen.* Let them come to Berlin.

Refrains both crystallize arguments and help to deliberately obscure certain aspects of a speech. Without explicitly stating that he is doing so, Kennedy uses this refrain to lay out a hard-line policy against the Soviets: Communism is not the wave of the future, it does not permit economic freedom, we cannot work with the communists. This rhetorical sleight of hand carries a bigger emotional punch than if Kennedy had declared an intention to take on the Soviets. Instead, Kennedy's refrain invites the audience to make up its own mind: "Let them come to Berlin."

Kennedy's speech illustrates how moving five minutes and two powerful refrains can be. His words are crafted to accomplish two ambitious goals: to rally the people and outline a controversial foreign policy stand against the Soviets. Kennedy's Logos is simple and therefore powerful: (1) you have reasons to be proud; (2) we are with you; (3) Berlin in microcosm tells the story of the mischief of communism. This attention to Logos keeps the speech short; all extraneous verbiage is omitted. The speech offers solidarity and hope to its audience through Kennedy's excellent use of communion and his ability to locate the Berliners' struggle into its place in history. Through brevity, crisp logic, attention to themes and refrains, and communion with the audience, this speech became 600 words that changed the world.

John F. Kennedy, Berlin Wall Speech,
June 26, 1963

I am proud to come to this city as the guest of your distinguished Mayor, who has symbolized throughout

*the world the fighting spirit of West Berlin. And
I am proud to visit the Federal Republic with your
distinguished Chancellor who for so many years has
committed Germany to democracy and freedom and
progress, and to come here in the company of my fellow
American, General Clay, who has been in this city
during its great moments of crisis and will come again
if ever needed.*

*Two thousand years ago the proudest boast was "civis
Romanus sum." Today, in the world of freedom, the
proudest boast is "Ich bin ein Berliner."*

I appreciate my interpreter translating my German!

*There are many people in the world who really don't
understand, or say they don't, what is the great issue
between the free world and the Communist world. Let
them come to Berlin. There are some who say that
communism is the wave of the future. Let them come to
Berlin. And there are some who say in Europe and
elsewhere we can work with the Communists. Let them
come to Berlin. And there are even a few who say that
it is true that communism is an evil system, but it
permits us to make economic progress. Lass' sie nach
Berlin kommen. Let them come to Berlin.*

*Freedom has many difficulties and democracy is not
perfect, but we have never had to put a wall up to keep
our people in, to prevent them from leaving us. I want
to say, on behalf of my countrymen, who live many
miles away on the other side of the Atlantic, who are
far distant from you, that they take the greatest pride
that they have been able to share with you, even from a
distance, the story of the last 18 years. I know of no*

town, no city, that has been besieged for 18 years that still lives with the vitality and the force, and the hope and the determination of the city of West Berlin. While the wall is the most obvious and vivid demonstration of the failures of the Communist system, for all the world to see, we take no satisfaction in it, for it is, as your Mayor has said, an offense not only against history but an offense against humanity, separating families, dividing husbands and wives and brothers and sisters, and dividing a people who wish to be joined together.

What is true of this city is true of Germany—real, lasting peace in Europe can never be assured as long as one German out of four is denied the elementary right of free men, and that is to make a free choice.
In 18 years of peace and good faith, this generation of Germans has earned the right to be free, including the right to unite their families and their nation in lasting peace, with good will to all people. You live in a defended island of freedom, but your life is part of the main. So let me ask you as I close, to lift your eyes beyond the dangers of today, to the hopes of tomorrow, beyond the freedom merely of this city of Berlin, or your country of Germany, to the advance of freedom everywhere, beyond the wall to the day of peace with justice, beyond yourselves and ourselves to all mankind.

Freedom is indivisible, and when one man is enslaved, all are not free. When all are free, then we can look forward to that day when this city will be joined as one and this country and this great Continent of Europe in a peaceful and hopeful globe. When that day finally comes, as it will, the people of West Berlin can take sober satisfaction in the fact that they were in the front lines for almost two decades.

All free men, wherever they may live, are citizens of Berlin, and, therefore, as a free man, I take pride in the words "Ich bin ein Berliner."

J. Making a Speech of Hope, Part 2: Ronald Reagan

How do you pay fitting homage to a day that was at once a tremendous military victory and a profound human tragedy? In his June 6, 1984, address commemorating the D-Day invasion of Normandy, U.S. President Ronald Reagan displayed mastery of rhetoric through memorable writing and delivery, with just the right dose of Pathos. Interestingly, once he had won the hearts of his listeners, Reagan converted his epideictic address into a deliberative public policy oration. His gifted performance ensured that his audience would listen.

When the Allies stormed the beaches on D-Day, they initiated the campaign to liberate Europe from the Nazis. At the same time, they endured staggering losses and brutal violence. Forty years later, in 1984, President Reagan and other heads of state gathered at Normandy to commemorate the invasion. The United States and the Soviet Union, allies during the days of World War II, were in the grip of the Cold War. Reagan set out with multiple objectives: to pay homage to the soldiers who have gathered to celebrate the day, to rally the international community by invoking the ghosts of Normandy, and to extend an olive branch to the Soviets.

His first attention is to the soldiers. Reagan paints a picture of D-Day chilling in its immediacy. He uses sensory language so that his audience can hear, smell, and see the scene that he describes:

> We stand on a lonely, windswept point on the northern shore of France. The air is soft, but 40 years ago at this moment, the air was dense with smoke and the cries of men, and the air was filled with the crack of rifle fire and the roar of cannon.

The action begins; Rangers take the cliffs. Reagan dwells on the description to build interest:

> At dawn, on the morning of the 6th of June, 1944, 225 Rangers jumped off the British landing craft and ran to the bottom of these cliffs. . . . The Rangers looked up and saw the enemy soldiers—the edge of the cliffs shooting down at them with machineguns and throwing grenades. And the American Rangers began to climb. They shot rope ladders over the face of these cliffs and began to pull themselves up. When one Ranger fell, another would take his place. When one rope was cut, a Ranger would grab another and begin his climb again. They climbed, shot back, and held their footing. Soon, one by one, the Rangers pulled themselves over the top, and in seizing the firm land at the top of these cliffs, they began to seize back the continent of Europe.

The speech is memorable for this vivid passage, but Reagan does not focus exclusively on the Americans. In order to achieve his other objectives, Reagan's address must be inclusive. D-Day is not strictly an American celebration or an American achievement; success was possible because the Allies worked together. Reagan builds support from the audience by praising the contributions of soldiers from England, France, Canada, Poland, and Scotland with the same attention to memorable detail that he has paid to the Americans:

> Lord Lovat of Scotland, who calmly announced when he got to the bridge, "Sorry I'm a few minutes late," as if he'd been delayed by a traffic jam, when in truth he'd just come from the bloody fighting on Sword Beach, which he and his men had just taken.

The invasion of Normandy was a global effort. Reagan needs the same global backing to confront the Soviet Union.

Reagan calls for this support in the next passages of his speech. The former alliance between the United States and Russia during the war now lies in tatters. They are sworn enemies, in ideological opposition, locked in the vise of Cold War. Reagan offers the actions of the Soviet Union and the other Allied countries in the aftermath of World War II as a microcosm of this conflict:

> In spite of our great efforts and successes, not all that followed the end of the war was happy or planned. . . . Soviet troops that came to the center of this continent did not leave when peace came. They're still there, uninvited, unwanted, unyielding, almost 40 years after the war. . . .
>
> We in America have learned bitter lessons from two World Wars: It is better to be here ready to protect the peace, than to take blind shelter across the sea, rushing to respond only after freedom is lost. We've learned that isolationism never was and never will be an acceptable response to tyrannical governments with an expansionist intent.

Reagan invokes the struggle of World War II to chide the Soviet Union, but also to offer hope for a dialogue:

> But we try always to be prepared for peace; prepared to deter aggression; prepared to negotiate the reduction of arms; and, yes, prepared to reach out again in the spirit of reconciliation. In truth, there is no reconciliation we would welcome more than a reconciliation with the Soviet Union, so, together, we can lessen the risks of war, now and forever.
>
> It's fitting to remember here the great losses also suffered by the Russian people during World War II: 20 million perished, a terrible price that testifies to all the world the necessity of ending war. I tell you from my heart that we in the United States do not want war. We want to wipe from the face of the Earth the terrible weapons that man now has in his hands. And I tell you, we are ready to seize that beachhead. We look for some sign from the Soviet Union

> that they are willing to move forward, that they share our
> desire and love for peace, and that they will give up the
> ways of conquest. There must be a changing there that
> will allow us to turn our hope into action.

Reagan knows that the world is listening. He seizes the moment
to say something important.

Finally, in order to appreciate the speech fully, one must study
Reagan's masterful delivery. A video of the speech has been made
available by the Reagan Foundation here: *http://www.youtube*
.com/watch?v=eEIqdcHbc8I. Notice his pacing, slow and confident at first, then building in order to bring the listeners into
the description of the Rangers taking the cliffs. He heightens
the excitement of the scene through his clear, powerful voice
and his deliberate attention to pacing and pausing. Even though
he relies on note cards in order to get the words right, he make a
point of looking up at his audience as much as he can, using eye
contact to project calm and control. He is at ease at the podium.
He sounds conversational in parts ("I think I know what you are
thinking right now"); in other sections, his poetry soars. He
honors the listeners by describing their exploits with admiration
and gravitas; watch for a shift in tone from grateful to powerful
when he delivers his message to the Soviets. He punctuates
important moments with pauses ("Why? Why did you do
it?") A less able speaker might rush through this address; Reagan
takes his time. His calm confidence establishes a strong Ethos;
he builds Pathos through attention to pacing, eye contact,
and tone.

Excerpts from Ronald Reagan's Remarks at a Ceremony Commemorating the 40th Anniversary of the Normandy Invasion, D-Day, June 6, 1984

*We're here to mark that day in history when the Allied
armies joined in battle to reclaim this continent to
liberty. For four long years, much of Europe had been*

under a terrible shadow. Free nations had fallen, Jews cried out in the camps, millions cried out for liberation. Europe was enslaved, and the world prayed for its rescue. Here in Normandy the rescue began. Here the Allies stood and fought against tyranny in a giant undertaking unparalleled in human history.

We stand on a lonely, windswept point on the northern shore of France. The air is soft, but 40 years ago at this moment, the air was dense with smoke and the cries of men, and the air was filled with the crack of rifle fire and the roar of cannon. At dawn, on the morning of the 6th of June, 1944, 225 Rangers jumped off the British landing craft and ran to the bottom of these cliffs. Their mission was one of the most difficult and daring of the invasion: to climb these sheer and desolate cliffs and take out the enemy guns. The Allies had been told that some of the mightiest of these guns were here and they would be trained on the beaches to stop the Allied advance.

The Rangers looked up and saw the enemy soldiers— the edge of the cliffs shooting down at them with machineguns and throwing grenades. And the American Rangers began to climb. They shot rope ladders over the face of these cliffs and began to pull themselves up. When one Ranger fell, another would take his place. When one rope was cut, a Ranger would grab another and begin his climb again. They climbed, shot back, and held their footing. Soon, one by one, the Rangers pulled themselves over the top, and in seizing the firm land at the top of these cliffs, they began to seize back the continent of Europe. Two hundred and twenty-five came here. After 2 days of fighting, only 90 could still bear arms.

Behind me is a memorial that symbolizes the Ranger daggers that were thrust into the top of these cliffs. And before me are the men who put them there.

These are the boys of Pointe du Hoc. These are the men who took the cliffs. These are the champions who helped free a continent. These are the heroes who helped end a war.

Gentlemen, I look at you and I think of the words of Stephen Spender's poem. You are men who in your "lives fought for life . . . and left the vivid air signed with your honor."

I think I know what you may be thinking right now— thinking "we were just part of a bigger effort; everyone was brave that day." Well, everyone was. Do you remember the story of Bill Millin of the 51st Highlanders? Forty years ago today, British troops were pinned down near a bridge, waiting desperately for help. Suddenly, they heard the sound of bagpipes, and some thought they were dreaming. Well, they weren't. They looked up and saw Bill Millin with his bagpipes, leading the reinforcements and ignoring the smack of the bullets into the ground around him.

Lord Lovat was with him—Lord Lovat of Scotland, who calmly announced when he got to the bridge, "Sorry I'm a few minutes late," as if he'd been delayed by a traffic jam, when in truth he'd just come from the bloody fighting on Sword Beach, which he and his men had just taken.

There was the impossible valor of the Poles who threw themselves between the enemy and the rest of Europe as the invasion took hold, and the unsurpassed courage of the Canadians who had already seen the horrors of war on this coast. They knew what awaited them there, but they would not be deterred. And once they hit Juno Beach, they never looked back.

All of these men were part of a roll-call of honor with names that spoke of a pride as bright as the colors they bore: the Royal Winnipeg Rifles, Poland's 24th Lancers, the Royal Scots Fusiliers, the Screaming Eagles, the Yeomen of England's armored divisions, the forces of Free France, the Coast Guard's "Matchbox Fleet" and you, the American Rangers.

Forty summers have passed since the battle that you fought here. You were young the day you took these cliffs; some of you were hardly more than boys, with the deepest joys of life before you. Yet, you risked everything here. Why? Why did you do it? What impelled you to put aside the instinct for self-preservation and risk your lives to take these cliffs? What inspired all the men of the armies that met here? We look at you, and somehow we know the answer. It was faith and belief; it was loyalty and love.

The men of Normandy had faith that what they were doing was right, faith that they fought for all humanity, faith that a just God would grant them mercy on this beachhead or on the next. It was the deep knowledge—and pray God we have not lost it—that there is a profound, moral difference between the use of force for liberation and the use of force for conquest. You were here to liberate, not to conquer, and so you and those others did not doubt your cause. And you were right not to doubt.

You all knew that some things are worth dying for. One's country is worth dying for, and democracy is worth dying for, because it's the most deeply honorable form of government ever devised by man. All of you loved liberty. All of you were willing to fight tyranny, and you knew the people of your countries were behind you.

The Americans who fought here that morning knew word of the invasion was spreading through the darkness back home. They fought—or felt in their hearts, though they couldn't know in fact, that in Georgia they were filling the churches at 4 a.m., in Kansas they were kneeling on their porches and praying, and in Philadelphia they were ringing the Liberty Bell. . . .

When the war was over, there were lives to be rebuilt and governments to be returned to the people. There were nations to be reborn. Above all, there was a new peace to be assured. These were huge and daunting tasks. But the Allies summoned strength from the faith, belief, loyalty, and love of those who fell here. They rebuilt a new Europe together.

There was first a great reconciliation among those who had been enemies, all of whom had suffered so greatly. The United States did its part, creating the Marshall plan to help rebuild our allies and our former enemies. The Marshall plan led to the Atlantic alliance—a great alliance that serves to this day as our shield for freedom, for prosperity, and for peace.

In spite of our great efforts and successes, not all that followed the end of the war was happy or planned.

*Some liberated countries were lost. The great sadness of
this loss echoes down to our own time in the streets of
Warsaw, Prague, and East Berlin. Soviet troops that
came to the center of this continent did not leave when
peace came. They're still there, uninvited, unwanted,
unyielding, almost 40 years after the war. Because of
this, allied forces still stand on this continent. Today,
as 40 years ago, our armies are here for only one
purpose—to protect and defend democracy. The only
territories we hold are memorials like this one and
graveyards where our heroes rest.*

*We in America have learned bitter lessons from two
World Wars: It is better to be here ready to protect the
peace, than to take blind shelter across the sea, rushing
to respond only after freedom is lost. We've learned that
isolationism never was and never will be an acceptable
response to tyrannical governments with an
expansionist intent.*

*But we try always to be prepared for peace; prepared to
deter aggression; prepared to negotiate the reduction of
arms; and, yes, prepared to reach out again in the spirit
of reconciliation. In truth, there is no reconciliation we
would welcome more than a reconciliation with the
Soviet Union, so, together, we can lessen the risks of
war, now and forever.*

*It's fitting to remember here the great losses also suf-
fered by the Russian people during World War II:
20 million perished, a terrible price that testifies to all
the world the necessity of ending war. I tell you from
my heart that we in the United States do not want
war. We want to wipe from the face of the Earth the
terrible weapons that man now has in his hands. And*

I tell you, we are ready to seize that beachhead. We look for some sign from the Soviet Union that they are willing to move forward, that they share our desire and love for peace, and that they will give up the ways of conquest. There must be a changing there that will allow us to turn our hope into action.

We will pray forever that some day that changing will come. But for now, particularly today, it is good and fitting to renew our commitment to each other, to our freedom, and to the alliance that protects it. . . .

K. Using a Refrain: Martin Luther King, Jr.

The words of Dr. Martin Luther King, Jr., are rightfully featured in many a "Greatest Speeches" list because of King's flair for memorable images, his finesse with themes and refrains ("I Have a Dream"), and the ability that his speeches have had to move audiences to action at the time they were given and beyond. Take, for example, Dr. King's final address, delivered on April 3, 1968, in Memphis, Tennessee. It is known by one of its memorable refrains, "I've Been to the Mountaintop," because of the eerily prophetic nature of the words: Dr. King tells his listeners that they are headed for the Promised Land, and while he has seen it from the mountaintop, "I may not get there with you." In the early morning hours after delivering this speech, King was assassinated.

The speech serves as a terrific model of excellent writing for speaking. For example, in the middle part of the address, King speaks of a time that he was hospitalized after being stabbed in the heart with a knife by a deranged woman. He explains that he received letters from any number of dignitaries and celebrities, but the most memorable was a note from a young, white girl from White Plains, New York. The girl had read that King's wound was so severe that, had he simply sneezed, he would have died. The child wrote, "I'm so happy that you did not sneeze."

King transforms her words into a central refrain: "If I had sneezed. . . ." He recounts the struggles of the civil rights movement from student sit-ins to freedom rides, voting rights protests, the Montgomery bus boycott, the march on Washington, and the Memphis garbage strike. King builds a timeline before our very eyes, and reminds us that he would have missed it all with one sneeze. The refrain is memorable because of the commonplace nature of a sneeze—something that we all do, such a small thing to stand between life and death. The word catches the ear because of the *sn* consonant blend and the long *ee* sound followed by the buzz of a *z*. King makes the refrain memorable by interlacing beautiful contrasting imagery amidst the refrain—students sitting in were really "standing up"; black people of Albany, Georgia, "decided to straighten their backs up. And whenever men and women straighten their backs up, they are going somewhere, because a man can't ride your back unless it is bent." He paints pictures with his words that listeners can imagine, and will recall long after the speech has ended.

King's delivery brings the images to life. As he recounts these seminal events of the civil rights movement, his voice rises. The ovation grows louder, more hopeful. King's words embolden: The accomplishments he lists are not his but the community's. He finishes on a surge of hope:

> Well, I don't know what will happen now. We've got some difficult days ahead. But it doesn't matter with me now. Because I've been to the mountaintop. . . . And I've looked over. And I've seen the promised land. I may not get there with you. But I want you to know tonight, that we, as a people, will get to the promised land. And so I'm happy, tonight. I'm not worried about anything. I'm not fearing any man. Mine eyes have seen the glory of the coming of the Lord.

King succeeds in turning a personal story into an evocative rallying cry. He uses it to inspire and deliver a potentially devastating message: that he may not be able to see the struggle through with them. But he has armed his listeners with pride in their accomplishments, faith in one another, and a way forward. A speech that could be remembered for the foreshadowing of death instead makes its mark as a hopeful symbol of unity. It is impossible not to be moved by the cadences, the refrain, the crisp telling of a chain of historical events. This is a speech of Pathos, empathy, a modern-day example of an Aristotelian epideictic address. It is even more memorable when one considers that "the sneeze" tragically came the very next day.

> *Excerpts from Dr. Martin Luther King, Jr., "I've Been to the Mountaintop," speaking at Mason Temple, Memphis, Tennessee, on April 3, 1968*

> *. . . Let us rise up tonight with a greater readiness. Let us stand with a greater determination. And let us move on in these powerful days, these days of challenge to make America what it ought to be. We have an opportunity to make America a better nation. And I want to thank God, once more, for allowing me to be here with you.*

> *You know, several years ago, I was in New York City autographing the first book that I had written. And while sitting there autographing books, a demented black woman came up. The only question I heard from her was, "Are you Martin Luther King?"*

> *And I was looking down writing, and I said yes. And the next minute I felt something beating on my chest. Before I knew it I had been stabbed by this demented woman. I was rushed to Harlem Hospital. It was a*

*dark Saturday afternoon. And that blade had gone
through, and the X-rays revealed that the tip of the
blade was on the edge of my aorta, the main artery.
And once that's punctured, you drown in your own
blood—that's the end of you.*

*It came out in the New York Times the next morning,
that if I had sneezed, I would have died. Well, about
four days later, they allowed me, after the operation,
after my chest had been opened, and the blade had
been taken out, to move around in the wheel chair in
the hospital. They allowed me to read some of the mail
that came in, and from all over the states, and the
world, kind letters came in. I read a few, but one of
them I will never forget. I had received one from the
President and the Vice-President. I've forgotten what
those telegrams said. I'd received a visit and a letter
from the Governor of New York, but I've forgotten
what the letter said. But there was another letter that
came from a little girl, a young girl who was a student
at the White Plains High School. And I looked at that
letter, and I'll never forget it. It said simply, "Dear
Dr. King: I am a ninth-grade student at the White
Plains High School." She said, "While it should not
matter, I would like to mention that I am a white girl.
I read in the paper of your misfortune, and of your
suffering. And I read that if you had sneezed, you
would have died. And I'm simply writing you to say
that I'm so happy that you didn't sneeze."*

*And I want to say tonight, I want to say that I am
happy that I didn't sneeze. Because if I had sneezed,
I wouldn't have been around here in 1960, when
students all over the South started sitting-in at lunch
counters. And I knew that as they were sitting in, they*

were really standing up for the best in the American dream. And taking the whole nation back to those great wells of democracy which were dug deep by the Founding Fathers in the Declaration of Independence and the Constitution. If I had sneezed, I wouldn't have been around in 1962, when Negroes in Albany, Georgia, decided to straighten their backs up. And whenever men and women straighten their backs up, they are going somewhere, because a man can't ride your back unless it is bent. If I had sneezed, I wouldn't have been here in 1963, when the black people of Birmingham, Alabama, aroused the conscience of this nation, and brought into being the Civil Rights Bill. If I had sneezed, I wouldn't have had a chance later that year, in August, to try to tell America about a dream that I had had. If I had sneezed, I wouldn't have been down in Selma, Alabama, been in Memphis to see the community rally around those brothers and sisters who are suffering. I'm so happy that I didn't sneeze.

And they were telling me, now it doesn't matter now. It really doesn't matter what happens now. I left Atlanta this morning, and as we got started on the plane, there were six of us, the pilot said over the public address system, "We are sorry for the delay, but we have Dr. Martin Luther King on the plane. And to be sure that all of the bags were checked, and to be sure that nothing would be wrong with the plane, we had to check out everything carefully. And we've had the plane protected and guarded all night."

And then I got to Memphis. And some began to say the threats, or talk about the threats that were out. What would happen to me from some of our sick white brothers?

Well, I don't know what will happen now. We've got some difficult days ahead. But it doesn't matter with me now. Because I've been to the mountaintop. And I don't mind. Like anybody, I would like to live a long life. Longevity has its place. But I'm not concerned about that now. I just want to do God's will. And He's allowed me to go up to the mountain. And I've looked over. And I've seen the promised land. I may not get there with you. But I want you to know tonight, that we, as a people, will get to the promised land. And I'm happy, tonight. I'm not worried about anything. I'm not fearing any man. Mine eyes have seen the glory of the coming of the Lord.

L. Discussing a Difficult Topic: Barack Obama

Then-Senator Barack Obama's address, "A More Perfect Union," tackled head-on one of the most divisive, discomfiting topics facing our nation—racial tensions in America. His insightful speech dealt squarely with passions and prejudices that swirled just below the surface throughout Obama's candidacy, offering instead genuine, nuanced dialogue about the topic. It is a skillful demonstration of how to defuse a political landmine.

In the period leading up to the address, the Reverend Jeremiah Wright, Obama's pastor, voiced anger about racial injustice via a number of inflammatory statements, including (most famously) "God damn America!" for its treatment of minorities. Videos of the provocative sermons spiraled through cable news and Internet sites, raising questions about Obama's own judgment and beliefs. The scandal threatened to derail his campaign as a transformative, post-racial candidate, painting him instead as an angry black man. Obama drafted "A More Perfect Union" in response.

In his address, Obama refuses to take the easy way out. He could simply express righteous indignation over the comments, forswearing Wright and his Chicago church, but he does not. He could decry the state of racial disunity and political Balkanization that gripped the country, pointing fingers or throwing up his hands in disgust, but he does not. Instead, he challenges conventional wisdom and political advice by disavowing Wright's comments but continuing to embrace the man, saying:

> I can no more disown him [Wright] than I can disown the black community. I can no more disown him than I can disown my white grandmother, a woman who helped raise me, a woman who sacrificed again and again for me, a woman who loves me as much as she loves anything in this world, but a woman who once confessed her fear of black men who passed her by on the street, and who on more than one occasion has uttered racial or ethnic stereotypes that made me cringe.

Rather than pretend that anger on both sides—both black and white—does not exist, Obama describes Sunday church service as "the most segregated [event] in America." He then offers the audience a glimpse inside the world of a predominantly African-American church to explain feelings of anger, isolation, and frustration within the black community. He ties these struggles to the frustrations of middle-class white families who decry programs like affirmative action. He turns a polarizing, controversial event into a cathartic self-exploration of race and politics in America.

Obama is uniquely positioned to offer these insights because he is not "the most conventional candidate." His personal story tells the tale of America:

> I am the son of a black man from Kenya and a white woman from Kansas. I was raised with the help of a white grandfather who survived a Depression to serve in Patton's Army during World War II and a white grandmother who worked on a bomber assembly line at Fort Leavenworth while he was overseas. I've gone to some of the best schools in America and lived in one of the world's poorest nations. I am married to a black

American who carries within her the blood of slaves and slaveowners—an inheritance we pass on to our two precious daughters. I have brothers, sisters, nieces, nephews, uncles and cousins, of every race and every hue, scattered across three continents, and for as long as I live, I will never forget that in no other country on Earth is my story even possible.

Obama's credibility is bolstered by his calm, measured tone; the care that he takes to accurately and respectfully describe both white and black points of view; and his own personal style. He does not sound like King or Kennedy; his language adopts a bit of both worlds and therefore can appeal to both sides while still assailing black anger and white privilege.

Most importantly, Obama offers hope. A reasonable tone, an approach that unifies rather than divides, a way forward—these themes appear time and again in the speeches that we have included in this "greatest hits" list, and Obama's is no exception. He tells his listeners that the power to write the history of America lies in their hands:

For we have a choice in this country. We can accept a politics that breeds division, and conflict, and cynicism. We can tackle race only as spectacle—as we did in the OJ trial—or in the wake of tragedy, as we did in the aftermath of Katrina—or as fodder for the nightly news. We can play Reverend Wright's sermons on every channel, every day and talk about them from now until the election, and make the only question in this campaign whether or not the American people think that I somehow believe or sympathize with his most offensive words. We can pounce on some gaffe by a Hillary supporter as evidence that she's playing the race card, or we can speculate on whether white men will all flock to John McCain in the general election regardless of his policies.

We can do that.

But if we do, I can tell you that in the next election, we'll be talking about some other distraction. And then another one. And then another one. And nothing will change.

That is one option. Or, at this moment, in this election, we can come together and say, "Not this time."

The voters' response demonstrates once again the power of a rhetoric of hope—they elected Obama President.

Excerpts from Remarks of Senator Barack Obama,
"A More Perfect Union," Constitution Center,
Tuesday, March 18, 2008, Philadelphia,
Pennsylvania

"We the people, in order to form a more perfect union."

Two hundred and twenty one years ago, in a hall that still stands across the street, a group of men gathered and, with these simple words, launched America's improbable experiment in democracy. . . .

This was one of the tasks we set forth at the beginning of this campaign—to continue the long march of those who came before us, a march for a more just, more equal, more free, more caring and more prosperous America. I chose to run for the presidency at this moment in history because I believe deeply that we cannot solve the challenges of our time unless we solve them together—unless we perfect our union by understanding that we may have different stories, but we hold common hopes; that we may not look the same and we may not have come from the same place, but we all want to move in the same direction—towards a better future for our children and our grandchildren.

This belief comes from my unyielding faith in the decency and generosity of the American people. But it also comes from my own American story.

I am the son of a black man from Kenya and a white woman from Kansas. I was raised with the help of a white grandfather who survived a Depression to serve in Patton's Army during World War II and a white grandmother who worked on a bomber assembly line at Fort Leavenworth while he was overseas. I've gone to some of the best schools in America and lived in one of the world's poorest nations. I am married to a black American who carries within her the blood of slaves and slaveowners—an inheritance we pass on to our two precious daughters. I have brothers, sisters, nieces, nephews, uncles and cousins, of every race and every hue, scattered across three continents, and for as long as I live, I will never forget that in no other country on Earth is my story even possible.

It's a story that hasn't made me the most conventional candidate. But it is a story that has seared into my genetic makeup the idea that this nation is more than the sum of its parts—that out of many, we are truly one....

On one end of the spectrum, we've heard the implication that my candidacy is somehow an exercise in affirmative action; that it's based solely on the desire of wide-eyed liberals to purchase racial reconciliation on the cheap. On the other end, we've heard my former pastor, Reverend Jeremiah Wright, use incendiary language to express views that have the potential not only to widen the racial divide, but views that denigrate both the greatness and the goodness of our nation; that rightly offend white and black alike....

But the truth is, that isn't all that I know of the
man. . . . In my first book, Dreams From My Father,
I described the experience of my first service at Trinity:

"People began to shout, to rise from their seats and clap
and cry out, a forceful wind carrying the reverend's
voice up into the rafters. . . . And in that single note—
hope!—I heard something else; at the foot of that cross,
inside the thousands of churches across the city,
I imagined the stories of ordinary black people merging
with the stories of David and Goliath, Moses and
Pharaoh, the Christians in the lion's den, Ezekiel's
field of dry bones. Those stories—of survival, and
freedom, and hope—became our story, my story; the
blood that had spilled was our blood, the tears our
tears; until this black church, on this bright day,
seemed once more a vessel carrying the story of a people
into future generations and into a larger world. Our
trials and triumphs became at once unique and
universal, black and more than black; in chronicling
our journey, the stories and songs gave us a means to
reclaim memories that we didn't need to feel shame
about . . . memories that all people might study and
cherish—and with which we could start to rebuild."

That has been my experience at Trinity. Like other
predominantly black churches across the country,
Trinity embodies the black community in its
entirety—the doctor and the welfare mom, the model
student and the former gang-banger. Like other black
churches, Trinity's services are full of raucous laughter
and sometimes bawdy humor. They are full of
dancing, clapping, screaming and shouting that may
seem jarring to the untrained ear. The church contains
in full the kindness and cruelty, the fierce intelligence
and the shocking ignorance, the struggles and successes,

*the love and yes, the bitterness and bias that make up
the black experience in America.*

*And this helps explain, perhaps, my relationship with
Reverend Wright. As imperfect as he may be, he has
been like family to me. He strengthened my faith,
officiated my wedding, and baptized my children. Not
once in my conversations with him have I heard him
talk about any ethnic group in derogatory terms, or
treat whites with whom he interacted with anything
but courtesy and respect. He contains within him the
contradictions—the good and the bad—of the community that he has served diligently for so many years.*

*I can no more disown him than I can disown the black
community. I can no more disown him than I can
disown my white grandmother—a woman who helped
raise me, a woman who sacrificed again and again for
me, a woman who loves me as much as she loves
anything in this world, but a woman who once
confessed her fear of black men who passed her by on
the street, and who on more than one occasion has
uttered racial or ethnic stereotypes that made me
cringe.*

*These people are a part of me. And they are a part of
America, this country that I love. . . .*

*But for all those who scratched and clawed their way to
get a piece of the American Dream, there were many
who didn't make it—those who were ultimately
defeated, in one way or another, by discrimination.
That legacy of defeat was passed on to future
generations—those young men and increasingly young
women who we see standing on street corners or*

*languishing in our prisons, without hope or prospects
for the future. Even for those blacks who did make it,
questions of race, and racism, continue to define their
worldview in fundamental ways. For the men and
women of Reverend Wright's generation, the memories
of humiliation and doubt and fear have not gone
away; nor has the anger and the bitterness of those
years.*

*That anger may not get expressed in public, in front of
white co-workers or white friends. But it does find
voice in the barbershop or around the kitchen table. At
times, that anger is exploited by politicians, to gin
up votes along racial lines, or to make up for a
politician's own failings.*

*And occasionally it finds voice in the church on Sunday
morning, in the pulpit and in the pews. The fact that
so many people are surprised to hear that anger in
some of Reverend Wright's sermons simply reminds us
of the old truism that the most segregated hour in
American life occurs on Sunday morning.*

*That anger is not always productive; indeed, all too
often it distracts attention from solving real problems;
it keeps us from squarely facing our own complicity in
our condition, and prevents the African-American
community from forging the alliances it needs to bring
about real change. But the anger is real; it is powerful;
and to simply wish it away, to condemn it without
understanding its roots, only serves to widen the chasm
of misunderstanding that exists between the races.*

*In fact, a similar anger exists within segments of the
white community. Most working- and middle-class*

*white Americans don't feel that they have been
particularly privileged by their race. Their experience
is the immigrant experience—as far as they're
concerned, no one's handed them anything, they've
built it from scratch. They've worked hard all their
lives, many times only to see their jobs shipped overseas
or their pension dumped after a lifetime of labor. They
are anxious about their futures, and feel their dreams
slipping away; in an era of stagnant wages and global
competition, opportunity comes to be seen as a zero sum
game, in which your dreams come at my expense. So
when they are told to bus their children to a school
across town; when they hear that an African American
is getting an advantage in landing a good job or a spot
in a good college because of an injustice that they
themselves never committed; when they're told that
their fears about crime in urban neighborhoods are
somehow prejudiced, resentment builds over time.*

*Like the anger within the black community, these
resentments aren't always expressed in polite company.
But they have helped shape the political landscape for
at least a generation. Anger over welfare and
affirmative action helped forge the Reagan Coalition.
Politicians routinely exploited fears of crime for their
own electoral ends. Talk show hosts and conservative
commentators built entire careers unmasking bogus
claims of racism while dismissing legitimate discussions
of racial injustice and inequality as mere political
correctness or reverse racism.*

*Just as black anger often proved counterproductive,
so have these white resentments distracted attention
from the real culprits of the middle class squeeze—a
corporate culture rife with inside dealing, questionable*

accounting practices, and short-term greed; a Washington dominated by lobbyists and special interests; economic policies that favor the few over the many. And yet, to wish away the resentments of white Americans, to label them as misguided or even racist, without recognizing they are grounded in legitimate concerns—this too widens the racial divide, and blocks the path to understanding.

This is where we are right now. It's a racial stalemate we've been stuck in for years. Contrary to the claims of some of my critics, black and white, I have never been so naïve as to believe that we can get beyond our racial divisions in a single election cycle, or with a single candidacy—particularly a candidacy as imperfect as my own.

But I have asserted a firm conviction—a conviction rooted in my faith in God and my faith in the American people—that working together we can move beyond some of our old racial wounds, and that in fact we have no choice if we are to continue on the path of a more perfect union.

For the African-American community, that path means embracing the burdens of our past without becoming victims of our past. It means continuing to insist on a full measure of justice in every aspect of American life. But it also means binding our particular grievances—for better health care, and better schools, and better jobs—to the larger aspirations of all Americans—the white woman struggling to break the glass ceiling, the white man who's been laid off, the immigrant trying to feed his family. And it means taking full responsibility for our own lives—by

*demanding more from our fathers, and spending more
time with our children, and reading to them, and
teaching them that while they may face challenges and
discrimination in their own lives, they must never
succumb to despair or cynicism; they must always
believe that they can write their own destiny.*

*Ironically, this quintessentially American—and yes,
conservative—notion of self-help found frequent
expression in Reverend Wright's sermons. But what my
former pastor too often failed to understand is that
embarking on a program of self-help also requires a
belief that society can change.*

*The profound mistake of Reverend Wright's sermons is
not that he spoke about racism in our society. It's that
he spoke as if our society was static; as if no progress has
been made; as if this country—a country that has
made it possible for one of his own members to run for
the highest office in the land and build a coalition of
white and black; Latino and Asian, rich and poor,
young and old—is still irrevocably bound to a tragic
past. But what we know—what we have seen—is that
America can change. That is true genius of this nation.
What we have already achieved gives us hope—the
audacity to hope—for what we can and must achieve
tomorrow.*

*In the white community, the path to a more perfect
union means acknowledging that what ails the
African-American community does not just exist in
the minds of black people; that the legacy of
discrimination—and current incidents of discrimination, while less overt than in the past—are real and
must be addressed. Not just with words, but with*

deeds—by investing in our schools and our communities; by enforcing our civil rights laws and ensuring fairness in our criminal justice system; by providing this generation with ladders of opportunity that were unavailable for previous generations. It requires all Americans to realize that your dreams do not have to come at the expense of my dreams; that investing in the health, welfare, and education of black and brown and white children will ultimately help all of America prosper.

In the end, then, what is called for is nothing more, and nothing less, than what all the world's great religions demand—that we do unto others as we would have them do unto us. Let us be our brother's keeper, Scripture tells us. Let us be our sister's keeper. Let us find that common stake we all have in one another, and let our politics reflect that spirit as well.

For we have a choice in this country. We can accept a politics that breeds division, and conflict, and cynicism. We can tackle race only as spectacle—as we did in the OJ trial—or in the wake of tragedy, as we did in the aftermath of Katrina—or as fodder for the nightly news. We can play Reverend Wright's sermons on every channel, every day and talk about them from now until the election, and make the only question in this campaign whether or not the American people think that I somehow believe or sympathize with his most offensive words. We can pounce on some gaffe by a Hillary supporter as evidence that she's playing the race card, or we can speculate on whether white men will all flock to John McCain in the general election regardless of his policies.

We can do that.

*But if we do, I can tell you that in the next election,
we'll be talking about some other distraction. And then
another one. And then another one. And nothing will
change.*

*That is one option. Or, at this moment, in this election,
we can come together and say, "Not this time."...*

*There is one story in particular that I'd like to leave
you with today—a story I told when I had the great
honor of speaking on Dr. King's birthday at his home
church, Ebenezer Baptist, in Atlanta.*

*There is a young, twenty-three year old white woman
named Ashley Baia who organized for our campaign
in Florence, South Carolina. She had been working to
organize a mostly African-American community since
the beginning of this campaign, and one day she was
at a roundtable discussion where everyone went
around telling their story and why they were there.*

*And Ashley said that when she was nine years old, her
mother got cancer. And because she had to miss days of
work, she was let go and lost her health care. They had
to file for bankruptcy, and that's when Ashley decided
that she had to do something to help her mom.*

*She knew that food was one of their most expensive
costs, and so Ashley convinced her mother that what she
really liked and really wanted to eat more than
anything else was mustard and relish sandwiches.
Because that was the cheapest way to eat.*

*She did this for a year until her mom got better, and
she told everyone at the roundtable that the reason she*

*joined our campaign was so that she could help the
millions of other children in the country who want and
need to help their parents too.*

*Now Ashley might have made a different choice.
Perhaps somebody told her along the way that the
source of her mother's problems were blacks who were
on welfare and too lazy to work, or Hispanics who
were coming into the country illegally. But she didn't.
She sought out allies in her fight against injustice.*

*Anyway, Ashley finishes her story and then goes around
the room and asks everyone else why they're supporting
the campaign. They all have different stories and
reasons. Many bring up a specific issue. And finally
they come to this elderly black man who's been sitting
there quietly the entire time. And Ashley asks him why
he's there. And he does not bring up a specific issue.
He does not say health care or the economy. He does
not say education or the war. He does not say that
he was there because of Barack Obama. He simply
says to everyone in the room, "I am here because of
Ashley."*

*"I'm here because of Ashley." By itself, that single
moment of recognition between that young white girl
and that old black man is not enough. It is not enough
to give health care to the sick, or jobs to the jobless, or
education to our children.*

*But it is where we start. It is where our union grows
stronger. And as so many generations have come to
realize over the course of the two-hundred and twenty
one years since a band of patriots signed that document
in Philadelphia, that is where the perfection begins.*

Epilogue

From Training Wheels to "Look, Ma, No Hands"

The "training wheels" to "Eureka!" transition in a student of public speaking can be astonishing to watch.

The speaker is likely to be the first to notice his own frustration with the "training wheels" of clinging to a script or hiding behind a podium. He frets when he misses a phrase and panics at the omitted paragraph. His eyes work his notes rather than the room. His arms and feet stay frozen because he is concentrating so hard to recite the text exactly as he wrote it. Public speaking, done like that, is not much fun.

Finally comes a rush of adrenaline. After repeated trials, coaching, much cogitating, it is time to take a shot: He knows the meat of his subject, he knows the order in which he wants to explain things, he has memorized a well-turned phrase or two. And so he puts down the script, even for just part of the speech. He ventures out from behind the podium.

Maybe the first time or two he achieves only modest success. But it feels better. Then Eureka! An audience member nods, interested. Several laugh at a joke. Some start to take notes. All are looking at him with interest now; all are engaged. It feels good. And he responds in kind—is warmer, more relaxed, and at the same time much more confident and powerful. He uses gestures without even realizing that he is doing so; some sentences come out with more energy; he is enjoying himself. People are listening. That is a proud moment.

This will happen to you if you take the time to learn the basics and practice.

Once you have felt the Eureka moment, it only gets better from there. *Comfort in speaking never regresses.* Once you've found your voice, there is no need resort to the prior panicky state. Nervousness may recur in flashes—a Supreme Court argument comes to mind—but you can manage it. It's the same feeling that you experience when you learn to ride a bicycle without training wheels—you never really forget how to do it. If you get up and try it again, it will all come back to you and soon you will find yourself soaring. The biggest obstacle is behind you: convincing *yourself* that you can do it, and the exhilaration of "Take the training wheels off, Mom."

❖

Once you shed the training wheels, we offer you one last challenge: "Look, Ma, no hands!"

You may find yourself faced with the occasion that demands the best speech you can give. Perhaps it is a speech commemorating someone dear to you; perhaps the career-making speech of your life; perhaps your first-ever court appearance.

In such a situation, you want to be more than simply competent. You aspire to be superb—to be memorable, moving, powerful, convincing. It is hard to do each of those things perfectly. But the desire to ascend those heights is what drives us to continue improving, so that we can achieve greatness one day, when the time is right.

And once you have mastered the ability to express yourself, you will find that it spills into other parts of your life as well. You are more confident. You are more likely to speak up, to share your ideas. You are more likely to be heard.

Our take-home message: Think about what you are saying and why you are saying it. Take the time to craft your speech well. Practice so that your delivery enhances your point. Make your words sing. Speak up, and we will listen.

A Suggested Curriculum

For those interested in designing a public speaking course, we include here a sample syllabus. This syllabus is meant for use at a law school, but can easily be adapted for a business school or college class. This Appendix can also be used by anyone as a practice guide: Try your hand at any of the assignments on this syllabus (videotaping yourself, if possible) in order to improve your public speaking skills.

An oral advocacy or public speaking class works best if the class size is limited so that each student is able to present a speech at each meeting of the class and receive feedback on her work. The class should be taught in a room that permits the students to use various visual aids, including an easel, a chalkboard, and a computer that can run a PowerPoint slide show. It will be helpful if the chairs in the room can be arranged in various ways in order to simulate different speaking environments (as a lecture hall, for example, or around a table as in a business meeting, or lined up to simulate a jury box).

If possible, students should be videotaped each time they make a speech so that they can watch and take notes on their performance in preparation for the next class. The professor should meet with each student individually midway through the semester in order to review the videotapes. This permits the professor to offer detailed feedback that he or she might not have time to give in class and to address any issues that might embarrass the student if they were raised in front of his classmates.

This syllabus could be used to teach a semester-long course meeting 2.5 hours per week. One hour of each meeting would be devoted to a lecture by the professor about public speaking, and the remaining 1.5 hours would be used as a workshop session, in which the participants present speeches (written by the students outside of class in advance) and are critiqued on them. (This schedule permits you 9 minutes per student, which means that your critique for each student should last no more than 5 minutes.) You will notice that the syllabus is designed for the professor to lecture on a topic a week or so before the student attempts to present a speech in that area (for example, a lecture about opening statements must precede the opening statement assignment so the students have some guidance before undertaking the exercise). The readings generally relate to the topic of the lecture.

If the class has one instructor, this syllabus would accommodate between 10-12 students. With two instructors who perhaps take turns lecturing, the class can hold 20 students if the students are split into two groups for the workshop portion of the class (which then requires using two classrooms, one for each group). The readings suggested here are all from this book.

	Lecture Topic	Speech Assignment	Reading Assignment
Class 1	Lessons from Classical Rhetoric	Decision Speech (3 minutes): Prepare a three-minute speech about a turning point in your life—a moment when you had to make an important decision.	Chapters 2 & 3, Appendix B
Class 2	How to Write a Speech	Historical Figure (3 minutes): Pretend that you have been asked to introduce the keynote speaker at a banquet. The speaker that you are introducing can be any historical figure, alive or dead, real or imagined. Prepare a three-minute speech to introduce this person.	Chapter 4
Class 3	Ethics and Persuasion	Epideictic, Deliberative, or Forensic Speech (4 minutes): Prepare a four-minute speech that is either epideictic, deliberative, or forensic, or that combines elements of each. The topic is up to you.	Chapter 15
Class 4	Performing a Speech	Public Policy Speech (4 minutes): Prepare a four-minute speech concerning any issue of public policy that interests you. Take a position and argue for it.	Chapter 5

Class 5	Voice Class	Drama Day: You will be assigned a speech from a play or a movie to perform. You do not need to memorize the speech. (Instructors: Pick your favorite dramatic monologues for this assignment. We've used speeches from *A Man for All Seasons, Henry V, To Kill a Mockingbird, Romeo & Juliet,* and *Pride and Prejudice* with good success. Look for a speech in which the stakes are high, such as Henry V's Crispin Crispian speech, delivered before going into battle. This exercise can help students break out of their shells. To find more dramatic monologues, see http://www.americanrhetoric.com/speechbank.htm.)	Chapter 6
Class 6	Gender, Age and Advocacy	Speech With No Notes (4 minutes): Prepare a four-minute speech about any topic that interests you. You must be able to deliver this speech with absolutely no notes in front of you.	Chapters 8 & 9
Class 7	Visual Aids	Complex Topic (5 minutes): Present a five-minute speech in which you distill a complex topic into something understandable to your audience.	Chapter 7

	Lecture Topic	Speech Assignment	Reading Assignment
Class 8	Opening Statements	Speech With Visual Aids (4 minutes): Prepare a four-minute speech on any topic. You must use some sort of visual aid as part of your speech. This visual aid could be PowerPoint, a blackboard, an overhead transparency, or any other thing that you think would be appropriate.	Chapter 11
Class 9	Direct and Cross Examinations	Opening Statements (5 minutes): You will be assigned to represent either the plaintiff or the defendant in the case of Smith v. Jones. Please present five minutes of an opening statement in the case. You will not be able to cover every single issue in that short amount of time, so just give us your best five minutes. (Instructors: Numerous practice "case files" are available for purchase at the National Institute of Trial Advocacy, http://www.nita.org/.)	Chapter 11
Class 10	Closing Arguments	Direct and Cross Examination (5 minutes): We will assign you a witness from Smith v. Jones to examine on direct and on cross. We will also assign you a character to play so that a classmate can examine you.	Chapter 11

Class 11	Oral Presentations at Work	Closing arguments (5 minutes): Present a closing argument for your side in Smith v. Jones. You will not be able to cover every issue, so please address the ones that you think are the most important.	Chapters 9, 12, 13
Class 12	What Makes a Great Speech Great?	Presentation to a Practice Group (5 minutes): Prepare a five-minute presentation to colleagues at an imaginary law firm about a legal matter on which you are working. You can pick a case that you studied about in law school and pretend that you are a lawyer involved in the case, or you could speak about something that you actually worked on or a legal topic that interests you. This assignment is intended to simulate the type of presentation that many young associates and summer associates are asked to make, in which they tell a group of colleagues about the status of a matter and perhaps educate them about some area of the law.	Part Four
Class 13	Rhetoric and Democracy	Greatest Speeches (8 minutes): Prepare an eight-minute presentation about a speech that you think is an important or significant one—give us an analysis of why it works. As part of the presentation (either incorporated into the presentation, or at the beginning or end) perform all or part of the speech. Use visual aids or technology of some kind.	Prologue, Chapter 14, Chapter 15

A Quick History of Rhetoric

Interest in the subject of rhetoric has waxed and waned through the centuries, as have views about how to go about doing it well.

A. The Ebbs and Flows of Rhetoric

Rhetoric has enjoyed several heydays over the years. There was much early focus: the writings of Corax,[169] the vast writing and teaching in Greece and Rome by the likes of Aristotle,[170] Demosthenes,[171] Cicero,[172] Quintilian,[173] Thucydides,[174] and the like; and study of advocacy during the first sophistry (Gorgias[175] and Isocrates[176]), as well as the second.

During the Middle Ages, as Christianity became increasingly powerful, rhetoric was condemned as a pagan art.[177] During the late Middle Ages there was a revival, inspired by St. Augustine's Sermons and his text *On Christian Doctrine*,[178] and the addition of rhetoric along with logic and grammar to the important trivium curriculum.[179] Interest rekindled during the Renaissance, especially led by the Italian humanists (especially Petrarch[180]). The writings and work of George Campbell[181] and Richard

Whately[182] spawned an eighteenth and nineteenth century resurgence.

Rhetoric was scarcely taught in the first half of the twentieth century in this country, but it commanded more interest during the second half of the twentieth century here, in a movement led by Cornell University.[183] In more recent times, colorful rhetoric has flourished in many churches, leading some to blanch at the oft fanatically extreme. Interest in the tools of oral persuasion has grown in recent decades among trial and appellate advocates, with instruction provided in major law firms. Rhetorically trained jury consultants have become a cottage industry.

B. Divergence of Views About Rhetoric

Just as cyclical as the level of interest in oral advocacy is the disparity of views among those taking the topic to heart about what they see as effective stuff.

1. The Doubters

Debates have raged about whether rhetoric is a serious matter to begin with. Chief among the skeptics was Plato himself, following the lead of his mentor Socrates.[184] He noted three bases for concerns about the value of rhetoric:

1. There was then no systematic study of the field; it seemed mushy to Plato, too unacademic.

2. A heavy dose of elitism underlay Plato's scorn: "Plato was influenced by the conviction of Socrates that the road to moral knowledge was narrow and steep; and he was led ultimately to an exaggerated form of the Socratic view that goodness is a special skill or branch of knowledge, accessible only to the gifted and highly trained philosopher."[185] To him, truth could be grasped only by the cognoscente, demonstrable by rigorous proofs. He found rhetoric squishy, not grist for the serious thinker.

3. Plato foresaw mischievous use, when the persuasive powers of the gifted and morally flawed oral advocate were unleashed on the malleable.[186] He thought it could lead to riots. Plato's disquiet reverberated in academia throughout centuries.[187]

2. Exponents of the Flowery

These speakers treasured flashy, poetic rhetoric. This type of rhetoric flourished in the *"altruistic movement,"* the **second sophistry**, and the so-called *"Belles-lettres"* movement ascendant in the eighteenth and nineteenth centuries. Professor Hugh Blair was a leader in this movement.[188] It had antecedents in Gorgias, in Isocrates, and in some of Cicero's showy orations.

3. Psychological Focus

The so-called "epistemologists" (George Campbell and Richard Whately, for example) paid central attention to the **psychology of persuasion**, focusing on tone of argument, arrangement of arguments, presumptions, and the clear, efficient demonstration of fallacies.[189]

4. The Elocutionists

Exponents of this school of rhetoric stressed **style of oral presentation**: cadence, delivery, body language. Gilbert Austin was the leading light several centuries ago.[190] Of course, drama schools heed this today, just as they have for centuries.

5. Written Advocacy

Over the centuries many have argued that the essence of rhetoric depends more on cogent writing than gifted delivery. In nineteenth century and early twentieth century America, the teaching of rhetoric turned almost exclusively to rigorous application of rules of grammar, said to be the bedrock of persuasion.

6. Rationalism

Throughout the post-Aristotelian years, many great philosophers argued that the essence of persuasion is achieving the high ground on clear logic, resting on explicated rational bases and clear proof of propositions. Plato ascribed to that. So, too, did Descartes,[191] Erasmus,[192] and Francis Bacon[193]: "The duty and office of Rhetoric is to apply Reason to Imagination," the latter wrote.[194]

7. The Multimodal

This movement is usually identified with Professor Henry Noble Day, who argued that persuasion lay in appealing to a collection of multi-discipline devices. Day said that the job of rhetoric is "to combine explanation, conviction, excitement and persuasion."[195] He derided style-focused disciples in the field, insisting on maintaining adherence to a rigid series of laws of discourse. This movement never flourished, chiefly because his expositions were turgidly written. His "laws" were his handcuffs.

8. The New Rhetoric

New Rhetoric is intensively focused on the psychology of listeners, what makes them similar and dissimilar, and what that has to do with persuasion. The so-called "New Rhetoricians" inject modern refinements in psychology, semantics, motivational research, and the behavioral sciences more deeply into the stuff of persuasion. Among the leading exponents were I.A. Richards[196] and Kenneth Burke,[197] who strove to expand the conception of rhetoric into more "*argumentative compositions*," with increased attention centered on the "*psychological enlightenment function*" and to inspiring passion by focusing on human senses, feeling, tone, and intentions, placing more stress on wordsmithing and symbols, and enhancing efforts to reach both the heart and mind of an audience.

The leading text in this movement, *The New Rhetoric*, co-authored by Chaim Perelman, instructs oral advocates to identify and repeat those segments of arguments warranting "presence," to make sure the listener gets the "take-away" message. He also advocated seeking psychological "communion" with the audience, both a hypothetical "universal audience" (requiring themes that should appeal to all rational listeners and were uncontroversial) and, separately, the "particular audience" to whom the speaker would be speaking. He wrote that the speaker should use of a variety of appeals to different segments of an audience, differentiating the appeals to assure the audience of the speaker's "conviction" to a cause as distinct from mere "persuasion" as to its soundness.[198]

While largely embracing of Aristotle, Perelman argued that the tools of persuasion run deeper, broader in their weaponry. Whereas Aristotle sought "convergence" of argumentation with the dialectic (arguing from generally accepted opinions), Perelman sought a merging of argumentation with an expanded view of rhetoric.

Teaching oral competence can be tough sledding. Even the masters disagree about how to achieve the desired results. The best lessons from the masters, in our estimation, are the ones that we have included in Part 1 of this book.

Appendix C

Poverty and Communication Skills

Throughout this book, we have argued that all of us profit from improving our ability to articulate our ideas. Perhaps for no other group is that more true than for the economically disadvantaged. If basic language skills are not mastered in early childhood, it can be impossible for a child to catch up in later years. When a young child is exposed to only a limited vocabulary, and when much of it is filled with slang or worse, the results are likely to be costly both for the child and for society.

The literature in a variety of subject areas—psychology, education, and criminal justice—attests to the overriding, inexorable connection between verbal impairment and social, economic, and psychological troubles. Indeed, it is difficult to think of anything more telling as a behavioral predictor than verbal impairment. Poverty is, of course, one such predictor, but once you merge poverty with serious verbal deficiencies, the results are devastating. Underprivileged children can be helped directly and immediately through intensive attention to their speaking skills.

A. The Need

A child's intelligence is influenced a great deal by environment. A child who grows up in an environment in which she is encouraged to learn new words and engage in conversation will have greater success in adult life than the child who does not have this same advantage.[199] According to Richard E. Nisbett, a cognitive psychologist and professor at the University of Michigan, this difference in background frequently falls along socioeconomic lines in America.

Nisbett writes that, on average, a professional parent speaks about 2,000 words per day to a young child; a working-class class parent speaks about 1,300 to his child; and children born to a parent on welfare hear only about 600 words per day. By the age of three, the child of a professional has heard 30 million words; the child of a welfare home is likely to have heard only about a third as many.[200]

According to Nisbett, wealthier parents are more likely than parents raising their children in poverty to provide cognitive stimulation to their children—for example, by asking their children questions to which the parents already know the answer in order to encourage their child to reason.[201] An impoverished child is less likely to grow up in an environment that offers conversation designed to trigger the process of reasoning, analyzing, and expressing ideas.

Nisbett's studies show that the average lower-income parent—likely to be a single parent struggling with the difficulties of poverty—typically does not stress cognitive development[202] and may not read much to her child.[203] These parents may not spend time simplifying concepts for their children, labeling objects or events, asking children to compare and evaluate, or asking questions for which the adult knows the answer.[204] The verbal exchanges in impoverished households tend to last less than a minute. As a result, children of the poor suffer academically.[205]

There is also a difference in the types of words to which many privileged and poor children are exposed. The words poor children hear are more likely to be words of reprimand. The children of professionals receive six encouraging words for every reprimand; in the working class, two encouraging words for every criticism. The children of welfare parents receive well more than two reprimands for every word of encouragement. By the time a child of professionals is three years old, she has heard 500,000 encouraging statements and 80,000 discouraging ones, whereas the child of a parent on welfare has heard 75,000 encouraging terms and 200,000 reprimands.[206]

So what happens to the young child thrown into the school system at kindergarten without an adequate grounding in how to express himself? He starts with a frustrating disadvantage, lagging behind his peers from day one. He will fall behind in school, more so every year, because peers will have more command of language skills and comprehend more of what is said to them. Alienation will set in. He will get no help in developing passable verbal skills at home. He will develop no proficiency in conflict resolution because he cannot articulate words of conciliation. His job prospects become more hopeless each year. Life at home will deteriorate by the year, a battle of inarticulate criticism and raging anger, terms of punishment and disdain. As the more verbally impaired child sinks deeper, it is any wonder that we face a raging epidemic of bad consequences?

B. A Possible Solution

The problem can be solved to some degree through education, although our schools must be improved to accomplish this.[207] Educational dollars aimed at increasing verbal literacy can offer the best bang for our bucks and our time. This does not have to be yet another billion-dollar bailout package. One experience offers hope:

A preschool/kindergarten teacher taught for 30 years in Alexandria, Virginia. Most of the children at her school came from well-educated parents. The kids received the necessary grounding in colors, the alphabet, and so forth, but what made this teacher's classroom special was her focus on communication skills. She offered lots of "show and tell" oral exercises, had discussions in "circle," and encouraged the children to express themselves in order to cope with anger or conflict. The recurring theme was "use your words"—explain what you mean. The kids thrived. This teacher found that even at such an early age, the children were eager to express themselves. They were not paralyzed by the fear so many adult speakers experience; they loved to speak up. She saw payoff for that early oral education, as many of her pupils went on to academic and other distinctions.

The Chief Judge of the Juvenile Court in Alexandria, Virginia, spent most of his time dealing with serious anti-social behavior—drugs, gangs, early criminal conduct. He found it striking how hard it was for him to communicate with many defendants. They could not express themselves or understand him. Most had little comprehension of English (despite its being their only language), no words to express just what they did, why they did it, or how they would change their behavior. Without profanity, words of hate and violence, and "umm" and "aahh" connectives, they were tongue-tied. Scary, he called it.

The teacher related to the Judge her successful efforts in encouraging and teaching early verbal skills. As the talk went on, both were struck by the disparity between what her students received and the paltry verbal training offered the children that the Judge encountered in court.

The teacher, with prompting from the Judge, organized one of the first preschools in the Alexandria housing projects. Before the inception of the preschool, few children from this community made it successfully through kindergarten. The causes were myriad: The families of these children often suffered from drug- and alcohol-related problems and other challenges of poverty; many of the parents were unable to consistently deliver their children to a far-away school; some panicked at the notion of connecting to a government education program (for fear it would lead to intrusive home visits, maybe even jail terms for drug possession or child neglect).

This new preschool succeeded because it was set up in the high-rise welfare project itself. The child only had to press a button on the elevator to get to school. The organizers of the school also paid mothers a modest wage to serve as "helpers" in the school as a way to teach the parents better language and parenting skills. Finally, they included children as young as three in the program, recognizing the importance of early intervention.

The effort spread. One such school became four, then six. Hundreds enrolled. The schools stressed communications skills: how to talk to other kids and to their teachers, how to resolve conflicts without hitting, screaming, threatening, or calling names. The founders of the school began to offer parenting classes and special courses for those parents for whom English was a second language, again, in the apartment buildings themselves.

Every child from these preschools after that first year graduated from public kindergarten. The Judge computerized the names of all the students in these schools and noticed a striking absence of the graduates from these preschools in his caseload. More than one of the "helping mothers" went back to school and prospered as well. One mother, some years later, was presented at an American Bar Association conference and proudly boasted that she had just received not just a college degree, but a Masters Degree.

This is only one experience. It was not expensive. It worked. All of this speaks to the need to impart verbal skills beginning at ages three and four. We are now reaching only a small fraction of those needing help through the underfunded and often unavailable Head Start program. We cannot imagine anything more cost-effective for our education dollars than this: teaching basic verbal skills to our very youngest, especially the disadvantaged.

High School or College Debate: A Modest Proposal

Many public speakers get their start by participating in high school or college debate. This extracurricular activity, if coached well, can offer a wonderful grounding in public speaking skills to those who participate in it. But too frequently, debaters are taught to argue in a style that is exactly the *opposite* of persuasive rhetoric. They are encouraged to speak as quickly as possible in order to cram in as many points as they can. They are rewarded in the scoring for quantity over quality, scoring higher for answers that touch briefly on each possible topic without properly developing any. They learn to adopt a dismissive tone when speaking of their opponent's point of view. These ill-considered lessons, once taught, are difficult to unlearn, and they creep into debate-like interactions in adulthood: courtroom battles between lawyers, political debates during election years, and even disputes between family members.

Perhaps you are a volunteer debate coach or judge, as many attorneys and law students are. Perhaps you teach debate. Perhaps your child is considering joining the debate team, or perhaps you are thinking of taking up debate yourself to hone your public speaking skills. To aid you, we offer this chapter about effective debating.

❖

It was the championship round of high school policy debate. The players: four of the top high school debaters in the Middle Atlantic Region. The subject: energy.

The debaters were gifted indeed. It was at once clear, especially from the cross-examination (in which the debaters questioned one another), that they were extraordinarily bright and articulate, with a detailed mastery of the subject. Moreover, it was clear from post-debate discussions with the debaters that each was warm, personable, and engaging.

So far, so good. What disturbed was this: At no time during the 80-minute debate did even the most educated audience member, who was in fact an expert on energy, have the foggiest notion of the substance of what was going on. The debate could have been conducted in Chinese. The energy expert in the audience sat, puzzled, understanding only isolated sentences here or there. It was clear to him that there was at issue a dispute about whether the earth was cooling or heating, and that this dispute was deemed significant by both sides, and that for some reason both sides had decided to waffle a bit on the subject. But despite giving the discussion his total attention, that was about all he understood.

Afterward, his young companions asked him who won. He replied that he had no idea. He turned the question on them and received the same response. They asked him what the major contentions had been, and once again he demurred. They asked him what the precise topic was. He said that he did not know and could not have given them even a ballpark answer until the third constructive speech. Then they asked the hard questions: Why was it necessary that the debaters talk so fast that the uninitiated ear simply could not make out the words? Why was it necessary that the language be cluttered with so much jargon and shop-talk that otherwise intelligent, reasonable, and well-read listeners could not follow the give-and-take? How was it possible that they could emerge from the debate without having been persuaded of anything, without having their store of knowledge on the subject enlarged, and without any sense as to who had been most persuasive?

❖

This is what is wrong with this style of debate: It is quite unintelligible to all but the debaters themselves (and perhaps a few—but not all—of the judges), and for that precise reason it fails to develop many of those qualities that are its objective. In the process, it teaches and then ingrains very bad habits. To be sure, even *this* form of debate imparts much that *is* valuable: research skills, mental quickness, mental discipline, and poise on one's feet. But it could teach a good deal more. It could teach the art of persuasiveness, or how to precisely and clearly use words, or how to synthesize an argument (one's own or the opposition's). It could teach students how to distinguish between those opposing arguments that require a response and those that can be left alone. It could teach them how to enhance the quality of their argument through better delivery skills, or when to use (or not use) sarcasm. But it does not impart any of those skills.

It is precisely these characteristics (persuasiveness, ability to synthesize an argument, and so forth) that are the hallmarks of the distinguished advocate. They are the qualities that are useful in almost all aspects of formal communication—and by that we mean everything from examination papers to courtroom advocacy to effective presentations in the community. Basic early instruction *can* begin with high school debate. In fact, we know no better place to begin the development of these skills. Our concern about the style of debate witnessed by the energy expert is that it fails to develop these skills and, what's worse, it could even *impair* their development.

Following are the deficiencies of the mile-a-minute approach:

1. Speed

The debaters speak at such a rate of speed that the unitiated ear cannot understand what they are saying. Many words, phrases, and sometimes sentences are blurted out so quickly that nothing is understood. Even where words here and there are grasped, the substance of the point is frequently lost. And if one manages to hear the words and takes the time to translate them into their substance and assess the force of the point, the listener may miss the next statement or two. An audience has the terrible choice of either attempting to hear all of the words and distilling their substance at some breaking point, or attempting to understand and assess the arguments at the cost of grasping only about every other point. An audience dilemma of this sort is a potentially catastrophic problem for a speaker. Machine-gun speech detracts from the persuasiveness of oral advocacy because it impedes the hearer's ability to concentrate on the argument. It can even suggest hysteria, eroding the listener's confidence in the speaker and in the force of the speaker's argument. Furthermore, the habit of lightning-speed speech, once fully ingrained, sometimes takes decades to undo.

So, on the downside, the high school style of debate imparts bad speaking habits. It also fails to develop an important and useful skill: the ability to enhance one's persuasiveness by using cadence effectively. All of the great oral advocates are masters of timing. It is essential to learn to pause for effect, and to impart emphasis by making especially important or difficult points in a deliberate style. These are skills that are developed only if the speaker ordinarily speaks at a normal speed and, from there, introduces inflections, tonal modulations, and speed variations to first grab the hearer's attention and then to persuade him.

2. Poor Delivery

Judges of debate tournaments do not reward good presentation skills, and consequently debaters have little incentive to develop those skills. Eye contact, posture, enunciation, methods of introducing emphasis, humor, warmth, sincerity, and the like, are nowhere in sight. Instead, there is limited eye contact, considerable reading, and a fair amount of stumbling over words (probably because of the speed).

3. Erroneous Strategies for Persuasion

In order to teach debaters the best habits for effective public speaking, debate competitions should be designed to reward the following:

- Ability to grasp and hold the listener's attention;

- Effective organization of both affirmative and rebuttal contentions;

- Ability to perceive what major points scored by the adversary are likely to trouble the listener, and the ability to deal effectively with those;

- Ability to summarize and hammer major themes of the speaker's own affirmative argument;

- Wisdom to make the narrowest argument necessary so that the listener does not feel compelled to accept dubious or overstated arguments in order to agree with the speaker's position;

- Willingness to concede a fair claim by an opponent if it does not destroy one's position; and

- Judgment to know what not to attempt to answer.

The machine-gun style of debate teaches the wrong lessons on most of these points. The emphasis seems to be on attempting to answer virtually every point made by the opposition, and to do so in the order in which the points originally were made. This approach erroneously ascribes the same approximate weight to each point and seems to reward (or at least not penalize) over-statement and over-argument. It is no surprise, then, that high school debaters often exhibit an unrealistic (and unpersuasive) determination to defend dubious propositions past their logical limits.

4. The Urge to Complicate

No skill is more difficult to master or more essential to effective advocacy than the ability to simplify and clarify an argument. It requires at once superior analytical skills, an economic use of words, and an ability to inspire the listener's confidence. "Flowchart" debating (in which judges keep score by counting the quantity of points each side makes) not only fails to develop this skill but flat-out impedes it. It leads not to clarity, but to confusion. It rivets attention on the trees but disguises the forest.

5. Anti-intellectualism

One necessary result of the participants' belief that they must respond to every point made by the other side is an erosion of logic. Participants do not consider which arguments are strong and which are weak; they treat all arguments equally, simply because someone on the other side has made them and they will earn more points if they refute each one. If debates are to be judged on the basis of "flowcharts," with an emphasis on scoring the most points and introducing the most evidence (even if the evidence is weak), that lessens the import given to the quality of the argument and the quality of supporting documentation.

The high school style of debating is preoccupied with quantity: quantity of words that can be squeezed into short presentations, quantity of arguments that can be recited, quantity of supporting evidence. What is most troublesome about this approach is that it is far removed from other forms of verbal persuasion. Teaching with this approach constitutes a disservice to young students and is far less valuable than a *qualitative* approach.

So what can be done to change the emphasis? Some of the following are possibilities:

1. Teachers and debate coaches should emphasize the *quality* of argumentation and public speaking. The failings of rapid-fire, scatter-gun debate should be flagged and addressed in class. Many teaching aids are available. For example, the American Bar Association offers superb audio-visual tapes on the art of effective oral advocacy which would be of great assistance to debaters.

2. The organizations supervising debates should organize clinics for debate coaches and judges to train them to teach with a more qualitative approach.

3. The judging criteria should include an assessment of speaking style, the ability to organize points and summarize information, and the like. If the students know they will be judged on the quality of their style and rhetoric, the zeal to excel in these areas will itself serve to be a great teacher.

4. Lay judges (those who do not have a particular expertise in debate or the subject matter of the debate) should be used more frequently. If the students know they are not being judged by those schooled in debate and intimately familiar with the debate topic, they will be forced to adjust their presentations and to discipline themselves to learn how to persuade the outsider.

5. There should be occasional tournaments that utilize some topic other than the national one. One of the incentives for speed and repeated rote presentations may be that the debaters tire of the national topic, thereby causing mental laziness. One way to avoid that problem is to announce, perhaps a month before a tournament, that the subject will be some issue of public significance, not requiring prolific research, and to make clear that the debate will be judged more on the quality of argumentation than on the number of points mentioned or bits of evidence included.

Competitive debate can provide a terrific foundation for someone who wants to become a fine public speaker, with the adjustments that we have described above. Many lawyers and others who speak for a living have fond memories of their experiences on the debate team. We hope that those who coach or judge these teams in the future will do all they can to ensure that the lessons they impart to the participants are consistent with the best practices of good public speakers.

Endnotes

Prologue

i Stephanie K. Gerding, The Accidental Technology Trainer 52 (2007) ("Glossophobia . . . is said to be the single most common phobia, affecting as many as 75 percent of all people."). *See also* Sandra F. Rief & Julie A. Heimburge, How to Reach and Teach All Children Through Balanced Literacy 101 (2007) ("Fear of speaking in public (glossophobia) is documented as the number-one fear in America. According to Richmond and McCroskey (1995a), 95 percent of the population reports some degree of anxiety about communicating with a person or in groups. The good news is that although some nervousness is normal, proper preparation and rehearsal can help reduce the fear by 75 percent (Laskowski, 1996).").

ii Edmund L. Andrews & Stephen Labaton, *Bailout Plan: $2.5 Trillion and a Strong U.S. Hand*, N.Y. Times, Feb. 11, 2009, at A1, *available at* http://www.nytimes.com/2009/02/11/business/economy/11bailout.html.

Chapter 1

1 Geoff Tibballs, The Mammoth Book of Zingers, Quips, and One-Liners 504 (2004).

2 U.S. Const. amend. I ("Congress shall make no law . . . abridging the freedom of speech, or of the press . . .").

3 Plato's Gorgias 23 (Albert A. Anderson ed., Benjamin Jowett trans., Agora Publications, Inc. 1994).

4 Jay Heinrichs, *Why Harvard Destroyed Rhetoric*, Harv. Mag., *available at* http://www.figarospeech.com/harvard/.

5 Harvard.edu, Derek Bok Center for Teaching and Learning: Program in Speaking and Learning, http://isites.harvard.edu/icb/icb.do?keyword=k1985&pageid=icb.page92143 (last visited July 2, 2010).

6 *See* Ron M. Aizen, Four Ways to Better 1L Assessments, 54 Duke L.J. 765 (2004).

7 William M. Sullivan et al., Carnegie Found. for the Advancement of Teaching, Educating Lawyers: Preparation for the Profession of Law (2007).

Chapter 2

8 *See* Sonja K. Foss et al., Contemporary Perspectives on Rhetoric 71-77 (3d ed. 2002).

9 *See id.* at 77-84.

10 CNN.com, *Dean: "We have just begun to fight,"* http://www.cnn.com/2004/ALLPOLITICS/01/20/elec04.prez.dean.tran/index.html (last visited June 4, 2010). You can see Dean's outburst on YouTube, http://www.youtube.com/watch?v=KDwODbl3muE (last visited July 20, 2010).

11 *See, e.g.,* Verne Gay, *Dean's Theatrics Draw Mixed Reviews,* Seattle Times, Jan. 21, 2004, http://seattletimes.nwsource.com/html/nationworld/2001840708_deantv21.html.

12 *See* Edward P.J. Corbett & Robert J. Connors, Classical Rhetoric for the Modern Student 32 (4th ed. 1999).

13 *See id.* ("[The rhetoricians] thought of rhetoric as an offshoot of logic....").

14 *See id.* at 38-52.

15 *See id.* at 52-58.

16 *See, e.g., id.* at 22 ("When Demosthenes, the greatest of the Greek orators, was asked what he considered to be the most important part of rhetoric, he replied, 'Delivery, delivery, delivery.' ").

17 *See id.* at 21 ("All rhetorical considerations of style involved some discussion of *choice of words*...."); *see also id.* at 337-339.

18 *See, e.g.*, Benjamin Frankel, Roots of Realism 189 (1996) ("Not only is Thucydides to be considered a minimalist, he is also a critic of the fundamentalism prevalent in the Athenian rhetoric of his day.").

19 Oyez.org, *Roe v. Wade*—Oral Argument, http://www.oyez.org/cases/1970-1979/1971/1971_70_18/argument (last visited June 4, 2010) ("It disrupts her body. It disrupts her education. It disrupts her employment. And it often disrupts her entire family life.").

20 *See* Corbett & Connors, *supra* note 12, at 17 ("By the time Cicero came to write his treatises on rhetoric, the study of rhetoric was divided, mainly for pedagogical convenience, into five parts....").

21 Anthony Everitt, Cicero 58 (2003).

22 *See, e.g., id.* at 59-61.

23 *See, e.g.*, Solomon Asch, *Forming Impressions of Personality*, 41 J. Abnormal & Soc. Psychol. 258-290 (1946).

24 *See, e.g.*, John T. Cacioppo & Richard E. Petty, *Effect of Message Repetition and Position on Cognitive Response, Recall, and Persuasion*, 37 J. Personality & Soc. Psychol. 97-109 (1979).

25 *See* U.S. Dept. of Labor, OSHA Office of Training & Educ., *Presenting Effective Presentations with Visual Aids* (1996), *available at* http://www.osha.gov/doc/outreachtraining/htmlfiles/traintec.html (last visited Aug. 26, 2010).

26 *See, e.g.*, Norman Miller & Donald T. Campbell, *Recency and Primacy in Persuasion as a Function of the Timing of Speeches and Measurements*, 59 J. Abnormal & Soc. Psychol. 1-9 (1959).

27 *See, e.g.*, William J. McGuire, *The Effectiveness of Supportive and Refutational Defenses in Immunizing and Restoring Beliefs Against Persuasion*, 24 Sociometry 184-197 (1961).

28 *See, e.g.*, Richard L. Miller, *Mere Exposure, Psychological Reactance, and Attitude Change*, 40 Pub. Op. Q. 229-233 (1976).

29 For a fine discussion of this topic, see Drew Westen, The Political Brain (2008).

Chapter 3

30 A transcript of the speech is available at http://www.talkingpointsmemo.com/news/2009/04/transcript_obama_speaks_on_economy.php (last visited Aug. 26, 2010).

31 *See*, for further discussion of the three types of speeches, Corbett & Connors, *supra* note 12, at 23.

32 Chaim Perelman & Lucie Olbrechts-Tyteca, The New Rhetoric 51 (John Wilkinson & Purcell Weaver trans., 1969) ("[Epideictic] discourse sets out to increase the intensity of adherence to certain values....").

33 November 19, 1863, *available at* http://avalon.law.yale.edu/19th_century/gettyb.asp (last visited Aug. 26, 2010).

34 March 4, 1865, *available at* http://avalon.law.yale.edu/19th_century/lincoln2.asp (last visited Aug. 26, 2010).

35 January 8, 2008 (after losing New Hampshire Primary), *available at* http://www.scribd.com/doc/3914389/Senator-Barack-Obamas-Yes-We-Can-Speech (last visited Aug. 26, 2010).

36 June 6, 1984, *available at* http://www.americanrhetoric.com/speeches/ronaldreaganddayaddress.html (last visited Aug. 26, 2010).

37 *See, e.g.*, YouTube clips: "It's Morning Again in America" http://www.youtube.com/watch?v=EU-IBF8nwSY; and "Peace," http://www.youtube.com/watch?v=jzfF6E-tx7o& feature=related.

38 May 13, 1940, *available at* http://www.winstonchurchill.org/learn/speeches/speeches-of-winston-churchill/92-blood-toil-tears-and-sweat; YouTube.com audio clip, *at* http://www.youtube.com/watch?v=gVg7rnRheK8 (last visited Aug. 26, 2010).

39 Edward R. Murrow, In Search of Light: Broadcasts of Edward R. Murrow 237 (Edward Bliss ed., 1997).

40 August 28, 1963, *available at* http://teacherlink.ed.usu.edu/tlresources/reference/ihaveadream.html; YouTube.com clip, http://www.youtube.com/watch?v=iEMXa TktUfA.

41 *See* Perelman & Olbrechts-Tyteca, *supra* note 32, at 51.

42 January 19, 2004, *available at* http://www.cnn.com/2004/ALLPOLITICS/01/20/elec04.prez.dean.tran/index.html (last visited Aug. 26, 2010).

43 Encarta Book of Quotations 306 (Bill Swainson ed., 2000).

44 June 6, 2009, *available at* http://www.cbsnews.com/stories/2009/06/06/world/main 5067743.shtml.

45 March 18, 2008, *available at* http://www.cnn.com/2008/POLITICS/03/18/obama .transcript.

46 May 17, 2009, *available at* http://www.nytimes.com/2009/05/17/us/politics/17text-obama.html.

47 June 4, 2008, *available at* http://www.whitehouse.gov/the_press_office/remarks-by-the-president-at-cairo-university-6-04-09.

48 December 1, 2009, *available at* http://www.nytimes.com/2009/12/02/world/asia/ 02prexy.text.html.

49 December 10, 2009, *available at* http://www.nytimes.com/2009/12/11/world/europe/ 11prexy.text.html.

50 *See, e.g.*, Daniel Gross, *BP—Blah Performance*, Slate, June 15, 2010, http://www.slate.com/ id/2257150.

Chapter 4

51 Brianna Rego, History of Sci. Socy., *The Polonium Brief: A Hidden History of Cancer, Radiation, and the Tobacco Industry*, 100 Isis 453, 454 (2009).

Chapter 5

52 For a terrific example of how important the space between beats is, watch *When Harry Met Sally* and look for the scene where Sally tells Harry the story of why she and Joe broke up. (It involves taking her friend's little girl to the zoo for the day.) Watch how her facial expressions change *in between* the lines. By the end of the scene, you know that she's not actually over Joe, nor (despite her statements to the contrary to Harry) is she certain that she did the right thing. You know this because of the skillful way that the actress moves from beat to beat. She uses the moments of transition to tell the true story.

53 American Presidency Project, John F. Kerry: Address Accepting the Presidential Nomination at the Democratic National Convention in Boston, http://www.presidency.ucsb.edu/ws/index.php?pid=25971 (last visited June 30, 2010).

54 You can hear Kerry's delivery of the speech here: http://www.americanrhetoric.com/speeches/convention2004/johnkerry2004dnc.htm (last visited Aug. 26, 2010).

55 Watch the speech on YouTube, http://www.youtube.com/watch?v=Fe751kMBwms; or on the Washington Post website, http://www.washingtonpost.com/wp-dyn/content/article/2008/01/08/AR2008010804032.html.

Chapter 6

56 1 Marvin Perry et al., Western Civilization: Ideas, Politics, and Society 68 (2006) (Vol. I: To 1789).

57 For this story we owe thanks to James J. Brosnahan, who told his version of it at a National Institute for Trial Advocacy Teacher Training session about vocal training.

58 These exercises are very basic vocal warm-ups that are widely used in theater circles; none of them are our own inventions, but we have tried them and found them to be useful, and have modified some after experimenting with them in the classes that we teach. We gathered them from theater programs at the North Carolina School of the Arts, Northwestern University, and Harvard University, as well as from actors of our acquaintance, including our dear friend, Becca Diaz-Bonilla. We are unsure of the original inventors of these exercises—they have been passed around so frequently that we suspect that many actors who use them could not tell you who first invented them.

59 From *Merrie England*, an opera by Edward German & Basil Hood (1902), *available at* http://www.archive.org/stream/merrieenglandnew00germuoft/merrieenglandnew00germuoft_djvu.txt.

60 From *The Mikado*, an opera by W.S. Gilbert & Arthur Sullivan (1885), *available at* http://math.boisestate.edu/gas/mikado/libretto.txt.

61 From *The Pirates of Penzance*, an opera by W.S. Gilbert & Arthur Sullivan (1879), *available at* http://math.boisestate.edu/gas/pirates/pirates_lib.txt.

Chapter 7

62 Richard Cohen, *A Campaign Gore Can't Lose*, Wash. Post, Apr. 18, 2006, at A19, *available at* http://www.washingtonpost.com/wp-dyn/content/article/2006/04/17/AR2006041701259.html.

63 Beginning around 14:50 in *An Inconvenient Truth*.

64 William Shakespeare, Henry V, act 3, sc. 3.

Chapter 8

65 *See, e.g.*, Marcella Bombardieri, *Some Think Ex-President Stooping on Campaign Trail*, Boston Globe, Jan. 24, 2008, http://www.boston.com/news/nation/articles/2008/01/24/some_think_ex_president_stooping_on_campaign_trail/.

66 *See, e.g.*, Robert N. Sayler, *Rambo Litigation: Why Hardball Tactics Don't Work*, 74 ABA J. 79 (Mar. 1, 1988). You can see counterexamples throughout our culture as well: Former Virginia Senator John Warner was revered on both sides of the political aisle because he refused to employ such needless aggression; he looked to solve problems, not pick fights. Former Arkansas Governor Mike Huckabee made a serious run for the Republican presidential nomination because his warm, gregarious, funny persona stood out in a field of extremely aggressive candidates.

67 William F. Buckley, Jr., *Torture on* 60 Minutes, Natl. Rev. Online, May 2, 2007, http://article.nationalreview.com/313807/torture-on-i60-minutesi/william-f-buckley-jr.

68 *See, e.g.*, John Buckley, *Let the Jury Draw the Conclusion*, 8 TortSource 2 (Fall 2005), *available at* http://www.abanet.org/tips/tortsource/tsfall05.pdf.

69 *See, e.g.*, Sarah Baxter, *"Jimmy Carter" Tag Has Obama Wincing*, Times Online, Feb. 1, 2009, http://www.timesonline.co.uk/tol/news/world/us_and_americas/us_elections/article5627534.ece.

70 *See, e.g.*, Ernest L. Boyer, College: The Undergraduate Experience in America 150 (1987) ("We were especially struck by the subtle yet significant differences in the way men and women participated in class.... In many classrooms, women are overshadowed. Even the brightest women often remain silent.... Not only do men talk more, but what they say often carries more weight."); Myra Sadker & David Sadker, Failing at Fairness: How Our Schools Cheat Girls 170 (4th ed. 1995) ("Women's silence is loudest at college.... In our research we have found that men are twice as likely to monopolize class discussions, and women are twice as likely to be silent.").

71 *See, e.g.*, Peggy Noonan, *What's Not to Like?*, Wall St. J., June 22, 2007, http://online.wsj.com/article/SB118254785028645232.html.

72 Patrick Healy, *The Clinton Sunday Show Blitz*, N.Y. Times, Sept. 23, 2007, http://thecaucus.blogs.nytimes.com/2007/09/23/the-clinton-sunday-show-blitz/; *see also* Howard Kurtz, *Hillary Chuckles; Pundits Snort*, Wash. Post, Oct. 3, 2007, at C01, *available at* http://www.washingtonpost.com/wp-dyn/content/article/2007/10/02/AR2007100201940.html.

73 You can see Senator Clinton's answer at http://www.youtube.com/watch?v=6qgWH89qWks.

74 *See* Karen Breslau, *Hillary Tears Up: A Muskie Moment, or a Helpful Glimpse of "the Real Hillary"?*, Newsweek, Jan. 7, 2008, http://www.newsweek.com/2008/01/06/hillary-tears-up.html.

Chapter 9

75 The architecture firm Gensler released an elegant report in 2002 called "Strategies for the Intergenerational Workplace," describing the ways that different generations interact and suggesting architectural elements in a workplace that could bring the generations together. The focus of Gensler's study was to develop a physical workplace that encouraged cross-generational collaboration. The generational differences that Gensler highlighted in its study also highlight issues that a speaker should consider when addressing his audience. Kate Kirkpatrick et al., Gensler, Strategies for the Intergenerational Workplace (2008), http://www.gensler.com/uploads/documents/IntergenerationalWorkplace_07_17_2008.pdf. The authors are also indebted to Peter Ronayne, Director of the Federal Executive Institute, for his thoughts about generational differences presented at a seminar at the University of Virginia in 2009.

76 Harriet Hankin, The New Workforce 51 (2004) ("The Boomers gave us hippies, communes, and free love. They also gave us the 80-hour workweek.").

77 Lisa Belkin, *Parents Who Can't Resist Smoothing Life's Bumps*, N.Y. Times, Feb. 11, 2007, http://www.nytimes.com/2007/02/11/business/yourmoney/11wcol.html?_r=1&src=tp.

78 See *id.*

79 See Kirkpatrick, *supra* note 75.

80 See, *e.g.*, Belkin, *supra* note 77.

81 See, *e.g.*, Jonathan D. Glater, To: Professor@University.edu Subject: Why It's All About Me, N.Y. Times, Feb. 21, 2006, http://www.nytimes.com/2006/02/21/education/21professors.html.

Chapter 11

82 University of Missouri-Kansas City School of Law, Closing argument of Johnnie Cochran in the O.J. Simpson case, http://www.law.umkc.edu/faculty/projects/ftrials/Simpson/cochranclose.html (last visited June 30, 2010).

83 For additional insight, see John W. Davis, *The Argument of an Appeal*, 26 ABA J. 895 (1940), and John Marshall Harlan, *What Part Does the Oral Argument Play in the Conduct of an Appeal?*, 41 Cornell L.Q. 6 (1955).

Chapter 12

84 This is true of anything that you post in cyberspace—read comments to blogs if you want to see some truly vicious discourse. Remember that anything you say online can come back to haunt you, so be careful when you post something on your Facebook page or on a blog. Make sure that your online persona is consistent with the persona that you hope to project in the real world.

Chapter 13

85 *Exactly How Much Are The Times A-Changin'?*, Newsweek, July 26, 2010, at 58, *available at* http://www.newsweek.com/feature/2010/by-the-numbers-how-the-digital-revolution-changed-our-world.html?gt1=43002.

86 William Powers, Hamlet's Blackberry 55 (2010).

87 *Id.* at 176.

88 *See, e.g.*, Matt Richtel, *Hooked on Gadgets, and Paying a Mental Price*, N.Y. Times, June 7, 2010, at A1, *available at* http://www.nytimes.com/2010/06/07/technology/07brain.html; Hilary Stout, *Antisocial Networking?*, N.Y. Times, May 2, 2010, at ST1, *available at* http://www.nytimes.com/2010/05/02/fashion/02BEST.html?ref=style&adxnnlx=1273082586-oSSwa11Zd0iHOAp1NpEA5g&pagewanted=all.

89 Powers, *supra* note 86, at 59 ("By some estimates, recovering focus can take ten to twenty times the length of the interruption.").

90 *See id.* at 177 ("[The] idea of the home as sanctuary [is] absent from most thinking and decision making about technology."); *see also* Richtel, *supra* note 88.

91 *See, e.g.*, Daniel de Vise, *Wide Web of Diversions Gets Laptops Evicted from Lecture Halls*, Wash. Post, Mar. 9, 2010, http://www.washingtonpost.com/wp-dyn/content/article/2010/03/08/AR2010030804915.html.

Chapter 14

92 CNN.com, Obama speech: "Yes, we can change," http://www.cnn.com/2008/POLITICS/01/26/obama.transcript/index.html (last visited June 17, 2010).

93 Landmark Speeches of the American Conservative Movement 39 (Peter Schweizer & Wynton C. Hall eds., 2007) (Full text: "I would remind you that extremism in the defense of liberty is no vice.").

94 National Archives, "Day of Infamy" Speech: Joint Address to Congress Leading to a Declaration of War Against Japan, http://www.archives.gov/historical-docs/document .html?doc=15&title_raw="Day of Infamy&quot (last visited June 17, 2010).

95 David E. Johnson & Johnny R. Johnson, A Funny Thing Happened on the Way to the White House 110 (2004).

96 Paul F. Boller, Presidential Anecdotes 283 (1996) ("About midnight . . . radio commentator H.V. Kaltenborn announced over the air: 'Mr. Truman is still ahead but these are returns from a few cities. When the returns come in from the country the result will show Dewey winning overwhelmingly.' ").

97 David McCullough, Truman 1057 (1993) ("He would not seek the presidency, Eisenhower said [to Truman]. Further, 'you know, far better than I, that the possibility that I will ever be drawn into political activity is so remote as to be negligible.' ").

98 Elvin T. Lim, The Anti-Intellectual Presidency 42 (2008) ("[S]peechwriters . . . have observed a Janus-like quality in their bosses, who are articulate, formal, and sophisticated in private, but decidedly casual and simplistic in public. According to his personal secretary, Ann Whitman, Eisenhower was 'deathly afraid of being considered highbrow.' His speechwriter, however, observed characteristics that could have branded him as such.' ").

99 Ted Sorensen, Counselor 156 (2008) ("Strange as it seems today, the chief obstacle to John F. Kennedy's nomination and election as president of the United States in 1960 . . . was based largely on his Roman Catholic faith.").

100 *Id.* at 108.

101 *New Administration: All He Asked...*, Time, Feb. 3, 1961, *available at* http://www.time .com/time/magazine/article/0,9171,872026,00.html.

102 Robert North Roberts & Scott Hammond, Encyclopedia of Presidential Campaigns, Slogans, Issues, and Platforms 219 (2004).

103 Lim, *supra* note 98, at 68-69.

104 Rhetorical Studies of National Political Debates, 1960-1992, at 110 (Robert V. Frieden-berg ed., 2d ed. 1993).

105 Jack Germond, *A Look at Presidential Contender Gaffes*, Washingtonian, Sept. 1, 2007, http://www.washingtonian.com/articles/people/5172.html.

106 *See, e.g.*, MSNBC.com, *Clinton Bores His Audience*, http://www.msnbc.msn.com/id/ 5470323/ (last visited June 18, 2010).

107 Michael Crowley, *The Democrats' Favorite Victim*, Slate, Apr. 2, 2004, http://slate.msn .com/id/2098171/.

108 Sheryl Gay Stolberg, *Daschle Defends Iraq Remarks*, N.Y. Times, Sept. 20, 2004, http:// www.nytimes.com/2004/09/20/politics/20dakota.html?_r=1.

109 *See, e.g.*, MSNBC.com, *Is John Kerry Fit for Command?*, http://www.msnbc.msn.com/id/ 5662329 (last visited June 18, 2010).

110 Steven V. Roberts, *Bush Intensifies Debate on Pledge, Asking Why It So Upsets Dukakis*, N.Y. Times, Aug. 25, 1988, http://www.nytimes.com/1988/08/25/us/bush-intensifies-debate-on-pledge-asking-why-it-so-upsets-dukakis.html?pagewanted=1?pagewanted=1.

111 *See, e.g.*, Michael Dobbs, *Was Obama Ever a Muslim?*, Wash. Post, June 13, 2008, http:// voices.washingtonpost.com/fact-checker/2008/06/was_obama_a_muslim.html.

112 Julie Bosman, *Clinton on Experience*, N.Y. Times, Mar. 1, 2008, http://www.nytimes .com/2008/03/01/us/01adbox.html. You can watch the ad at http://www.youtube.com/ watch?v=7yr7odFUARg.

113 James T. Patterson, Grand Expectations: The United States, 1945-1974, at 560 (1997). You can watch the ad at http://www.youtube.com/watch?v=IkWAhuXtalw.

114 *See, e.g.*, Editorial, *What David Duke Owes Willie Horton*, N.Y. Times, Feb. 22, 1989, http://www.nytimes.com/1989/02/22/opinion/what-david-duke-owes-willie-horton.html. You can watch the ad at http://www.youtube.com/watch?v=Io9KMSSEZ0Y.

115 *See, e.g.*, Robin Toner, *Ad Seen as Playing to Racial Fears*, N.Y. Times, Oct. 26, 2006, http://www.nytimes.com/2006/10/26/us/politics/26tennessee.html; Alex Johnson, *Tennessee Ad Ignites Internal GOP Squabbling*, MSNBC.com, Oct. 25, 2006, http:// www.msnbc.msn.com/id/15403071/. You can watch the ad at http://www.youtube.com/ watch?v=24rM3—IIv8.

116 *See, e.g.*, Gary A. Donaldson, The Making of Modern America: The Nation from 1945 to the Present 244 (2009) ("In 1984 Reagan's campaign slogan struck a chord with the nation: 'It's morning again in America.' For a nation that had been dragged through Vietnam, Watergate, urban riots, the energy crisis, and the failed presidencies of Ford and Carter, Reagan seemed something of a ray of sunshine. He was confident, clearly a leader, and he seemed to want to take the nation back to a better time—or at least what

Americans thought was a better time."). You can see the ad at http://www.youtube.com/watch?v=EU-IBF8nwSY.

Chapter 15

117 Corbett & Connors, *supra* note 12, at 490-491.

118 *Id.* at 492.

119 William Norwood Brigance, Speech: Its Techniques and Disciplines in a Free Society 5 (2d ed. 1961).

120 *Id.* at 423.

121 *Id.* at 12 (quoting Wallace Carroll).

122 *Id.* at 4 ("[D]emocracy and the system of speechmaking were born together, and grew up together. Since that early day we have never had a successful democracy unless a large part, a very large part, of its citizens were effective, intelligent, and responsible speakers.").

123 U.S. Const. amend. I ("Congress shall make no law . . . abridging the freedom of speech, or of the press. . . .").

124 274 U.S. 357, 375 (1927) (Brandeis, J., concurring).

125 *Abrams v. United States*, 250 U.S. 616, 630 (1919) (Holmes, J., dissenting) ("But when men have realized that time has upset many fighting faiths, they may come to believe even more than they believe the very foundations of their own conduct that the ultimate good desired is better reached by free trade in ideas—that the best test of truth is the power of the thought to get itself accepted in the competition of the market, and that truth is the only ground upon which their wishes safely can be carried out. That at any rate is the theory of our Constitution.").

126 John Stuart Mill, On Liberty 48-49 (Nabu Press 2010) (1859) ("First, if any opinion is compelled to silence, that opinion may, for aught we can certainly know, be true. To deny this is to assume our own infallibility. Secondly, though the silenced opinion be in error, it may, and very commonly does, contain a portion of the truth; and since the general or prevailing opinion on any subject is rarely or never the whole truth, it is only by the collision of adverse opinions that the remainder of the truth has any chance of being supplied. Thirdly, even if the received opinion be not only true, but the whole truth; unless it is suffered to be, and actually is, vigorously and earnestly contested, it will, by most of those who receive it, be held in the manner of a prejudice, with little comprehension or feeling of its rational grounds. And not only this but, fourthly, the meaning of the doctrine itself will be in danger of being lost, or enfeebled.").

127 *Reno v. ACLU*, 521 U.S. 844, 897 (1997).

128 Corbett & Connors, *supra* note 12, at 492.

129 *See, e.g.*, Plato's Gorgias, *supra* note 3, at 23, in which Plato argues that a skilled rhetorician can prove more convincing than an expert because he knows how to persuade and flatter an audience, which does not care much about facts. ("[R]hetoric is part of a practice created not by art but by the habit of a bold and clever mind, which knows how to act in the eyes of the world. I would call it flattery.") Plato preferred dialectics, in which debaters advance arguments and counter-arguments to arrive at a truth.

130 George A. Kennedy, *Chapters 1-3: Introduction, in* Aristotle, On Rhetoric: A Theory of Civil Discourse 27, 28 (George A. Kennedy trans., 2d ed. 2007). ("The [first] chapter [of Book One] continues with a discussion of why rhetoric is useful—remarks that can be thought of as addressed to students of philosophy who, under the influence of Plato, may be indifferent or hostile to rhetoric.").

131 *See, e.g.*, David Folkenflik, *Talk of the Nation: What's the Value of Extreme Rhetoric?* (NPR radio broadcast Oct. 5, 2009) (transcript available at http://www.npr.org/templates/story/ story.php?storyId=113506887).

132 Gerald Gunther, Constitutional Law 994 (12th ed. 1991).

133 Kent Sinclair, Trial Handbook §§ 3.08, 5.05 (2d ed. 1990).

134 Gunther, supra note 132, at 994; *see also Brandenburg v. Ohio*, 395 U.S. 444, 447 (1969) ("[T]he constitutional guarantees of free speech and free press do not permit a State to forbid or proscribe advocacy of the use of force or of law violation except where such advocacy is directed to inciting or producing imminent lawless action and is likely to incite or produce such action."); *Chaplinsky v. New Hampshire*, 315 U.S. 568, 571-572 ("There are certain well-defined and narrowly limited classes of speech, the prevention and punishment of which have never been thought to raise any Constitutional problem. These include the lewd and obscene, the profane, the libelous, and the insulting or 'fighting' words—those which by their very utterance inflict injury or tend to incite an immediate breach of the peace. It has been well observed that such utterances are no essential part of any exposition of ideas, and are of such slight social value as a step to truth that any benefit that may be derived from them is clearly outweighed by the social interest in order and morality."); Matthew Shepard and James Byrd, Jr. Hate Crimes Prevention Act, Pub. L. No. 111-84, § 4710(6), 123 Stat. 2835, 2842 (2009) ("The Constitution of the United States does not protect speech, conduct or activities consisting of planning for, conspiring to commit, or committing an act of violence.").

135 Brigance, *supra* note 119, at 522 ("You can get rid of an idea only by replacing it with a better one.").

136 An exception: lawyers are prohibited from making prejudicial or inflammatory remarks during opening statements and closing arguments. Sinclair, *supra* note 133, at §§ 3.08, 5.05.

137 *See, e.g.*, James Madison, *Federalist No. 10, in* The Federalist Papers 42, 48 (Buccaneer Books 1992) (1788) ("The smaller the society, the fewer probably will be the distinct parties and interests composing it; the fewer the distinct parties and interests, the more frequently will a majority be found of the same party; and the smaller the number of individuals composing a majority, and the smaller the compass within which they are placed, the more easily will they concert and execute their plans of oppression. Extend the sphere, and you take in a greater variety of parties and interests; you make it less probable that a majority of the whole will have a common motive to invade the rights of other citizens....").

138 *N.Y. Times v. Sullivan*, 376 U.S. 254, 270 (1964).

139 David Welch, Propaganda and the German Cinema, 1933-1945, at 198 (2001) (quoting Joseph Goebbels).

140 Adolf Hitler, Mein Kampf 182 (Ralph Manheim trans., Houghton Mifflin 1971) (1925).

141 This is similar to Lenin and the Soviet state. Lenin once said: "A lie told often enough becomes the truth."

142 Hitler, *supra* note 140, at 180-183.

143 *See* USHMM.org (United States Holocaust Memorial Museum), *Nazi Propaganda and Censorship*, http://www.ushmm.org/outreach/en/article.php?ModuleId=10007677 (last visited June 10, 2010); USHMM.org, *Book Burning*, http://www.ushmm.org/wlc/en/article.php?ModuleId=10005852 (last visited June 10, 2010).

144 Brigance, *supra* note 119, at 424-425.

145 PBS.org, *The Man Behind Hitler: Hitler and Goebbels, A Deadly Partnership*, http://www.pbs.org/wgbh/amex/goebbels/peopleevents/p_hitler.html (last visited June 10, 2010).

146 *See, e.g.*, Terry Smith, *A State of Seeing, Unsighted . . . ; Notes on the Visual in Nazi War Culture, in* War/Masculinity 11, 23 (Paul Patton & Ross Poole ed., 1985) ("[T]he Nuremberg rallies were reportedly visible at Frankfurt, over 100 miles away."). *See also* Clyde R. Miller et al., *Propaganda Techniques of German Fascism, in* Modern English Readings 312, 316 (Roger Sherman Loomis & Donald Lemen Clark eds., 5th ed. 1942) (describing "a vivid picture of one of the thousands of carefully planned great mass meetings: the waiting, the expectancy, the late hour when people's resistance is low, the decorations, the company of storm troopers drilling, the dramatic torchlight parade, the bands, the singing, finally the hush, a crash of drums and trumpets, the slow solemn entrance of a well disciplined procession to stirring martial music or perhaps Richard Wagner's 'Entry of the Gods into Valhalla'; at the end a special bodyguard, the uniformed party leaders, and then, 'the centre of all eyes, Der Führer—in his tan raincoat, hatless, smiling, and affably greeting those to right and left. A man of the people! Germany's Savior!' 'Heil! Heil!' and the third 'HEIL!' swells into a great ovation. Speeches, spotlights, cheers, waving of arms. The audience responds at the end with an overwhelming chorus, 'Heil! Heil! Heil! Hitler!' . . . . [An audience member at one of Hitler's speeches is quoted as saying,] 'He could play with that audience just as he wished. As I looked down at the sea of faces from the platform, the 30,000 in the auditorium seemed to be subjects of mass hypnotism.' ").

147 1 The Speeches of Adolf Hitler 737-741 (Norman H. Baynes ed., 1942).

148 More recently, the militant Islamist group al Qaeda inspired followers to violence and jihad through a similar misuse of Pathos. For example, in an address aired on Al-Jazeera on October 7, 2001, shortly after hijackers murdered thousands of people at the World Trade Center, Osama bin Laden (the leader of the group) labeled the United States the aggressors and invoked religion and the promise of paradise to inspire his followers. *See* BBC News, Bin Laden's Warning: Full Text, http://news.bbc.co.uk/2/hi/south_asia/1585636.stm (last visited June 11, 2010).

149 *See, e.g.*, Daniel Goldhagen, Hitler's Willing Executioners (1997) (arguing that the Holocaust was made possible by a particularly virulent, German strain of anti-Semitism);

Christopher Browning, Ordinary Men (1993) (arguing that the men responsible for killing the Jews—"ordinary men"—performed the deeds out of peer pressure, cowardice, and obedience to authority).

150 Richard Hofstadter, The Paranoid Style in American Politics 4 (Vintage Books 2008) (1952).

151 For more information on why we love conspiracies, see Michael Shermer, *Why People Believe in Conspiracies*, Sci. Am., http://www.scientificamerican.com/article.cfm?id= why-people-believe-in-conspiracies, and Arthur Goldwag, Cults, Conspiracies, and Secret Societies (2009).

152 Hofstadter, *supra* note 150, at 27.

153 *Id.* at 7.

154 *Id.* at 28.

155 *See* David Maraniss, *First Lady Launches Counterattack*, Wash. Post, Jan. 28, 1998, at A01, *available at* http://www.washingtonpost.com/wp-srv/politics/special/clinton/ stories/hillary012898.htm.

156 *See, e.g.*, CNN.com, *Falwell Apologizes to Gays, Feminists, Lesbians*, http://archives.cnn .com/2001/US/09/14/Falwell.apology/ (last visited June 14, 2010).

157 *See, e.g.*, Randall Bennett Woods, LBJ: Architect of American Ambition 764 (2006).

158 PBS.org, *The Weather Underground*, http://www.pbs.org/independentlens/weather underground/ (last visited Aug. 4, 2010).

159 *See, e.g.*, DailyKos.com, *Bush Authoritarianism*, http://www.dailykos.com/storyonly/ 2007/10/7/202253/460 (last visited June 12, 2010) (comparing the Bush administration to National Socialism and fascism); HuffingtonPost.com, *Limbaugh: "Adolf Hitler, Like Barack Obama, Ruled by Dictate,"* http://www.huffingtonpost.com/2009/08/06/ limbaugh-adolf-hitler-lik_n_253412.html (last visited June 12, 2010).

160 *See* Raymond Hernandez, *Clinton Calls Comments on Widows Mean-Spirited*, N.Y. Times, June 8, 2006, http://www.nytimes.com/2006/06/08/nyregion/08feud.html?_r=1.

161 *See* Colbert I. King, *A Dangerous Kind of Hate*, Wash. Post, Sept. 12, 2009, at A17, *available at* http://www.washingtonpost.com/wp-dyn/content/article/2009/09/11/AR2009 091103274.html?sid=ST2009091103433.

162 For a humorous example, see http://www.theonion.com/articles/area-man-passionate-defender-of-what-he-imagines-c,2849/.

163 Hofstadter, *supra* note 150, at 31.

164 For example, as David Folkenflik said in *Talk of the Nation: What's the Value of Extreme Rhetoric?* (NPR radio broadcast Oct. 5, 2009) (transcript available at http://www.npr.org/ templates/story/story.php?storyId=113506887), the angry rhetoric of today sounds much like the rhetoric that arose during the Great Depression in reaction to Roosevelt's New Deal initiatives.

Chapter 16

165 1 History of Woman Suffrage: 1848-1861, at 115 (Elizabeth Cady Stanton, Susan B. Anthony, & Matilda Joslyn Gage eds., 1881).

166 Carleton Mabee, Sojourner Truth: Slave, Prophet, Legend 81 (1995).
167 Buchanan.org (Homepage of Patrick J. Buchanan), *1992 Republican National Convention Speech*, http://buchanan.org/blog/1992-republican-national-convention-speech-148 (last visited July 31, 2010).
168 Norman Mailer wrote, "When Mary Fisher spoke like an angel that night, the floor was in tears and conceivably the nation as well." MaryFisher.com (Homepage of Mary Fisher), *About Mary Fisher*, http://www.maryfisher.com/subjects/about-mary/about-mary.htm (last visited July 31, 2010).

Appendix B

169 *See, e.g.*, Corbett & Connors, *supra* note 12, at 490.
170 *See id.* at 492-494.
171 *See, e.g.*, Ian Worthington, *Introduction: Demosthenes, then and now, in* Demosthenes: Statesman and Orator 1, 1 (Ian Worthington ed., 2001) ("[Demosthenes] was highly productive and is regarded as the best of the Greek orators whose works have survived today.").
172 *See* Corbett & Connors, *supra* note 12, at 495.
173 *See id.*
174 *See, e.g.*, Harvey Unis, *How Do the People Decide?: Thucydides on Periclean Rhetoric and Civic Instruction*, 112 Am. J. Philology 179, 179-180 (1991).
175 *See* Corbett & Connors, *supra* note 12, at 490-491.
176 *See id.* at 491-492.
177 *See* Foss, *supra* note 8, at 8.
178 *See* Corbett & Connors, *supra* note 12, at 498.
179 *See* Foss, *supra* note 8, at 9 ("[R]hetoric played a role in education in the Middle Ages as one of the three great liberal arts. Along with logic and grammar, rhetoric was considered part of the *Trivium* of learning. . . .").
180 *See, e.g.*, Brian Vickers, *The Recovery of Rhetoric: Petrarch, Erasmus, and Perelman, in* The Recovery of Rhetoric 25, 29 (J.M.M. Good & R.H. Roberts eds., 1993) ("The recovery of rhetoric in the Renaissance was brought about by a rediscovery of [educational and religious] sources. . . . The person responsible for inaugurating this process of recovery was Francesco Petrarca. . . .").
181 *See* Corbett & Connors, *supra* note 12, at 515-516.
182 *See id.* at 517.
183 *E.g., id.* at 537 ("It was the Speech Department at Cornell University that fostered the resuscitation of classical rhetoric in our time.").
184 *See id.* at 492.
185 Renford Bambrough, *Ethics: Introduction, in* The Philosophy of Aristotle 307 (J.L. Creed & A.E. Wardman trans., 2003).
186 *See, e.g.*, Foss, *supra* note 8, at 6-7 ("The first two speeches [in Plato's *Phaedrus*] illustrate the faults of rhetoric as practiced in contemporary Athens. Either a speech fails to move listeners at all, or it appeals to evil or base motives.").

187 *E.g.*, Corbett & Connors, *supra* note 12, at 492 ("[A]ll the derogatory things that men have said about this art down through the ages have their roots in Plato's strictures.").

188 *See id.* at 516-517.

189 *See, e.g.*, James L. Golden & Edward P.J. Corbett, The Rhetoric of Blair, Campbell, and Whately 3 (1990) ("[T]he British rhetoricians, especially George Campbell, made a significant contribution to the psychology of persuasion through the emotions.").

190 *See, e.g.*, Gilbert Austin, Choronomia; or a Treatise on Rhetorical Delivery (1806).

191 *See* Foss, *supra* note 8, at 10 ("[Descartes] rejected truths established in discourse, relegating language to the role of communicating the truth once it was discovered.").

192 *See* Corbett & Connors, *supra* note 12, at 499-500.

193 *See id.* at 506-507.

194 *Id.* at 507.

195 *See id.* at 522-523.

196 *See id.* at 538.

197 *See id.* at 538-539.

198 *See, e.g.*, Foss, *supra* note 8, at 87 ("Perelman['s] . . . concern with argumentation as opposed to demonstration leads [him] to focus on the audience. All argumentation must be planned in relation to an audience. . . .").

Appendix C

199 Richard Nisbett, Intelligence and How to Get It: Why Schools and Cultures Count 31 (2009) ("If you were to average the contribution of genetics to IQ over different social classes, you would probably find 50 percent to be the maximum contribution of genetics.").

200 *Id.* at 111-112.

201 *Id.* at 89.

202 *Id.* at 85.

203 *Id.* at 87 ("The middle-class parent reads to the child much more than does the working-class parent.").

204 *Id.* at 88-89 ("Although working-class children are asked questions about what is read to them, there is not much effort to connect what is on the page with the outside world. A book might have a picture of a duckling, and the mother might ask the child if he remembers the duck he saw at the lake, but then she might not explain the connection between the fuzzy yellow duckling on the page and the full-grown mallards at the lake.").

205 *Id.* at 114.

206 *Id.* at 116.

207 *Id.* at 77 ("We know that schools can do a lot better job at educating than most are doing.").

Index